The Transformation of the American Pension System

The Transformation of the American Pension System

Was It Beneficial for Workers?

Edward N. Wolff

2011

W.E. Upjohn Institute for Employment Research
Kalamazoo, Michigan

Library of Congress Cataloging-in-Publication Data

Wolff, Edward N.
  The transformation of the American pension system : was it beneficial for workers? /
Edward N. Wolff.
    p. cm.
  Includes bibliographical references and index.
  ISBN-13: 978-0-88099-379-1 (pbk. : alk. paper)
  ISBN-10: 0-88099-379-0 (pbk. : alk. paper)
  ISBN-13: 978-0-88099-380-7 (hardcover : alk. paper)
  ISBN-10: 0-88099-380-4 (hardcover : alk. paper)
  1. Pensions—United States. 2. Old age pensions—United States. 3. Social
security—United States. 4. Retirement income—United States. I. Title.
  HD7125.W57 2011
  331.25'220973—dc23
                            2011041271

The facts presented in this study and the observations and viewpoints expressed are
the sole responsibility of the author. They do not necessarily represent positions of
the W.E. Upjohn Institute for Employment Research.

Cover design by Alcorn Publication Design.
Index prepared by Diane Worden.
Printed in the United States of America.
Printed on recycled paper.

Contents

Figures

Tables

x

Preface

My work on retirement wealth and retirement adequacy was originally stimulated by two articles by Martin Feldstein (1974, 1976), which introduced the concept of Social Security wealth and developed its methodology, and considered the effects of Social Security wealth on the overall distribution of wealth. The latter paper was based on the 1962 Survey of Financial Characteristics of Consumers. My work up until that point focused on the inequality of household wealth, beginning with a 1980 paper using the so-called Measurement of Economic and Social Performance (MESP) database, a 1969 synthetic database on household wealth constructed from a statistical match of the 1970 Decennial Census Public Use Microdata Sample and the 1969 Internal Revenue Service Statistics of Income tax file.

Feldstein (1976) found that the inclusion of Social Security wealth had a major effect on lowering the inequality of total household wealth (including Social Security wealth). The Gini coefficient—a measure of inequality that ranges from zero (complete equality) to one (total inequality)—for the sum of net worth and Social Security wealth among families in the age class 35–64 was 0.51, compared to a Gini coefficient of 0.72 for net worth.

My first article in this area, Wolff (1987b), followed up Feldstein (1976) by examining the distributional implications of both Social Security and defined benefit private pension wealth. I was particularly interested in whether Feldstein's results on the equalizing effects of Social Security wealth persisted when private pension wealth was also included. Did retirement wealth as a whole lower measured wealth inequality to the same degree that Feldstein found for just Social Security wealth?

Wolff (1987b) used the 1969 MESP database. His was perhaps the first paper to add estimates of private pension wealth to standard household net worth and examine its effects on the overall distribution of wealth. The paper, like that of Feldstein (1976), showed that Social Security wealth had a pronounced equalizing effect on the distribution of augmented wealth (the sum of marketable wealth and retirement wealth). However, pension wealth had a disequalizing effect on augmented wealth. In particular, while the addition of Social Security wealth to net worth reduced the overall Gini coefficient from 0.73 to 0.48, the addition of pension wealth to the sum of net worth and Social Security wealth raised the Gini coefficient back to 0.66. The sum of Social Security and pension wealth had, on net, an equalizing effect on the distribution of augmented wealth but substantially less than did Social Security wealth alone. I also followed up this work with Wolff (1992), which provided a discussion of some of the methodological issues involved in estimating both Social Security and pension wealth.

In the early 1990s, I turned my attention to the redistributional effects of the Social Security system. Wolff (1993a,b), using the 1962 Survey of Financial Characteristics of Consumers and the 1983 Survey of Consumer Finances, examined the *intra-cohort* distributional effects of Social Security benefits relative to contributions into the Social Security system. The papers considered which groups were net gainers and which were net losers from the Social Security system as a whole.

I first divided Social Security benefits into two components: 1) an annuity component, which is the benefit level that would be strictly determined by the person's contributions into the Social Security system, and 2) the remainder, the transfer component. The transfer component, as its name indicates, is the additional benefit paid to retirees over and above the amount strictly justified as an annuity payment. The results indicated that the Social Security system is highly redistributive, paying out higher benefits relative to accumulated contributions for lower- than for upper-income families. Moreover, the paper also found that the transfer component of Social Security benefits fell over time, from an overall ratio of 0.85 in 1969 to 0.73 in 1973, and to 0.66 in 1983.

After an almost decade-long hiatus, I returned to the issue of retirement wealth. In my presidential address to the Eastern Economics Association at its 2003 annual conference, held in New York, I called attention to the remarkable transformation of the American pension system. In particular, I reported on the rapid decline in pension coverage from traditional defined benefit plans and the equally stunning rise in coverage from newer defined contribution plans. My main focus was again on the effects of pension wealth on overall wealth inequality. Using data from the 1983, 1989, and 1998 Survey of Consumer Finances, I charted changes in the share of households in the age group 47–64 with each type of pension coverage from 1983 to 1998, and reported that the share with a defined contribution pension plan climbed from 12 to 60 percent while the share with a defined benefit plan fell from 69 to 46 percent. I also found that defined contribution wealth was distributed much more unequally than defined benefit pension wealth. As a result, the switchover in pension systems raised the inequality of pension wealth overall, and the inequality of total wealth, including pension wealth, advanced from 1983 to 1998 at a pace greater than that of standard net worth alone. This work was later updated to the year 2001 in Wolff (2007c).

In two books for the Economic Policy Institute, Wolff (2002b) and Weller and Wolff (2005), I focused on time trends in pension wealth, retirement wealth, and total or augmented wealth, which is the sum of standard net worth and retirement wealth. I also investigated the issue of retirement income adequacy—that is, whether future retirees will have enough financial resources to provide an adequate standard of living. The results indicated strong growth in pension wealth, retirement wealth, and augmented wealth from 1983 to 2001, and an improvement in retirement adequacy as measured by expected retirement income. However, there were still some important gaps in this picture, particularly for minorities and single females, who had much lower augmented wealth and expected retirement income than their counterparts.

On a somewhat different topic, in Wolff (2007a) I compared the well-being of the baby boom generation (ages 40–55) in 2001 with the same age group in 1983 to see how their fortunes had changed over time. The paper found little evidence that their relative position had deteriorated over the period. By some indicators, this generation actually saw an improvement. In terms of income, the 40–55 age group was at about the same relative position in 2001 as in 1983, though in terms of conventional wealth, there was some slippage over the period. In terms of mean augmented wealth (net worth plus pension and Social Security wealth), their relative position improved somewhat, but in terms of median augmented wealth there was again some relative decline.

The present volume both updates and expands my earlier work on these issues. I once again look at time trends in pension coverage, the value of pension plans, retirement wealth, and augmented wealth, as well as changes in wealth inequality and retirement adequacy over time. I also look at differences between demographic groups as defined by age, race, marital status, and education. My particular focus here is on the period from 2001 to 2009. As we shall see, there was a marked reversal in the fortunes of most Americans in regard to these factors in the first decade of the twenty-first century as compared to the "booming" 1980s and 1990s.

1
Introduction

The last three decades have witnessed the radical transformation of the American pension system. In Wolff (2003), I call attention to this change which had been occurring since the early 1980s. I report that the share of households in the age group 47–64 with a defined contribution (DC) pension plan soared from 12 percent in 1983 to 60 percent in 1998, while the share with a defined benefit (DB) plan plummeted from 69 to 46 percent. Subsequently, in Wolff (2007c), I calculate that the share with a DC plan rose to 62 percent in 2001, while the share with a DB plan fell to 45 percent. I sometimes refer to this changeover as the "great transformation."

This volume focuses primarily on changes in the U.S. pension system from 1983 to 2009. However, attention is paid to the entire retirement system, including the role of Social Security. In earlier papers, estimates were provided for the years 1983 to 2001 on the basis of the Federal Reserve Board's Survey of Consumer Finances (SCF) (see Weller and Wolff 2005; Wolff 2002b, 2003, 2007a,b,c). With the availability of the 2004 and 2007 SCF, estimates of retirement wealth and retirement adequacy are updated here to 2007.

The primary question of interest is who gained from and who was hurt by the "great transformation." Five major developments will be addressed: First, how has the transformation affected the pension holdings of workers? Second, how has it impacted both the pension wealth and the total retirement wealth (the sum of pension and social security wealth) of the average median household? Third, which demographic and income groups in particular gained in terms of pension and total retirement wealth, and which lost out? Fourth, has the transformation of the pension system led to greater overall inequality in pension wealth, in total retirement wealth, and in augmented wealth (the sum of net worth and retirement wealth)? Fifth, what implications does the transformation have for the adequacy of retirement income, as measured by the absolute level of expected retirement income, its replacement rate of preretirement income, and the expected poverty rate of future retirees?

Though the empirical analysis contained in the book concerns exclusively the *consequences* of the transformation of the pension system on the wealth and retirement adequacy of U.S. households, it might be useful to speculate on some of the *causes* behind this rapid transformation. There are three reasons why employers might prefer DC plans to DB plans: 1) DC plans allow firms to shift the risk to workers, 2) firms no longer have long-term pension liabilities, and 3) employers generally make lower contributions to DC plans than DB plans.[1]

There were some pulls and pushes as well. With regard to the "pull," the main reason was the availability of DC plans. Individual Retirement Accounts were first established in 1974. This was followed by 401(k) plans in 1978 for profit-making companies (403[b] plans for nonprofits are much older). Another reason was the option to convert DB pension plans to so-called cash balance plans (effectively, DC accounts). In 1999, a lawsuit was initiated by older IBM employees when IBM tried to convert its DB pension plan to a cash balance plan. Though the court initially ruled in favor of the employees, this decision was overturned on appeal, and regulations issued by the Internal Revenue Service (IRS) made such conversions legal. This probably helped to further expedite the elimination of DB plans.[2]

With regard to the "push," the first reason for it was likely the passage of the Employee Retirement Income Security Act (ERISA) in 1974, which increased regulatory burdens on DB plans and made DB plans more costly. ERISA put restrictions on how companies could manage and administer their pension assets: it mandated that companies must put money into pension funds to meet future liabilities and must pay out benefits. ERISA also required companies to pay premiums to the Pension Benefit Guaranty Corporation, which was created in 1974 to insure their pension plans. A second was the Omnibus Budget Reconciliation Act of 1987, which established even tighter funding limits on DB plans. A third push came from the decline of unions in the United States. According to Current Population Survey data, the unionization rate fell from 20 percent in 1983 to 13 percent in 2001. Unions had been one of the bulwarks supporting the traditional DB pension system.[3]

A PRÉCIS OF THE BOOK

This section provides a brief synopsis of the book's principal findings in order to help the reader navigate through the rather dense set of empirical research presented in the ensuing chapters. There are six major questions in the book:

1) With the "great transformation," did pension coverage expand or contract over time?

2) Did the value of pension wealth increase or decline?

3) Did overall wealth inequality rise or fall?

4) Did the retirement prospects of middle-aged Americans improve or worsen?

5) How did the "great transformation" affect different demographic groups?

6) How did these effects vary between the 1980s, the 1990s, and particularly the 2000s?

The results are very sensitive to time periods and particularly to movements in the stock market. The stock market boomed during the 1980s and especially the 1990s but softened during the 2000s. The elimination of DB plans in the 1980s hurt workers in terms of pension coverage, particularly among the elderly, but because of the rapid growth of DC plans in the 1990s, overall pension coverage expanded. In contrast, during the 2000s, pension coverage suffered a mild contraction. However, at least among current workers, the pension coverage rate for females increased from 1989 to 2007, while the rate for men declined.

The value of DC pension plans is especially sensitive to stock market developments, and the defined contribution pension system works very well when the stock market booms. DC pension wealth gained in the 1980s and then grew enormously in the 1990s as coverage expanded and the stock market roared. However, as coverage slackened in the 2000s and the stock market weakened, gains in DC pension wealth slowed down. When the stock market tanked from 2007 to 2009, DC pension wealth actually plummeted. The period 2001–2009 was indeed a "lost decade" in terms of DC pension wealth, with absolutely no net gains over the decade.

Despite the elimination of many DB plans, overall pension wealth (the sum of DB and DC pension wealth) continued to grow in the 1980s, 1990s, and even during the years 2001–2007, though gains during the early and mid-2000s were much smaller than those in the preceding decades. However, overall pension wealth during the entire decade of the 2000s showed a sizable decline. One group that did well over that decade was the elderly, mainly because many of them remained "legacies" of the traditional DB pension system, in which by law their pension benefits could not be reduced.

The story is not complete without considering the ancillary role of the Social Security system. Social Security fills many holes in the rather porous private pension system. Social Security wealth, like (private) pension wealth, grew strongly in the 1990s. However, during the 2000s, its gain slowed markedly. Retirement wealth, the sum of pension and Social Security wealth, showed marked improvement in the 1990s but, again, much slower advances in the 2000s.

When standard net worth is added to retirement wealth to produce augmented wealth, this addition creates the most comprehensive measure of retirement resources. The results show that mean augmented wealth grew very strongly in the 1990s but that gains were much weaker in the 2000s. Indeed, *median* augmented wealth showed almost no change among middle-aged and elderly households and actually declined in absolute terms among younger households. Indeed, younger households were found to be particularly vulnerable as a group, and their retirement prospects appear to have faded over time.

In the case of inequality trends, there is not much differentiation between the 1980s, 1990s, and 2000s. One notable finding is that DC pension wealth is distributed much more unequally than traditional DB pension wealth. As a result, the transition from the DB system to the DC system resulted in higher levels of inequality of pension wealth, retirement wealth, and augmented wealth. In particular, there was an increase in the overall inequality of augmented wealth between 1989 and 2007. This result contrasts with almost no change in the inequality of net worth over these years.

In 2007, there were large gaps in pension wealth, retirement wealth, and augmented wealth between minority households and the white majority, between single females and married couples, and between college graduates and other educational groups. However, minority households generally showed strong progress in terms of pension, retirement, and augmented wealth relative to white households. Likewise, single female households generally showed gains relative to married couples in these three dimensions. In contrast, less educated households generally lost out relative to college graduates in terms of pension, retirement, and augmented wealth.

CHAPTER OUTLINE

Chapter 2 provides an update of wealth trends on the basis of the standard definition of net worth: marketable assets less debts. This sets the stage for the remainder of the book. The chapter first discusses the sources and methods for the data used in this study. The data sources used for this study are the 1983, 1989, 2001, and 2007 SCF conducted by the Federal Reserve Board. Each survey consists of a core representative sample combined with a high-income supplement. The SCF provides considerable detail on both pension plans and Social Security contributions. The SCF also gives detailed information on expected pension and Social Security benefits for both spouses.

Chapter 2 then analyzes trends in median and mean wealth, the inequality of wealth, wealth composition, stock ownership, and wealth by race, ethnicity, and age group. An update of household wealth to mid-2009 is also provided on the basis of movements in stock and housing prices. The chapter will thus serve as a backdrop to the analysis of retirement wealth and enable us to see what differences in wealth trends are engendered by the introduction of both pension wealth and Social Security wealth to the definition of household wealth.

As will be seen, there was very strong growth in both mean and median net worth during the 2000s (2001–2007), as there was during the 1990s (1989–2001). There was a dramatic shift in the household portfolio away from liquid assets like savings accounts and money market funds and into DC plans instead. The early and mid-2000s also witnessed sharply rising family indebtedness, as the debt-to-income ratio by 2007 reached its highest level in almost 25 years, particularly among the middle class. In contrast, wealth inequality remained flat during the 1990s as well as from 2001 to 2007. An update to mid-2009 indicates a very sharp drop in mean net worth and, particularly, median net worth, as well as a sharp rise in wealth inequality.

Chapter 3 reviews some of the relevant literature on pensions and Social Security, which is important in order to provide a context for my later empirical findings. It focuses on the evolution of pension coverage rates, pension and Social Security wealth, and replacement rates for each. The chapter also discusses how pensions and Social Security wealth affect inequality, both overall and between different demographic groups.

The chapter is divided into six parts. The first part reviews studies that have documented changes in pension coverage in the United States, particularly the decline in DB and the corresponding rise in DC pension coverage among workers since the early 1980s. It asks, did the great transformation raise or lower the level of pension wealth and retirement wealth in general? The second part surveys work on trends in both the level of retirement wealth as well as its degree of inequality.

One ongoing controversy is whether DC plans such as 401(k) plans have, on net, added to total household savings, or whether they have simply substituted for other forms of savings. These studies are reviewed in the third part. Have workers saved enough (or will they save enough) to meet their needs during retirement? The fourth section delves into the literature on measuring retirement adequacy. In more general terms, how have the elderly fared over time? The next section reviews some of the studies that have attempted to measure the economic status of the elderly. How did families fare during the "great recession" of 2007–2009? The final part of Chapter 3 reviews studies that have tried to measure the effects of the 2007–2009 recession on the pension wealth holdings of households and their anticipated retirement behavior.

In Chapter 4 I turn to the empirical analysis of pension and Social Security wealth. How did the great transformation affect pension coverage in general? I first analyze how pension coverage developed over the period 1989–2007 among individual workers and then investigate trends in pension coverage on the household level over the more extended time interval, 1983–2007. If we now add pension wealth to standard net worth to obtain what I call "private accumulations," how has the level of private accumulations and its degree of inequality changed over time?

In Chapter 5, I extend the empirical results reported in Chapter 4 by considering Social Security wealth, retirement wealth in general, and augmented wealth. Did Social Security wealth grow over time? What happened to total retirement wealth, the sum of pension and Social Security wealth? These are the first two topics considered in the chapter.

I next introduce the concept of total (augmented) household wealth, the sum of net worth, pension wealth, and Social Security wealth. While net worth is a limited measure of resource availability, augmented wealth provides the most comprehensive measure of the full set of resources available to families for retirement. When I later consider retirement adequacy, I shall once again rely on the concept of augmented wealth. How then did augmented wealth and its degree of inequality change from 1983 to 2007? This is the next set of topics to occupy us in the chapter. Finally, what happened to pension wealth and augmented wealth during the great recession? The last section of Chapter 5 provides an update on these estimates to mid-2009 on the basis of changes in stock and housing prices.

The results of Chapters 4 and 5 show a huge increase in pension wealth during the 1990s despite the collapse of the DB pension system, mainly because of the enormous take-up rate in DC pension plans (as discussed above) and extremely robust gains in the stock market (as we see in Chapter 2). However, in the 2000s, there was a marked slowdown in advances in pension wealth, as both the share of households with pensions declined a bit and stock prices advanced more slowly. Private accumulations, which also showed substantial gains in the 1990s, showed smaller increases in the 2000s. Social Security wealth, likewise, jumped in the 1990s but was largely unchanged in the 2000s. As a result, both total retirement wealth and augmented wealth climbed sharply in the 1990s but showed only very modest gains in the 2000s. Finally, while the inequality of net worth remained largely unchanged from 1989 to 2007, the inequality of augmented wealth rose over the period, as more unequal DC wealth replaced more equal DB wealth.

How did different demographic groups fare with regard to relative gains in pensions, retirement wealth, and augmented wealth? Chapter

6 investigates these issues for the period 1989–2007. For purposes of analysis, three divisions of the population are made: 1) race/ethnicity, 2) marital status, and 3) educational attainment. As will be seen in this chapter, there was a remarkable turnaround in the relative fortunes of minorities, though significant gaps between them and the white majority still remained in 2007. Differentials in retirement wealth and augmented wealth also generally narrowed between single females and married couples, though once again very large gaps remained in 2007. In contrast, differences in retirement and augmented wealth by educational group splayed out over the years, with college graduates in particular increasing their lead over the other educational groups.

What was the level of retirement adequacy among households close to retirement in 2007, and how did this change over time from 1989 to 2007? These are the subjects of Chapter 7. Retirement adequacy is measured in three different ways: 1) by calculating the stream of retirement income that today's older workers can expect at retirement from their accumulated wealth at the time of retirement, 2) by comparing their expected retirement income to the poverty line in order to measure the expected poverty rate at retirement, and 3) by the so-called replacement rate, which calculates the ratio of expected retirement income to preretirement income. All three measures of retirement adequacy are computed for individual age groups and by race/ethnicity, marital status, and educational attainment.

The results of Chapter 7 show strong gains in expected retirement income for the age group 47–64 during the 1990s but a marked slowdown in its growth from 2001 to 2007, even before the financial meltdown of 2007–2009. These findings are consistent with the pronounced decline in the rate of advance of augmented wealth between the 1990s and the 2000s (see Chapter 5). Households in this age group also saw a large reduction in their expected poverty rate at retirement from 1989 to 2001. However, there was no further reduction in the expected poverty rate from 2001 to 2007. In contrast, the percentage of households with at least a 75 percent replacement rate rose somewhat more in the 2000s than it had in the 1990s, though the gains were quite modest in both periods.

The last chapter, Chapter 8, presents a summary of the principal findings of this study, considers the policy implications of the study, and offers pertinent policy recommendations. I argue in favor of universal pension coverage. For current workers, I propose guaranteed employer pension coverage for all workers in the company. For non-workers below the age of retirement, I advocate a mixture of Individual Retirement Accounts and Individual Development Accounts supported by the federal government. I also make the case that the current Social Security system should be left largely intact.

Notes

1. Ghilarducci, Sun, and Nyce (2004) estimate that DC plans, on average, cost the employer less than traditional DB pension plans. They investigate the pension choices of over 800 firms between 1988 and 1996 using data on pension plan finances from the Internal Revenue Service Form 5500 and on firm finances from Compustat. They calculate that a 10 percent increase in the use of 401(k) plans reduced pension costs per worker by 1.8 to 2.0 percent. However, it is not clear whether this reduction in pension costs could be reflected in higher wages paid to workers. See also Wolman and Colamosca (2002) for more discussion of these points.
2. However, Gustman and Steinmeier (1992), examining the 1977–1985 period, conclude that regulatory changes could account for no more than half of the shift from DB to DC plans, at least over this period.
3. Another factor that has been mentioned is greater worker mobility in the 1990s than in the 1980s. The argument is that because DB pensions are not portable between employers, workers who switch jobs may prefer DC to DB plans. Such an argument is made by Friedberg and Owyang (2004) using a contract-theoretic matching model with moral hazard. In their work, they show that a decline in the value of existing jobs relative to new jobs reduces the expected match duration and therefore the desirability of DB pensions. They find that this explanation is consistent with observed trends in DB pension coverage. However, according to Farber (2001), there was virtually no change, on average, in the degree of job tenure between the 1980s and the 1990s, casting some doubt on the increased worker mobility argument.

2
Recent Trends in Household Wealth, 1983–2009

Robust Growth Followed by Collapse

It is useful to begin the empirical part of the book with a presentation of wealth trends based on the standard definition of wealth. This will serve as a backdrop for the rest of the book. In particular, we will see how our basic findings on wealth trends change when we include retirement wealth in the definition of household wealth. Moreover, we will be able to see some of the reasons for the plunge in wealth during the "great recession" of 2007–2009.

The 1990s witnessed some remarkable events: the stock market boomed, stock ownership spread, and real wages, after stagnating for many years, finally grew. The prices of stocks listed on Standard & Poor's (S&P) 500 index surged 171 percent between 1989 and 2001, and by 2001 over half of U.S. households owned stock either directly or indirectly. According to Bureau of Labor Statistics (BLS) figures, real mean hourly earnings gained 8.3 percent between 1995 and 2001 (Council of Economic Advisers 2009a).[1]

However, 2001 saw a recession, albeit a short one. Moreover, the stock market, which had peaked in 2000, dropped steeply from 2000 to 2003 but recovered in 2004, so that between 2001 and 2004 the S&P 500 was down by "only" 12 percent in real terms (Council of Economic Advisers 2009b).[2] Real wages rose very slowly from 2001 to 2004: the BLS real mean hourly earnings rose by only 1.5 percent, while median household income dropped in real terms by 1.5 percent (Council of Economic Advisers 2009c). On the other hand, housing prices rose steeply. The median sales price of existing one-family homes rose by 18 percent in real terms nationwide (U.S. Census Bureau 2009). The other big story was household debt, particularly that of the middle class, which skyrocketed during these years, as we shall see below.

From 2004 to 2007, the stock market rebounded. The S&P 500 rose 19 percent in real terms. Over the period 2001–2007, the S&P 500 was up 24 percent (6 percent in real terms). Real wages remained stagnant, as the BLS real mean hourly earnings rose by only 1.0 percent. Median household income in real terms showed some growth over this period, rising by 3.2 percent. From 2001 to 2007 it gained 1.6 percent. From 2004 to 2007, housing prices slowed, as the median sales price of existing one-family nationwide advanced only 1.7 percent over these years in real terms. Over the years 2001 to 2007, real housing prices gained 19 percent.

Updating previous studies (Wolff 1994, 1996, 1998, 2001, 2002a, 2007d), I find that median net worth, the wealth of the average household, demonstrated robust growth over the years 1983–2007. In fact, the growth rate of median wealth accelerated from the 1980s to the 1990s and into the 2001–2007 period. However, the gains of that period were based largely on rising home prices financed by increasing mortgage debt. This growth came to an abrupt end in 2007 with the collapse in home prices, and median wealth plummeted from 2007 through 2009.

Household wealth inequality increased sharply between 1983 and 1989. However, in a surprising development, this increase was followed by a period of almost no change in household wealth inequality from 1989 to 2007. This trend during those years was unexpected because the two factors normally associated with wealth inequality, income inequality and the ratio of stock prices to home prices, both showed a marked rise over the same years.

Between 1983 and 2007, and particularly from 1989 to 2001, there was a striking shift in the portfolio composition of household wealth: out of liquid assets like savings accounts and money market funds and into DC pension accounts. There was also a noticeable expansion of stock ownership from 1989 to 2001, followed by a mild contraction between 2001 and 2007. Furthermore, DC pension accounts became more heavily invested in equities, making them vulnerable to the stock market downturn in 2007–2009.

Moreover, despite the buoyant economy over the 1980s and 1990s, overall indebtedness continued to rise among American families and then skyrocketed in the early and mid 2000s. Among the middle class, the debt-income ratio reached its highest level in 24 years. The high level of indebtedness made the middle class particularly vulnerable to the collapse of the housing market.

The ratio of mean wealth between African American and white families was very low in 1983, at 0.19, and barely budged over the years from 1983 to 2007. However, Hispanics did show some relative gains over the 2001–2007 period. Young households (those with a head of household under the age of 45), after some relative gains from 1983 to 1989, saw their relative wealth position deteriorate between 1989 and 2007. This development made young households particularly exposed to the joint collapse of the stock and housing markets.

These results on traditional net worth will set the stage for later analysis of trends in what I call *augmented wealth*, the sum of net worth, DB pension wealth, and Social Security wealth. How did average pension wealth and augmented wealth grow over the period from 1983 to 2007 (Chapters 4 and 5)? What happened to the inequality of augmented wealth over this period? Is the racial divide smaller or larger once retirement wealth (the sum of pension and Social Security wealth) is included in household wealth (Chapter 6)? How did different age groups fare with regard to augmented wealth? Did young households, in particular, see their relative wealth position deteriorate once retirement wealth was added to net worth (Chapter 5)? What were the relative developments in augmented wealth by income class and wealth class (Chapter 6)? Moreover, I will also look at trends in net worth, retirement wealth, and augmented wealth by marital status, particularly between female-headed households and married couples, and by level of educational attainment (Chapter 6).

I begin the next section with a discussion of the measurement of household wealth and a description of the data sources used for this study. After that I present results on time trends in median and average wealth holdings, changes in the concentration of household wealth, and the composition of household wealth. I then investigate changes in wealth holdings by race and ethnicity, and report on changes in the age-wealth profile. The last three sections of the chapter provide details on stock ownership, a partial update of household wealth trends to 2009, and a summary of results.

DATA SOURCES AND METHODS

The data sources used for this study are the 1983, 1989, 2001, and 2007 SCF conducted by the Federal Reserve Board.[3] Each survey consists of a core representative sample combined with a high-income supplement. In 1983, for example, the supplement was drawn from the Internal Revenue Service's Statistics of Income data file. For the 1983 SCF, an income cutoff of $100,000 of adjusted gross income was used as the criterion for inclusion in the supplemental sample. Individuals were randomly selected for the sample within predesignated income strata. In later years, the high-income supplement was selected as a list sample from statistical records (the Individual Tax File) derived from tax data by the Statistics of Income Division of the IRS (SOI). This second sample was designed to disproportionately select families that were likely to be relatively wealthy (see, for example, Kennickell [2001] for a more extended discussion of the design of the list sample in the 2001 SCF). The advantage of the high-income supplement is that it provides a much richer sample of high-income (and therefore potentially very wealthy) families. However, the presence of a high-income supplement creates some complications, because weights must be constructed to meld the high-income supplement with the core sample.[4]

The principal wealth concept used here is marketable wealth (or net worth), which is defined as the current value of all marketable or fungible assets less the current value of debts. Net worth is thus the difference in value between total assets and total liabilities or debt. Total assets are defined as the sum of

- the gross value of owner-occupied housing;
- other real estate owned by the household;
- cash and demand deposits;
- time and savings deposits, certificates of deposit, and money market accounts;
- government bonds, corporate bonds, foreign bonds, and other financial securities;
- the cash surrender value of life insurance plans;

- the cash surrender value of pension plans, including IRAs, Keogh, and 401(k) plans;
- corporate stock and mutual funds;
- net equity in unincorporated businesses; and
- equity in trust funds.

Total liabilities are the sum of

- mortgage debt;
- consumer debt, including auto loans; and
- other debt.

This measure reflects wealth as a store of value and therefore a source of potential consumption. I believe that this is the concept that best reflects the level of well-being associated with a family's holdings. Thus, only assets that can be readily converted to cash (that is, those that are fungible) are included. As a result, consumer durables such as automobiles, televisions, furniture, household appliances, and the like are excluded here, since these items are not easily marketed, with the possible exception of vehicles, or their resale value typically far understates the value of their consumption services to the household. Another justification for their exclusion is that this treatment is consistent with the national accounts, where purchase of vehicles is counted as expenditures, not savings. Also excluded here is the value of future Social Security benefits the family may receive upon retirement (usually referred to as Social Security wealth), as well as the value of DB pension benefits from private pension plans (DB pension wealth). In Chapters 4 and 5, we shall add these two components to standard wealth to create a concept I call augmented wealth.

Another concept that we will make use of later on is housing wealth. This is defined as net home equity, the difference between the (gross) market value of a home and its outstanding mortgage debt.

MEDIAN WEALTH ROSE BRISKLY DURING THE 2000s

Table 2.1 documents a robust growth in wealth during the 1990s (also see Figure 2.1). After rising 7 percent between 1983 and 1989, median wealth (the wealth of a household in the middle of the distribution) was 16 percent greater in 2001 than in 1989. As a result, median wealth grew slightly faster between 1989 and 2001, 1.3 percent per year, than between 1983 and 1989, at 1.1 percent per year. However, between 2001 and 2007, median wealth grew even faster, by 19 percent overall or 2.9 percent per year. Most of the increase (63 percent) in median net worth emanated from the pronounced rise in home prices.

Mean net worth also showed a sharp increase of 15 percent from 1983 to 1989 and then, buoyed largely by rising stock prices, surged 44 percent by 2001. There was an additional rise of 20 percent in 2007. Overall, its 2007 value was almost double its value in 1983 and about three quarters larger than in 1989. Mean wealth grew quite a bit faster between 1989 and 2001 (3.0 percent per year) than between 1983 and 1989 (2.3 percent per year). There was then a slight increase in wealth growth from 2001 to 2007 (3.1 percent per year). This modest acceleration was largely due to rapid increase in housing prices of 19 percent

Table 2.1 Mean and Median Household Wealth and Income, 1983–2007 (in thousands, 2007$)

					Percentage change			
Wealth concept	1983	1989	2001	2007	1983–1989	1989–2001	2001–2007	1983–2007
Net worth								
Median	69.5	74.3	86.1	102.5	7.0	15.8	19.1	47.5
Mean	270.4	309.8	445.1	536.1	14.6	43.7	20.4	98.2
Income[a]								
Median	43.5	48.3	49.4	50.2	11.2	2.3	1.6	15.5
Mean	52.9	61.1	68.1	67.6	15.5	11.6	−0.8	27.9

[a] Source for household income data: U.S. Census Bureau, Current Population Surveys. Available at http://www.census.gov/hhes/www/income/data/historical/household/index.html (accessed April 2011).
SOURCE: Author's computations from the 1983, 1989, 2001, and 2007 SCF. Wealth figures are deflated using the Consumer Price Index. See Appendix A for sources and methods.

**Figure 2.1 Mean and Median Household Wealth, 1983–2007
          (in thousands, 2007$)**

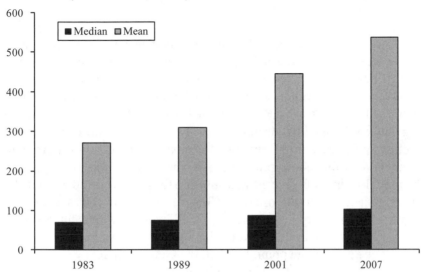

SOURCE: Author's computations from the 1983, 1989, 2001, and 2007 SCF.

in real terms over the six years, counterbalanced by a reduced growth in stock prices between 2001–2007 and 1989–2001, and to the fact that housing comprised 28 percent and (total) stocks made up 25 percent of total assets in 2001. Another point of note is that mean wealth grew about twice as fast as the median between 1983 and 2007, indicating widening inequality of wealth over these years.

Median household income (based on Current Population Survey [CPS] data), after gaining 11 percent between 1983 and 1989, grew by only 2.3 percent (total) in 1989–2001 and by another 1.6 percent in 2001–2007, for a net change of 16 percent in 1983–2007. In contrast, mean income rose by 16 percent from 1983 to 1989, by another 12 percent from 1989 to 2001, and then fell by 0.8 percent from 2001 to 2007, for a total change of 28 percent from 1983 to 2007. Between 1983 and 2007, mean income grew about twice as fast as median income.

In sum, while household income virtually stagnated for the average American household over the 1990s and 2000s, median net worth grew strongly over this period. In the 2000s in particular, mean and median income changed very little, while mean and median net worth grew strongly.

WEALTH INEQUALITY SHOWS LITTLE CHANGE OVER THE EARLY AND MID-2000s

The figures in Table 2.2 also show that wealth inequality, after rising steeply between 1983 and 1989, remained virtually unchanged from 1989 to 2007. The share of wealth held by the top 1 percent rose by 3.6 percentage points from 1983 to 1989, and the Gini coefficient increased from 0.80 to 0.83. Between 1989 and 2007, the share of the top percentile actually declined sharply, from 37.4 to 34.6 percent, though an increase in the share of the next four percentiles more than compensated for the drop. As a result, the share of the top 5 percent increased from 59.0 percent in 1989 to 61.9 percent in 2007, and the share of the top quintile rose from 83.5 to 85.0 percent. The share of the fourth and middle quintiles each declined by about a percentage point from 1989 to 2007, while that of the bottom 40 percent increased by almost one percentage point. Overall, the Gini coefficient was virtually unchanged—0.832 in 1989 and 0.834 in 2007.

The top 1 percent of families (as ranked by income on the basis of the SCF data) earned 21 percent of total household income in 2006, and the top 20 percent accounted for 61 percent—large figures but lower than the corresponding wealth shares.[5] The time trend for income inequality also contrasts with that of net worth. Income inequality increased sharply between 1982 and 1988, with the Gini coefficient rising from 0.48 to 0.52 and the share of the top one percent from 12.8 to 16.6 percent. There was again a pronounced increase in income inequality between 1988 and 2000, with the share of the top 1 percent rising from 16.6 to 20.0 percent, that of the top quintile from 55.6 to 58.6 percent, and the Gini coefficient from 0.52 to 0.56.[6]

The years between 2000 and 2006 saw a slight abatement in the rise of income inequality. Over these years, the Gini coefficient for income rose from 0.56 to 0.57, the share of the top 1 percent from 20.0 to 21.3 percent, and that of the top quintile from 15.2 to 15.9 percent. All in all, the 2000s witnessed a moderate increase in income inequality and a very slight rise in wealth inequality.[7]

Table 2.2 The Size Distribution of Wealth and Income, 1983–2007

Year	Gini coefficient	Percentage share of wealth or income held by:								
		Top 1.0%	Next 4.0%	Next 5.0%	Next 10.0%	Top 20.0%	4th 20.0%	3rd 20.0%	Bottom 40.0%	All
Net worth										
1983	0.799	33.8	22.3	12.1	13.1	81.3	12.6	5.2	0.9	100.0
1989	0.832	37.4	21.6	11.6	13.0	83.5	12.3	4.8	-0.7	100.0
2001	0.826	33.4	25.8	12.3	12.9	84.4	11.3	3.9	0.3	100.0
2007	0.834	34.6	27.3	11.2	12.0	85.0	10.9	4.0	0.2	100.0
Income										
1982	0.480	12.8	13.3	10.3	15.5	51.9	21.6	14.2	12.3	100.0
1988	0.521	16.6	13.3	10.4	15.2	55.6	20.6	13.2	10.7	100.0
2000	0.562	20.0	15.2	10.0	13.5	58.6	19.0	12.3	10.1	100.0
2006	0.574	21.3	15.9	9.9	14.3	61.4	17.8	11.1	9.6	100.0

NOTE: For the computation of percentile shares of net worth, households are ranked according to their net worth; and for percentile shares of income, households are ranked according to their income. Totals may not sum to 100.0 because of rounding.
SOURCE: Author's computations from the 1983, 1989, 2001, and 2007 SCF.

HOUSEHOLD PORTFOLIOS SHOW A PRONOUNCED SHIFT INTO DC PENSION ACCOUNTS

The portfolio composition of household wealth shows the forms in which households save. This aspect is important when we try to understand how wealth changes over time and the exposure of household wealth to asset price changes.

In 2007, owner-occupied housing was the most important household asset in the breakdown shown in Table 2.3, accounting for 33 percent of total assets. However, net home equity—the value of the house minus any outstanding mortgage—amounted to only 21 percent of total assets. Real estate, other than owner-occupied housing, comprised 11 percent, and business equity another 20 percent.

Demand deposits, time deposits, money market funds, CDs, and the cash surrender value of life insurance made up 7 percent and pension accounts 12 percent. Bonds and other financial securities amounted to 2 percent; corporate stock, including mutual funds, to 12 percent; and trust equity to 2 percent. Debt as a proportion of gross assets was 15 percent, and the debt-equity ratio (the ratio of total household debt to net worth) was 18 percent.

There have been some notable changes in the composition of household wealth over the period 1983–2007. From the point of view of this work, the most important is the pronounced growth of DC pension accounts, which rose moderately from 1.5 percent of total assets in 1983 to 2.9 percent in 1989 and then shot up to 12 percent in 2001, where they remained in 2007. This increase largely offset the decline in the share of liquid assets in total assets, from 17 percent in 1983 to 7 percent in 2007, so it is reasonable to conclude that households have to a large extent substituted tax-deferred DC pension accounts for taxable savings deposits.

A second notable change is that the share of (gross) housing wealth in total assets, after fluctuating between 28 and 30 percent from 1983 to 2001, jumped to 33 percent in 2007. There were two factors behind this. The first was the rise in the homeownership rate, which, according to the SCF data, climbed from 63 percent in 1983 to 69 percent in 2007. The second was the sharp rise in housing prices, noted above. Between 2001 and 2004, the median house price for existing one-family homes

**Table 2.3 Composition of Total Household Wealth, 1983–2007
             (percentage of gross assets)**

	1983	1989	2001	2007
Wealth component				
Principal residence (gross value)	30.1	30.2	28.2	32.8
Other real estate (gross value)[a]	14.9	14.0	9.8	11.3
Unincorporated business equity[b]	18.8	17.2	17.2	20.1
Liquid assets[c]	17.4	17.5	8.8	6.6
Pension accounts[d]	1.5	2.9	12.3	12.1
Financial securities[e]	4.2	3.4	2.3	1.5
Corporate stock and mutual funds	9.0	6.9	14.8	11.8
Net equity in personal trusts	2.6	3.1	4.8	2.3
Miscellaneous assets[f]	1.3	4.9	1.8	1.7
Total	100.0	100.0	100.0	100.0
Debt				
Debt on principal residence	6.3	8.6	9.4	11.4
All other debt[g]	6.8	6.4	3.1	3.9
Total debt	13.1	15.0	12.5	15.3
Selected ratios in percent				
Debt/equity ratio	15.1	17.6	14.3	18.1
Debt/income ratio	68.4	87.6	81.1	118.7
Net home equity/total assets[h]	23.8	21.6	18.8	21.4
Principal residence debt/house value	20.9	28.6	33.4	34.9
Stocks, directly or indirectly owned/ total assets[i]	11.3	10.2	24.5	16.8

NOTE: Totals may not sum to 100.0 because of rounding.
[a] In 2001 and 2007 this equals the gross value of other residential real estate plus the net equity in nonresidential real estate.
[b] Net equity in unincorporated farm and nonfarm businesses and closely held corporations.
[c] Checking accounts, savings accounts, time deposits, money market funds, certificates of deposit, and the cash surrender value of life insurance.
[d] IRAs, Keogh plans, 401(k) plans, the accumulated value of defined contribution pension plans, and other retirement accounts.
[e] Corporate bonds, government bonds (including savings bonds), open-market paper, and notes.
[f] Gold and other precious metals, royalties, jewelry, antiques, furs, loans to friends and relatives, future contracts, and miscellaneous assets.
[g] Mortgage debt on all real property except principal residence; credit card, installment, and other consumer debt.
[h] Ratio of gross value of principal residence less mortgage debt on principal residence to total assets.
[i] Includes direct ownership of stock shares and indirect ownership through mutual funds, trusts, IRAs, Keogh plans, 401(k) plans, and other retirement accounts.
SOURCE: Author's computations from the 1983, 1989, 2001, and 2007 SCF.

rose by 19 percent in real terms. The rise in housing prices by itself would have caused the share of housing in total assets to rise by 5.3 percentage points, compared to the actual increase of 4.6 percentage points.

A third and related trend is that net equity in owner-occupied housing (the difference between the market value and outstanding mortgages on the property), after falling from 24 percent in 1983 to 19 percent in 2001, picked up to 21 percent in 2007. The difference between the two series (gross versus net housing values as a share of total assets) is attributable to the changing magnitude of mortgage debt on homeowners' property, which increased from 21 percent in 1983 to 35 percent in 2007. Moreover, mortgage debt on a principal residence climbed from 9.4 to 11.4 percent of total assets between 2001 and 2007. The fact that net home equity as a proportion of assets increased during that period reflected the strong gains in real estate values over these years.

Fourth, the debt-equity ratio fell slightly, from 15 percent in 1983 to 14 percent in 2001; however, it then jumped to 18 percent in 2007. In contrast, the ratio of debt to total income increased from 68 percent in 1983 to 81 percent in 2001 and then skyrocketed to 119 percent in 2007, its high for this period. If mortgage debt on principal residence is excluded, then the ratio of other debt to total assets fell off from 6.8 percent in 1983 to 3.9 percent in 2007. One implication is that over the 1990s and 2000s, families used tax-sheltered mortgages and home equity loans rather than consumer loans and other forms of consumer debt to finance consumption.

Fifth, the share of corporate stock and mutual funds in total assets rose rather briskly, from 9 percent in 1983 to 15 percent in 2001, before plummeting to 12 percent in 2007. If we include the value of stocks indirectly owned through mutual funds, trusts, IRAs, 401(k) plans, and other retirement accounts, then the value of total stocks owned as a share of total assets more than doubled, from 11 percent in 1983 to 25 percent in 2001, and then tumbled to 17 percent in 2007. The rise during the 1990s reflected the bull market in corporate equities as well as increased stock ownership, while the decline in the 2000s was a result of the relatively small rise in the stock market over this period (particularly relative to housing prices), as well as a drop in stock ownership (see Table 2.10a). The change in stock prices by itself would have caused the share of stocks in total assets to rise by 1.4 percentage points between 2001 and 2007, compared to the actual decline of 7.6 percentage points. The decline in the share of stocks in total assets was due to sales of stocks and withdrawals from stock funds.

PORTFOLIO COMPOSITION BY WEALTH CLASS

Table 2.3 provides a picture of the average holdings of all families in the economy, but there are marked class differences in how middle-class families and the rich invest their wealth. These differences in portfolio composition are important because they affect how wealth changes over time for different parts of the wealth distribution and thus how overall wealth inequality develops.

As shown in Table 2.4, the richest 1 percent of households (as ranked by wealth) invested over three-quarters of their savings in investment real estate, businesses, corporate stock, and financial securities in 2007. Corporate stocks, either directly owned by the households or indirectly owned through mutual funds, trust accounts, or various pension accounts, comprised 21 percent by themselves. Housing accounted for only 10 percent of their wealth (and net equity in housing only 9 percent), liquid assets another 5 percent, and pension accounts another 6 percent. Their ratio of debt to net worth was only 3 percent, their ratio of debt to income was 39 percent, and the ratio of mortgage debt to house value was 15 percent.

Among the next richest 19 percent of U.S. households, housing comprised 32 percent of their total assets (and net home equity 24 percent), liquid assets another 7 percent, and pension assets 16 percent. Forty-four percent of their assets took the form of investment assets—real estate, business equity, stocks, and bonds—and 19 percent was in the form of stocks directly or indirectly owned. Debt amounted to 12 percent of their net worth and 110 percent of their income, and the ratio of mortgage debt to house value was 26 percent.

In contrast, almost two-thirds of the wealth of the middle three wealth quintiles of households was invested in their own home in 2007. However, home equity amounted to only 35 percent of total assets, a reflection of their large mortgage debt. Another 21 percent went into monetary savings of one form or another and pension accounts.

**Table 2.4 Composition of Household Wealth by Wealth Class, 2007
(percent of gross assets)**

	All households	Top 1%	Next 19%	Middle 3 quintiles
Asset				
Principal residence	32.8	10.2	31.8	65.1
Liquid assets (bank deposits, money market funds, and cash surrender value of life insurance)	6.6	4.5	7.3	7.8
Pension accounts	12.1	5.8	15.9	12.9
Corporate stock, financial securities, mutual funds, and personal trusts	15.5	25.2	15.0	3.6
Unincorporated business equity, other real estate	31.3	52.3	28.5	9.3
Miscellaneous assets	1.7	2.0	1.6	1.3
Total assets	100.0	100.0	100.0	100.0
Selected ratios (%)				
Debt/equity ratio	18.1	2.8	12.1	61.1
Debt/income ratio	118.7	39.4	109.8	156.7
Net home equity/total assets[a]	21.4	8.7	23.6	34.8
Principal residence debt/ house value	34.9	15.2	25.6	46.6
All stocks/total assets[b]	16.8	21.4	18.6	7.0

NOTE: Households are classified into wealth class according to their net worth. Brackets for 2007 are as follows:
• Top 1%: Net worth of $8,232,000 or more.
• Next 19%: Net worth between $473,000 and $8,232,000.
• Quintiles 2–4: Net worth between $200 and $473,000.
[a] Ratio of gross value of principal residence less mortgage debt on principal residence to total assets.
[b] Includes direct ownership of stock shares and indirect ownership through mutual funds, trusts, and IRAs, Keogh plans, 401(k) plans, and other retirement accounts.
SOURCE: Author's computations from the 2007 SCF.

Together, housing, liquid assets, and pension assets accounted for 86 percent of the total assets of the middle class. The remainder was about evenly split among nonhome real estate, business equity, and various financial securities and corporate stock. Stocks directly or indirectly owned amounted to only 7 percent of their total assets. The ratio of debt to net worth was 61 percent, substantially higher than for the richest 20 percent, and their ratio of debt to income was 157 percent, also much higher than for the top quintile. Finally, their mortgage debt amounted to almost half the value of their principal residences.

The rather staggering debt level of the middle class in 2007 raises the question of whether this accumulation of debt is a recent phenomenon or whether it has been going on for some time. The overall debt-equity ratio in 2007 was only slightly above its level in 1989, while the overall debt-income ratio has generally trended upward since 1983 and actually took a big jump from 2001 to 2007.

Table 2.5 compares the wealth composition of the three wealth classes in 1983 and 2007. There is remarkable stability in the composition of wealth by wealth class between 1983 and 2007. The most notable exception is a substitution of pension assets for liquid assets—a transition that occurred for all three wealth classes but that was particularly marked for percentiles 81–99 and for the middle three quintiles. The debt-equity ratio actually fell for the top 1 percent from 1983 and 2007, as did the debt-income ratio. The debt-income ratio increased slightly for the next 19 percent, while the debt-income ratio rose sharply, from 73 to 110 percent.

Among the middle three wealth quintiles, pension accounts rose as a share of total assets by almost 12 percentage points (and the proportion of households with a pension account surged by 41 percentage points) from 1983 to 2007, while liquid assets declined as a share by 14 percentage points. This set of changes paralleled that of all households. The share of all stocks in total assets mushroomed from 2.4 percent in 1983 to 13 percent in 2001, and then fell off to 7 percent in 2007 as stock prices stagnated.

Changes in debt, however, were much more dramatic. There was a sharp rise in the debt-equity ratio of the middle class, from 37 percent in 1983 to 61 percent in 2007. The rise was much steeper than at the aggregate level. The debt-income ratio skyrocketed over this period, more than doubling. Here, too, much of the increase happened between

Table 2.5 Composition of Household Wealth by Wealth Class, 1983 and 2007 (percent of gross assets)

Component	Top 1%		Next 19%		Middle 3 quintiles	
	1983	2007	1983	2007	1983	2007
Principal residence	8.1	10.2	29.1	31.8	61.6	65.1
Liquid assets (bank deposits, money market funds, and cash surrender value of life insurance)	8.5	4.5	21.4	7.3	21.4	7.8
Pension accounts	0.9	5.8	2.0	15.9	1.2	12.9
Corporate stock, financial securities, mutual funds, and personal trusts	29.5	25.2	13.0	15.0	3.1	3.6
Unincorporated business equity, other real estate	52.0	52.3	32.8	28.5	11.4	9.3
Miscellaneous assets	1.0	2.0	1.6	1.6	1.3	1.3
Total assets	100.0	100.0	100.0	100.0	100.0	100.0
Debt/equity ratio	5.9	2.8	10.9	12.1	37.4	61.1
Debt/income ratio	86.8	39.4	72.8	109.8	66.9	156.7

NOTE: Totals may not sum to 100.0 due to rounding.
SOURCE: Author's computations from the 1983 and 2007 SCF.

2001 and 2007. Moreover, the increase was much steeper than in the aggregate. In fact, in 1983, the debt-income ratio was about the same for middle-class as for all households, but by 2007 the ratio was much larger. As for all households, net home equity as a percentage of total assets fell for the middle class from 1983 to 2007, and mortgage debt as a proportion of house value rose. Middle-class households were using their homes as a virtual ATM, withdrawing equity to sustain their normal consumption.

The rising indebtedness of the middle class, particularly in the form of mortgage debt, made it very vulnerable to the home price collapse of 2007–2009. As we shall see below, there was a large reduction in median wealth over this period, as well as a substantial increase in the share of homeowners whose mortgage debt was greater than their home values (so-called underwater mortgages). Though the rich were more heavily invested in stocks than the middle class, stocks did not constitute nearly as high a percentage of their wealth as homes did for the middle class, and the stock market meltdown of 2007–2009 did not hurt the rich as much as the home price collapse hurt the middle class.

THE RACIAL DIVIDE REMAINS LARGELY UNCHANGED OVER TIME

Striking differences are found in the wealth holdings of different racial and ethnic groups. In Tables 2.6 and 2.7, households are divided into three groups: 1) non-Hispanic whites, 2) non-Hispanic African Americans, and 3) Hispanics.[8] In 2007, while the ratio of mean incomes between (non-Hispanic) white and (non-Hispanic) black households was an already-low 0.48 and the ratio of median incomes was 0.60, the ratios of mean and median wealth holdings were even lower, at 0.19 and 0.06, respectively.[9] The homeownership rate for black households was 49 percent in 2007, a little less than two-thirds the rate among whites, and the percentage of black households with zero or negative net worth stood at 33.4, more than double the corresponding percentage among whites.

Between 1982 and 2006, while the average real income of non-Hispanic white households increased by 42 percent and the median by 10 percent, the former rose by only 28 percent for non-Hispanic black households but the latter by 18 percent. As a result, the ratio of mean income slipped from 0.54 in 1982 to 0.48 in 2006, while the ratio of median income rose from 0.56 to 0.60.

Between 1983 and 2001, average net worth (in 2001 dollars) rose by a whopping 73 percent for whites but only by 31 percent for black households, so that the net worth ratio fell from 0.19 to 0.14. Most of the slippage occurred between 1989 and 2001, when white net worth surged by a spectacular 46 percent and black net worth advanced by only a respectable 24 percent. Indeed, mean net worth growth among black households was actually much higher in the 1989–2001 years than in the years from 1983 to 1989 (only a 5 percent gain). The difference in the 1989–2001 period was the huge increase in household

**Table 2.6 Household Income and Wealth by Race, 1983–2007
(in thousands, 2007$)**

Year	Means			Medians		
	Non-Hispanic whites	Non-Hispanic African Americans	Ratio	Non-Hispanic whites	Non-Hispanic African Americans	Ratio
Income						
1982	64.8	34.9	0.54	45.6	25.4	0.56
1988	71.0	31.6	0.45	47.3	17.9	0.38
2000	88.9	43.0	0.48	51.5	29.3	0.57
2006	92.3	44.6	0.48	50.0	30.0	0.60
Net worth						
1983	316.0	59.5	0.19	91.0	6.1	0.07
1989	373.9	62.7	0.17	108.1	2.8	0.03
2001	545.3	77.7	0.14	124.6	12.5	0.10
2007	652.1	122.7	0.19	143.6	9.3	0.06
Homeowner-ship rate (%)						
1983	68.1	44.3	0.65			
1989	69.3	41.7	0.60			
2001	74.1	47.4	0.64			
2007	74.8	48.6	0.65			

NOTE: Households are divided into four racial/ethnic groups: 1) non-Hispanic whites, 2) non-Hispanic blacks, 3) Hispanics, and 4) American Indians, Asians, and others. For 1995, 1998, and 2001, the classification scheme does not explicitly indicate non-Hispanic whites and non-Hispanic blacks for the first two categories, so some Hispanics may have classified themselves as either whites or blacks.
SOURCE: Author's computations from the 1983, 1989, 2001, and 2007 SCF.

wealth among white households. However, between 2001 and 2007, mean net worth among black households gained an astounding 58 percent while white wealth advanced only 29 percent, so that by 2007 the net worth ratio was back to 0.19, the same level as in 1983.

It is not clear how much of the sharp increase in the racial wealth gap between 1989 and 2001 and the turnaround between 2001 and 2007 is due to actual wealth changes in the African American community and how much is due to sampling variability (since the sample sizes of non-Hispanic African Americans are relatively small in all years). However,

Table 2.7 Family Income and Wealth for Non-Hispanic Whites and Hispanics, 1983–2007 (in thousands, 2007$)

Year	Means			Medians		
	Non-Hispanic whites	Hispanics	Ratio	Non-Hispanic whites	Hispanics	Ratio
Income						
1982	64.8	39.2	0.60	45.6	30.2	0.66
1988	71.0	32.4	0.46	47.3	22.7	0.48
2000	88.9	44.0	0.50	51.5	28.1	0.55
2006	92.3	46.4	0.50	50.0	35.0	0.70
Net worth						
1983	316.0	51.4	0.16	91.0	3.5	0.04
1989	373.9	61.5	0.16	108.1	2.3	0.02
2001	545.3	93.8	0.17	124.6	3.5	0.03
2007	652.1	170.4	0.26	143.6	9.1	0.06
Homeowner-ship rate (%)						
1983	68.1	32.6	0.48			
1989	69.3	39.8	0.57			
2001	74.1	44.3	0.60			
2007	74.8	49.2	0.66			

NOTE: Households are divided into four racial/ethnic groups: 1) non-Hispanic whites, 2) non-Hispanic blacks, 3) Hispanics, and 4) American Indians, Asians, and others. For 1995, 1998, and 2001, the classification scheme does not explicitly indicate non-Hispanic whites and non-Hispanic blacks for the first two categories, so some Hispanics may have classified themselves as either whites or blacks.
SOURCE: Author's computations from the 1983, 1989, 2001, and 2007 SCF.

one salient difference between the two groups is the much higher share that stocks constituted in the white portfolio and the much higher share that homes constituted in the portfolio of black households. In 2001, the gross value of principal residences formed 46 percent of the gross assets of black households and only 27 percent that of white households, while (total) stocks were 25 percent of the total assets of whites and only 15 percent that of black households.[10] Moreover, while the debt-to-asset ratio was higher for black than white households in 2001 (0.32 versus 0.12), the ratio among black households rose to 0.36 in 2007. For whites the debt-to-asset ratio increased slightly, to 0.13, in 2007.

In the case of median wealth, the black-white ratio first increased from 7 to 10 percent between 1983 and 2001 but then slipped to 6 percent in 2007. In this case, median wealth for white households grew by 15 percent between 2001 and 2004 but median wealth dropped by 26 percent among black households, reflecting in part the rising share of black households with zero or negative net worth.

The homeownership rate of black households grew from 44 to 47 percent between 1983 and 2001, but, relative to white households, the homeownership rate fell off a bit, from a ratio of 0.65 in 1983 to 0.64 in 2001. The change over these years primarily reflected a big jump—6 percentage points—in the white homeownership rate. However, from 2001 to 2007, the black homeownership rate gained 1.2 percentage points and the white homeownership rate 0.7 percentage points, so by 2007 the homeownership rate ratio had recovered a bit, to 0.65.

The picture is somewhat different for Hispanics (see Table 2.7). The ratio of mean income between Hispanics and non-Hispanic whites in 2007 was 0.50, almost the same as that between African American and white households. However, the ratio of median income was 0.70, much higher than the 0.60 ratio between black and white households. The ratio of mean net worth was 0.26, compared to a ratio of 0.19 between blacks and whites. However, the ratio of medians was 0.06, almost identical to the ratio between blacks and whites. The Hispanic homeownership rate was 49 percent, almost identical to that of non-Hispanic black households.

Developments among Hispanic households over the period from 1983 to 2007 were generally a positive story. Mean household income for Hispanics grew by 18 percent and median household income by 16 percent, so that while the ratio of mean income between Hispanics and non-Hispanic whites slid from 60 to 50 percent, that of median income advanced from 66 to 70 percent. In fact, from 2001 to 2007 median income for Hispanics grew by an astonishing 25 percent while that for non-Hispanic whites declined by 3 percent.

Between 1983 and 2001, mean wealth almost doubled for Hispanic households, and the ratio of mean net worth between Hispanics and non-Hispanic whites improved slightly, from 16 percent in 1983 to 17 percent in 2001. However, from 2001 to 2007, mean net worth among Hispanics climbed by another 82 percent, while that of whites gained

20 percent, so the corresponding wealth ratio advanced to 26 percent, quite a bit higher than that between black and white households.

On the other hand, from 1983 to 2007, median wealth among Hispanics remained extremely low and largely unchanged, so the ratio of median wealth between Hispanics and non-Hispanic whites stayed virtually the same. The homeownership rate among Hispanic households climbed from 33 to 44 percent between 1983 and 2001, and the ratio of homeownership rates between Hispanics and non-Hispanic whites likewise rose from 0.48 to 0.60. Between 2001 and 2007, the Hispanic homeownership rate rose once again, to 49 percent, about the same as for black households, and the homeownership ratio surged to 0.66.

Despite some progress from 2001 to 2007, the respective wealth gaps between blacks and whites and between Hispanics and non-Hispanic whites were still much greater than the corresponding income gaps in 2007. While mean income ratios were on the order of 50 percent, mean wealth ratios were on the order of 20 to 25 percent. While blacks and Hispanics were left out of the wealth surge of the years 1989 to 2001 because of relatively low stock ownership (see the subsequent section on stock ownership), they actually benefited from this (and the relatively high share of houses in their portfolio) in the 2001–2007 period.[11]

WEALTH SHIFTS FROM THE YOUNG TO THE OLD

As shown in Table 2.8, the cross-sectional age-wealth profiles of 1983, 1989, 2001, and 2007 generally follow the predicted hump-shaped pattern of the life-cycle model (see, for example, Modigliani [1954]). Mean wealth increases with age up through age 65 or so and then falls off (see Figure 2.2). Homeownership rates also have a similar profile, though the falloff after the peak age is much more attenuated than for the wealth numbers. In 2007, the wealth of elderly households (age 65 and over) averaged 75 percent higher than that of the nonelderly, and their homeownership rate was 21 percentage points higher.

Despite the apparent similarity in the profiles, there have been notable shifts in the relative wealth holdings of age groups between 1983

Table 2.8 Age-Wealth Profiles and Homeownership Rates by Age, 1983–2007

Age	1983	1989	2001	2007
Mean net worth (ratio to overall mean)				
Overall	1.00	1.00	1.00	1.00
Under 35	0.21	0.29	0.19	0.17
35–44	0.71	0.72	0.64	0.58
45–54	1.53	1.50	1.25	1.19
55–64	1.67	1.58	1.86	1.69
65–74	1.93	1.61	1.72	1.86
75+	1.05	1.26	1.20	1.16
Homeownership rate (%)				
Overall	63.4	62.8	67.7	68.6
Under 35	38.7	36.3	40.2	40.8
35–44	68.4	64.1	67.6	66.1
45–54	78.2	75.1	76.1	77.3
55–64	77.0	79.2	83.2	80.9
65–74	78.3	78.1	82.5	85.5
75+	69.4	70.2	76.2	77.0

NOTE: Households are classified according to the age of the householder.
SOURCE: Author's computations from the 1983, 1989, 2001, and 2007 SCF.

and 2007. The relative wealth of the youngest age group, under 35, expanded from 21 percent of the overall mean in 1983 to 29 percent in 1989 but then collapsed to only 17 percent in 2007. In 2007, the mean wealth of the youngest age group was $91,200, which was only slightly more than the mean wealth of this age group in 1989 ($88,500). The mean net worth of the next-youngest age group, 35–44, relative to the overall mean showed a slight increase from 1983 to 1989 and then tumbled from 0.72 in 1989 to 0.58 in 2007. The relative wealth of the third-youngest age group, 45–54, also declined rather steadily over time, from 1.53 in 1983 to 1.19 in 2007. The relative wealth of age group 55–64, after falling between 1983 and 1989, advanced from 1.58 in 1989 to 1.69 in 2007. The relative net worth of age group 65–74 plummeted from 1.93 in 1983 to 1.61 in 1989 but then regained most of the lost ground, reaching 1.86 in 2007. The wealth of the oldest age group, aged 75 and over, advanced from a ratio of 1.05 in 1983 to 1.16

Figure 2.2 Age-Wealth Profiles, 2007 (ratio to overall mean wealth by age group)

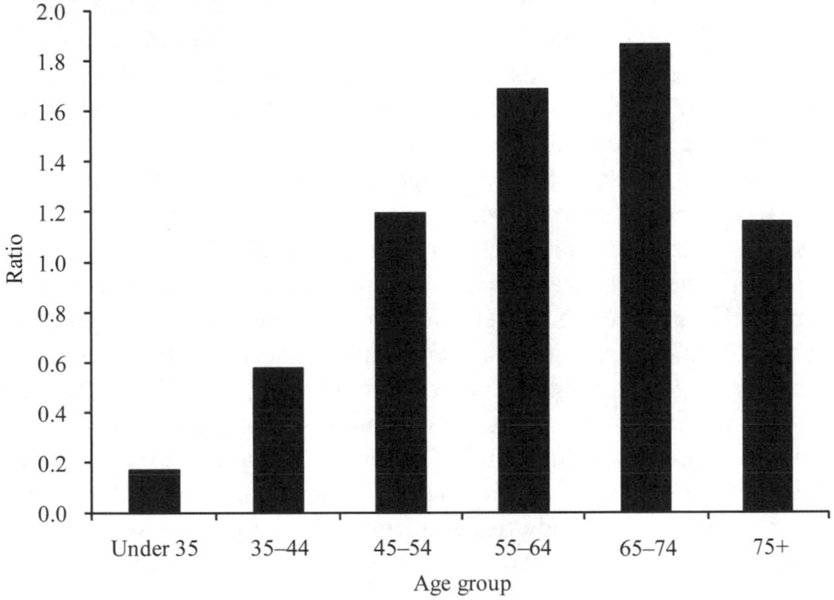

SOURCE: Author's computations from the 2007 SCF.

in 2007. At least over the period from 1989 to 2007, there was a clear shift in relative wealth holdings away from younger households (under age 55) and toward those in age group 55–64.

Changes in homeownership rates tend to mirror these trends. While the overall ownership rate increased by 5.2 percentage points, from 63.4 to 68.6 percent, between 1983 and 2007, the share of households in the youngest age group owning their own home increased by only 2.1 percentage points. The homeownership rate of households between ages 35 and 44 actually fell by 2.3 percentage points, and that of age group 45–54 declined by 0.9 percentage points. Big gains in homeownership were recorded by the older age groups: 3.9 percentage points for age group 55–64, 7.1 percentage points for age group 65–74, and 7.6 percentage points for the oldest age group. By 2007, homeownership rates rose monotonically with age up to age group 65–74 and then dropped for the oldest age group. The statistics point to a relative shifting of homeownership away from younger toward older households between 1983 and 2007.

Changes in the relative wealth position of different age groups depend in large measure on differences in asset composition and relative asset price movements. The latter are highlighted in Table 2.9 for the year 2007. The gross value of the principal residence comprised over half the value of total assets for age group 35 and under, and its share of total assets fell off with age to about a quarter for age group 55–64 and then rose to 30 percent for age group 75 and over. Liquid assets as a share of total assets remained relatively flat with age group at around 6 percent except for the oldest group, for whom it was 11 percent, perhaps reflecting the relative financial conservativeness of older people. Pension accounts as a share of total assets rose from 4 percent for the youngest group to 16 percent for age group 55–64 and then fell off to 5 percent for the oldest age group. This pattern likely reflects the buildup of retirement assets until retirement age and then a decline as these retirement assets are liquidated.[12] Corporate stock and financial securities showed a steady rise with age, from a 4 percent share for the youngest group to a 26 percent share for the oldest. A similar pattern was evident for total stocks as a percentage of all assets. Unincorporated business equity and nonhome real estate was relatively flat as a share of total assets with age, at about 30 percent.

There was a pronounced falloff of debt with age. The debt-to-equity ratio declined from 93 percent for the youngest group to 2 percent for the oldest, the debt-income ratio from 168 percent to 30 percent, and principal residence debt as a share of house value from 65 to 5 percent. As a result of the latter, net home equity as a proportion of total assets rose from 19 to 29 percent from the youngest to the oldest age group.

Younger households were thus more heavily invested in homes and more heavily in debt, whereas the portfolio of older households was more heavily skewed to financial assets, particularly corporate stock. As a result, younger households benefit relatively when housing prices rise and inflation is strong, while older households benefit relatively from rising stock prices. Conversely, younger households were much more exposed to the home price collapse of 2007–2008 than older ones, while older households were more vulnerable to the stock market crisis of 2007–2009 than younger ones. Changes in the relative net worth position of age groups over the 1983–2007 period were thus largely due to these relative asset price movements.

Table 2.9 Composition of Household Wealth by Age Class, 2007 (percentage of gross assets)

Asset	All	Under 35	35–44	45–54	55–64	65–74	75+
Principal residence	32.8	54.3	43.7	33.8	25.6	28.2	30.2
Liquid assets (bank deposits, money market funds, and cash surrender value of life insurance)	6.6	5.7	5.4	6.4	6.3	6.1	10.5
Pension accounts	12.1	6.0	10.7	13.0	15.8	12.9	5.0
Corporate stock, financial securities, mutual funds, and personal trusts	15.5	4.2	8.6	13.1	16.4	20.5	25.6
Unincorporated business equity, other real estate	31.3	28.7	30.1	32.0	34.4	30.2	27.1
Miscellaneous assets	1.7	1.2	1.5	1.7	1.5	2.1	1.6
Total assets	100.0	100.0	100.0	100.0	100.0	100.0	100.0
Selected ratios (%)							
Debt/equity ratio	18.1	92.7	41.3	20.2	11.9	7.1	2.1
Debt/income ratio	118.7	167.5	156.5	118.2	100.0	79.7	29.9
Net home equity/total assets[a]	21.4	18.8	21.3	20.9	18.1	23.4	28.7
Principal residence debt/house value	34.9	65.4	51.4	38.3	29.2	16.9	4.9
All stocks/total assets[b]	16.8	5.9	11.2	15.1	19.4	21.5	20.0

NOTE: Households are classified into age class according to the age of the household head. Totals may not sum to 100.0 due to rounding.
[a] Ratio of gross value of principal residence less mortgage debt on principal residence to total assets.
[b] Includes direct ownership of stock shares and indirect ownership through mutual funds, trusts, IRAs, Keogh plans, 401(k) plans, and other retirement accounts.
SOURCE: Author's computations from the 2007 SCF.

STOCK OWNERSHIP FIRST RISES AND THEN FALLS

Table 2.10a reports on overall stock ownership trends from 1989 to 2007.[13] The years 1989–2001 saw a substantial increase in stock ownership. The share of households with direct ownership of stock climbed from 13 percent in 1989 to 21 percent in 2001, while the share with some stock owned either outright or indirectly through mutual funds, trusts, or various pension accounts surged from 32 to 52 percent. Much of the increase was fueled by the growth in pension accounts like IRAs, Keogh plans, and 401(k) plans (see Chapter 4 for more details on this). Between 1989 and 2001, the share of households owning stock through a pension account more than doubled, accounting for the bulk of the overall increase in stock ownership. Indirect ownership of stocks through mutual funds also greatly expanded over the 1989–2001 period, from 6 to 17 percent, as did indirect ownership through trust funds, from 1.6 to 5.1 percent. All told, the share of households with indirect ownership of stocks doubled, from 24 percent in 1989 to 48 percent in 2001.

In contrast, the next six years, 2001–2007, saw a retrenchment in stock ownership. This trend probably reflected the sharp drop in the stock market from 2000 to 2001, its rather anemic recovery through 2004, and its modest rebound from 2004 to 2007. Direct stock ownership plummeted from 21 percent in 2001 to 18 percent. Indirect stock ownership fell by 3.3 percentage points from 2001 to 2007. This decrease was largely due to a sharp decline in stock ownership through mutual funds (down by 6 percentage points). Stock ownership through pension accounts was down by 1.2 percentage points from 2001 to 2007.

By 2007 the share of households who owned stock directly or indirectly dipped below half, down to 49 percent from its peak of 52 percent in 2001. Moreover, many of these families had only a minor stake in the stock market in 2007: only 35 percent owned total stock holdings worth $5,000 (in 1995 dollars) or more, down from 40 percent in 2001; only 30 percent owned $10,000 or more of stock, down from 35 percent in 2001; and only 22 percent owned $25,000 or more of stock, down from 27 percent six years earlier.

Direct plus indirect ownership of stocks as a percentage of total household assets more than doubled, increasing from 10 in 1989 to 25

Table 2.10a Stock Ownership, 1989, 2001, and 2007 (percentage of households holding stocks)

Stock type	1989	2001	2007
Direct stock holdings only	13.1	21.3	17.9
Indirect stock holdings only	23.5	47.7	44.4
Through mutual funds	5.9	16.7	10.6
Through pension accounts	19.5	41.4	40.2
Through trust funds	1.6	5.1	4.1
All stock holdings[a]			
Any holdings	31.7	51.9	49.1
Stock worth $5,000 or more[b]	22.6	40.1	34.6
Stock worth $10,000 or more[b]	18.5	35.1	29.6
Stock worth $25,000 or more[b]	10.5	27.1	22.1
Direct plus indirect stocks as a percentage of total assets	10.2	24.5	16.8

[a] Includes direct ownership of stock shares and indirect ownership through mutual funds, trusts, IRAs, Keogh plans, 401(k) plans, and other retirement accounts.
[b] 1995 dollars.
SOURCE: Author's computations from the 1983, 1989, 2001, and 2007 SCF.

in 2001. This increase may reflect in large measure the 171 percent surge in stock prices over these years. However, between 2001 and 2007, the share plummeted to 17 percent. This change is a result not only of the relative stagnation of the stock market over these years but also of the withdrawal of many families from the stock market.

Table 2.10b shows the distribution of total stocks owned, by vehicle of ownership. Here there are very marked time trends. Direct stock holdings as a share of total stock holdings fell almost continuously over time, from 54 percent in 1989 to 37 percent in 2007. In contrast, stock held in mutual funds as a share of total stock rose almost continuously over time, from 9 percent in 1983 to 21 percent in 2007, while that held in trust funds declined by 6 percentage points.

The most interesting pattern is with regard to stock held in DC pension accounts (including IRAs). Its share of total stocks first increased from 24 percent in 1989 to 34 percent in 2001 but then fell off to 31 percent in 2007. The trend from 2001 to 2007 seems to reflect a substitution of stock holdings in mutual funds for those in pension plans as investors looked for safer retirement accounts (see below). Likewise, the share of

Table 2.10b Distribution of Stock Ownership by Asset Type, 1989–2007 (percentage of total stock held in each asset type)

Stock type	1989	2001	2007	1989–2007
Direct stock holdings	54.0	38.5	37.1	−16.9
Indirect stock holdings only	46.0	61.5	62.9	16.9
Through mutual funds	8.5	16.0	21.3	12.8
Through pension accounts	24.4	33.5	31.4	7.0
Through trust funds	13.2	12.0	7.2	−6.0
Stocks held in pension accounts/ total value of pension accounts	32.6	66.3	43.6	11.1

[a] Includes direct ownership of stock shares and indirect ownership through mutual funds, trusts, IRAs, Keogh plans, 401(k) plans, and other retirement accounts.
SOURCE: Author's computations from the 1983, 1989, 2001, and 2007 SCF.

the total value of pension plans held as stock doubled between 1989 and 2001, from 33 to 66 percent, and then plummeted to 44 percent in 2007. The sharp tail-off in stock ownership in pension plans after 2001 likely reflects both the lethargic performance of the stock market over this period and the search for more secure investments among plan holders.

Stock ownership is also highly skewed by wealth and income class. As shown in Table 2.11a, 93 percent of the very rich (the top 1 percent) reported owning stock either directly or indirectly in 2007, compared to 48 percent of the middle quintile and 16 percent of the poorest 20 percent. While 88 percent of the very rich also reported stocks worth $10,000 or more, only 22 percent of the middle quintile and 2 percent of the bottom quintile did so. The top 1 percent of households owned 38 percent of all stocks, the top 5 percent 69 percent, the top 10 percent 81 percent, and the top quintile over 90 percent.

Stock ownership also tails off by income class (see Table 2.11b). Whereas 94 percent of households in the top 3.6 percent of income recipients (those who earned $250,000 or more) owned stock in 2007, 39 percent of the middle class (incomes between $25,000 and $50,000), 23 percent of the lower middle class (incomes between $15,000 and $25,000), and only 11 percent of poor households (income under $15,000) reported stock ownership. The comparable ownership figures for stock holdings of $10,000 or more are 91 percent for the top income class, 19 percent for the middle class, 12 percent for the lower middle class, and 4 percent for the poor. Moreover, 84 percent of all stocks were owned by households earning $75,000 or more (the top 30 percent) and 92 percent by those earning $50,000 or more in terms of income.

Another notable development in the 2000s was an increase in the concentration of stock ownership, as shown in the last column of Tables 2.11a–b. The share of total stock owned by the richest 1 percent in terms of wealth increased from 34 percent in 2001 to 38 percent in 2007, and that of the richest 5 percent from 62 to 69 percent. In terms of income, the share of total stock owned by the top income class jumped from 41 to 54 percent (though it should be noted the top income class's share of total households also rose, from 2.7 to 3.6 percent) and that of the top two income classes from 69 to 75 percent. One result of the stock market bust of the early 2000s was a withdrawal from the market by middle-class families.

Thus, in terms of wealth or income, substantial stock holdings have still not penetrated much beyond the reach of the rich and the upper middle class. The big winners from the stock market boom of the late 1990s (as well as the big losers in the early 2000s) were these groups, while the middle class and the poor did not see sizable benefits from the bull market (or losses when the stock market tanked in 2000–2002). It is also apparent which groups were most exposed to the 2007–2009 stock market crash.

AN UPDATE TO 2009

A complete update of the wealth figures to 2009 is beyond the scope of the present study. However, it is possible to provide a partial update of the wealth figures to July 1, 2009, based on two notable developments. The first is that house prices fell by 24 percent in real terms, and the second is that the S&P 500 index was down by 41 percent in real terms.[14] A somewhat rough update, based on the change in housing and stock prices, shows a marked deterioration in middle-class wealth.[15] According to my estimates, while mean wealth (in 2007 dollars) fell by 17.3 percent between 2007 and 2009 to $443,600, median wealth plunged by an astounding 36.1 percent to $65,400 (about the same level as in 1992!).

Table 2.11a Concentration of Stock Ownership by Wealth Class, 2007 (in 2007$)

| Wealth class | Percentage of households owning stock worth more than | | | Percentage of stock owned | | | |
	Zero	$4,999	$9,999	Shares	Cumulative	Cumulative—2001
Top 1%	92.6	89.1	88.4	38.3	38.3	33.5
Next 4%	92.2	90.7	89.5	30.8	69.1	62.3
Next 5%	86.8	85.0	81.4	12.1	81.2	76.9
Next 10%	82.1	77.1	71.2	9.9	91.1	89.3
Second quintile	65.4	54.3	47.1	6.4	97.5	97.1
Third quintile	47.7	28.9	22.1	1.9	99.4	99.3
Fourth quintile	30.3	12.3	8.7	0.5	99.9	99.8
Bottom quintile	16.3	3.5	2.0	0.1	100.0	100.0
All	49.1	36.3	31.6	100.0		

NOTE: Includes direct ownership of stock shares and indirect ownership through mutual funds, trusts, IRAs, Keogh plans, 401(k) plans, and other retirement accounts.

SOURCE: Author's computations from the 2007 SCF.

Table 2.11b Concentration of Stock Ownership by Income Class, 2007 (in 2007$)

Income level ($)	Share of households	Percentage of households owning stock worth more than			Percentage of stock owned		
		Zero	$4,999	$9,999	Shares	Cumulative	Cumulative—2001
250,000 or more	3.6	95.4	93.4	91.3	53.7	53.7	40.6
100,000–249,999	15.5	84.5	71.0	63.7	21.5	75.2	68.6
75,000–99,999	10.4	71.1	55.6	49.6	9.0	84.3	77.4
50,000–74,999	17.5	58.1	40.7	34.9	7.7	92.0	89.3
25,000–49,999	27.1	39.3	23.6	19.0	5.7	97.7	97.6
15,000–24,999	12.7	23.1	15.7	11.9	1.1	98.8	98.9
Under $15,000	13.3	11.2	5.0	4.3	1.2	100.0	100.0
All	100.0	49.1	36.3	31.8	100.0		

NOTE: Includes direct ownership of stock shares and indirect ownership through mutual funds, trusts, IRAs, Keogh plans, 401(k) plans, and other retirement accounts.

SOURCE: Author's computations from the 2007 SCF.

Trends in inequality are also important. According to previous research (Wolff 2002a), wealth inequality is very sensitive and positively related to the ratio of stock prices to housing prices, since the former is heavily concentrated among the rich and the latter is the chief asset of the middle class (see the following section). The fact that stock prices fell more than housing prices, at least from 2007 to mid-2009, should lead to a decline in wealth inequality over these two years. However, instead, the results show a fairly steep rise in wealth inequality, with the Gini coefficient climbing from 0.834 to 0.865. The share of wealth for the top 1 percent advanced from 34.6 to 37.1 percent, that of the top 5 percent from 61.8 to 65.0 percent, and that of the top quintile from 85.0 to 87.7 percent, while that of the second quintile fell from 10.9 to 10.0 percent, that of the middle quintile from 4.0 to 3.1 percent, and that of the bottom two quintiles from 0.2 to −0.8 percent. There was also a large expansion in the share of households with zero or negative net worth, from 19 to 24 percent.

On the surface, these results appear somewhat surprising in light of the earlier regression results. However, while stock prices fell more than house prices, houses were a much larger share of the gross assets of the middle class than stocks were of the rich. As shown in Table 2.5, homes comprised 65 percent of the gross assets of the three middle wealth quintiles in 2007, whereas stocks made up 21 percent of the gross assets of the top 1 percent and 19 percent of the gross assets of the next richest 19 percent of households. As a result, the middle class took a bigger relative hit from the decline in home prices on their net worth than the top 20 percent did from the stock market decline. This is also reflected in the fact that median wealth dropped much more in percentage terms than mean wealth. Moreover, the rapid decline in house prices over these two years left 17 percent of homeowners "underwater," with greater mortgage debt than the value of their homes.

A WEALTH INEQUALITY PUZZLE

A puzzle about wealth inequality trends was encountered in my earlier work (Wolff 2002a). In particular, the share of total household wealth held by the richest 1 percent of households increased only a bit between 1989 and 1998, and the Gini coefficient for total household wealth actually declined slightly. I expected both the share of the top 1 percent and the Gini coefficient to have shown a considerable increase.

I expected wealth inequality to increase because in this work I identify two factors that seem to underlie much of the change in the share of wealth held by the top 1 percent. The first is the change in basic income inequality, and the second is the change in the ratio of stock prices to housing prices (see Figure 2.3). In a simple regression of the share of the top 1 percent on these two factors, both variables proved positive and statistically significant, and the goodness of the fit of the equation was quite high.[16] Over the period 1989–1998, income inequality, as measured by the share of the top 5 percent, increased by 2.8 percentage points, and the ratio of share prices to housing prices surged by a factor of 2.5. Extrapolating on the basis of the regression estimates, I would have expected a 9.9 percentage point increase in the share of the top 1 percent between 1989 and 1998, compared to its actual gain of 0.7 percentage points (see Figure 2.4).[17]

Figure 2.3 Wealth Inequality, Income Inequality, and the Ratio of Stock Prices to House Prices, 1922–1998

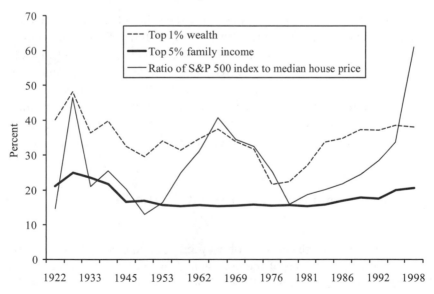

SOURCE: Wolff (2002a).

Figure 2.4 Predicted versus Actual Wealth Inequality, 1922–1998

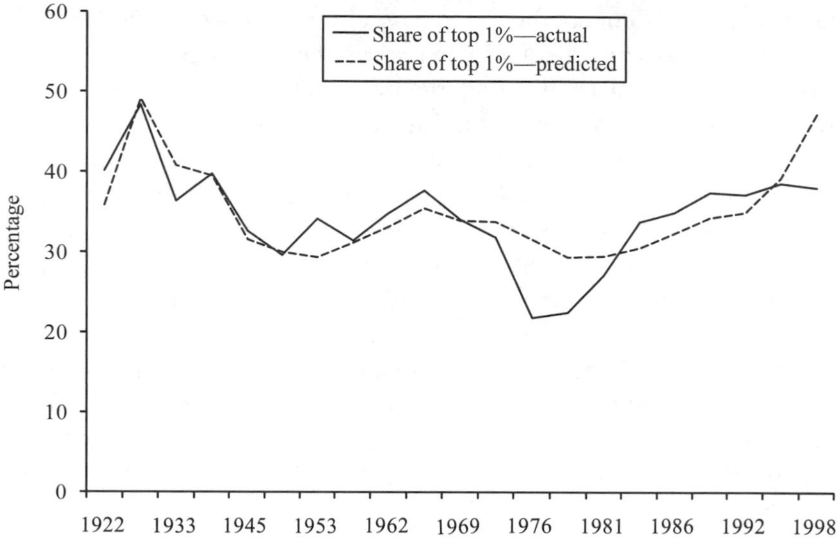

SOURCE: Wolff (2002a).

We shall see in Chapter 5 that this puzzle is largely resolved once we extend the concept of household wealth to include DB pension wealth. Once we include DB pension wealth in our measure, we find that the inequality of this extended measure does, in fact, show an increase between 1989 and 1998 (and indeed through 2007). The reason, as we shall see later, is that DB pension wealth is more equally distributed than conventional household wealth, and its shrinkage over time led to a rise in wealth inequality. This is discussed more in Chapter 5.

SUMMARY AND CONCLUDING COMMENTS

Median net worth showed robust gains over the period 1983–2007. In fact, the growth rate of median wealth accelerated from the 1980s to the 1990s and into the 2001–2007 period. However, the gains of the 2001–2007 period were based largely on rising home prices financed by increasing mortgage debt. This growth came to an abrupt end in 2007 with the collapse in home prices, and median wealth plummeted from 2007 through 2009.

Household wealth inequality showed a sharp increase from 1983 to 1989. However, from 1989 to 2007 there was almost no change in the degree of wealth inequality. This trend was surprising because the two factors normally positively associated with wealth inequality, income inequality and the ratio of stock prices to home prices, both showed a marked rise over the same years, 1989 to 2007. However, according to my projections, there was a fairly steep rise in wealth inequality from 2007 to 2009, as the collapse in housing prices hurt the middle class more than the decline in stock prices affected the rich.

A striking shift occurred in the portfolio composition of household wealth out of liquid assets and into DC pension accounts over the years 1989–2001, though pension accounts as a share of total assets also fell off a bit from 2001 to 2007. There was also a noticeable expansion of stock ownership from 1989 to 2001, but this was followed by a mild contraction between 2001 and 2007. Defined contribution pension accounts, moreover, became more heavily invested in equities, making them vulnerable to the stock market downturn of 2007 to 2009. We shall see more about this in Chapters 4 and 5.

Moreover, despite the buoyant economy over the 1980s and 1990s, overall indebtedness continued to rise among American families and then shot up in the 2000s. Among the middle class in particular, the debt-income ratio reached its highest level in 24 years. Mortgage debt on middle-class homeowners' property exploded from 29 percent in 1983 to 47 percent in 2007 (and among all homeowners from 21 to 35 percent). The high level of mortgage indebtedness made the middle class particularly vulnerable to the collapse of the housing market at the end of the decade of the 2000s. In fact, I estimate that 17 percent of homeowners were "underwater" by 2009.

The mean wealth of African Americans was only 19 percent that of white families in 1983, and that ratio barely budged during 1983–2007. The black homeownership rate did climb from 44 percent in 1983 to 49 percent in 2007, but relative to white households it was the same in 2007 (a ratio of 0.65) as in 1983. The mean wealth of Hispanic households was also very low compared to non-Hispanic whites in 1983, a ratio of 0.16, but Hispanics did show some gains in mean wealth relative to non-Hispanic whites, particularly in 2001–2007, and the ratio advanced to 0.26. The homeownership rate among Hispanic households also ascended, from a meager 33 percent in 1983 to 49 percent in 2007, the same level as African Americans, and the ratio of homeownership rates between Hispanics and non-Hispanic whites advanced from 48 percent in 1983 to 66 percent in 2007.

Young households (under the age of 45), after some relative gains from 1983 to 1989, saw their relative wealth position deteriorate between 1989 and 2007. This development made young households particularly exposed to the joint collapse of the stock and housing markets at the end of the decade of the 2000s.

These results on traditional net worth will set the stage for the later analysis of wealth trends once we include DB pension wealth and Social Security wealth in the definition of (augmented) wealth. In Chapters 4 and 5, we will see how pension wealth and augmented wealth grew over the years 1983–2007 and how the inequality of augmented wealth changed over this period. In Chapter 6, we will also reexamine the racial divide and age class differences once retirement wealth is included in household wealth. In the same chapter we will also look at relative developments in augmented wealth by income class and wealth class.

Notes

1. These figures are based on the BLS hourly wage series. The BLS wage figures are converted to constant dollars on the basis of the CPI-U.
2. The Census Bureau uses the newer CPI-U-RS series to convert to constant dollars. However, for this period, there is virtually no difference between the CPI-U and the CPI-U-RS.
3. I choose these years to be consistent with the later chapters on pension and Social Security wealth. However, the SCF was also conducted in the years 1992, 1995, and 2004.
4. For a discussion of some of the issues involved in developing these weights, see, for example, Kennickell and Woodburn (1999) for the 1989 SCF, or Kennickell (2001) for the 2001 SCF.
5. It should be noted that the income in each survey year (for instance, 2007) is for the preceding year (2006 in this case).
6. The SCF data show a much higher level of income inequality than the CPS data. In the year 2000, for example, the CPS data show the share of the top 5 percent as being 22.1 percent and the Gini coefficient as being 0.462. The difference is primarily due to three factors. First, the SCF oversamples the rich (as noted above),

while the CPS is a representative sample. Second, the CPS data are top-coded (that is, there is an open-ended interval at the top, typically at $75,000 or $100,000), whereas the SCF data are not. Third, the income concepts differ between the two samples. In particular, the SCF income definition includes realized capital gains whereas the CPS definition does not. However, the CPS data also show a large increase in inequality between 1989 and 2000, with the share of the top 5 percent rising from 18.9 to 22.1 percent and the Gini coefficient from 0.431 to 0.462. Further analysis of the difference in income figures between the two surveys is beyond the scope of this chapter.

7. The slight rise in wealth inequality between 2001 and 2007 appears to be due to two offsetting effects. As shown in my previous work (Wolff 2002a), wealth inequality is positively related to both income inequality and the ratio of stock prices to house prices (also see the section titled "A Wealth Inequality Puzzle"). Between 2001 and 2007, the Gini coefficient for household income, as noted above, rose modestly, from 0.562 to 0.574, while the ratio of the S&P 500 stock index to the median sales price of existing one-family homes fell from 8.1 to 7.1. These two effects generally offset each other, resulting in a small rise in wealth inequality.

8. The residual group, American Indians and Asians, is excluded here because of its small sample size.

9. It should be stressed that the unit of observation is the household, which includes families (two or more related individuals living together) as well as single adults. As is widely known, the share of female-headed households among African Americans is much higher than that among whites. This difference partly accounts for the relatively lower income and wealth among African American households.

10. Also, see Gittleman and Wolff (2004) for additional evidence from the Panel Study of Income Dynamics (PSID).

11. One important reason for the wealth gap is differences in inheritances. According to my calculations from the SCF data, 24.1 percent of white households in 1998 reported receiving an inheritance over their life time, compared to 11.0 percent of black households, and the average bequest among white inheritors was $115,000 (present value in 1998) and only $32,000 among black inheritors. Thus, inheritances appear to play a vital role in explaining the large wealth gap, particularly in light of the fact that black families appear to save more than white families at similar income levels (see, for example, Blau and Graham [1990]; Oliver and Shapiro [1997]; and Gittleman and Wolff [2004]).

12. This pattern may also be partly a cohort effect, since 401(k) plans and other DC plans were not widely introduced into the workplace until after 1989.

13. The 1983 data do not permit an estimation of indirect stock ownership, so I exclude 1983 from the table.

14. This figure is based on the National Association of Realtors Median Sales Price of Existing Single-Family Homes for Metropolitan Areas. In Chapter 5 we will examine the implications of the recent stock market crash on pension wealth holdings.

15. I assume that there are no additional savings (or dissavings) and no portfolio adjustments (except those caused by price changes of homes and stock).

16. A regression of a wealth inequality index, measured by the share of marketable wealth held by the top 1 percent of households (WLTH), on income inequality, measured by the share of income received by the top 5 percent of families (INC), and the ratio of stock prices (the S&P index) to housing prices (RATIO), with 21 data readings between 1922 and 1998, yields

$$WLTH = 5.10 + 1.27\ INC + 0.26\ RATIO,\ R^2 = 0.64,\ N = 21,$$
$$\qquad\ (0.9)\quad (4.2)\qquad\quad (2.5)$$

with t-ratios shown in parentheses. Both variables are statistically significant (INC at the 1 percent level and RATIO at the 5 percent level) and carry the expected (positive) sign. Also, the fit is quite good, even for this simple model.
Sources are as follows:

- Share of income of the top 5 percent: The basic data source is the Current Population Report series on shares of income held by families that runs from 1947 to 1998. The data are available at http://www.census.gov/hhes/income/ histinc. The earlier data, from 1922 to 1949, are from Kuznets's (1953) series on the percentage share of total income received by the top percentiles of tax units. This series is benchmarked against the census figure for 1949.

- S&P 500 Composite Stock Index: From 1922 to 1969: U.S. Census Bureau (1975a, p. 1004). From 1970 to 1998: Council of Economic Advisers (2001, Table B-93, p. 406).

- Median house prices: From 1922 to 1969: U.S. Census Bureau (1975b, Series N 259 and 261, p. 647). From 1970 to 1998: U.S. Census Bureau (1999, Table No. 1203, p. 725).

17. Kopczuk and Saez (2004), using U.S. estate tax data from 1916 to 2000, also find very little change in the shares of wealth held by the top wealth groups in the 1990s. Indeed, they find very little change in the 1980s as well. The share of the top 1 percent was 21.1 percent in 1983 and 20.8 percent in 2000, according to their data.

3
Review of the Literature on Retirement Wealth and Retirement Adequacy

We now turn our attention to the main topic of the book: retirement wealth and retirement adequacy. Before showing my own results on the subject, it is helpful to see what previous research has found. This review of the previous literature on these topics will provide a context for my later empirical findings.

I divide the survey into six parts. My own work will cover much of the same ground. The survey begins with a focus on trends in pension coverage. As will be seen, several previous studies have reported on the "great transformation" of the pension system away from DB plans and toward DC plans, which is a focus of the present volume. Has the pension transformation improved or worsened the level of pension wealth in the U.S. and its degree of inequality? The next section will present a review of studies on the level of retirement wealth as well as its distribution. Have pensions, particularly DC pension plans, added to household savings and wealth and, if so, by how much? After that I will survey the studies that have considered the effects of pensions on household savings.

Retirement adequacy is a key subject in this field. Has the great transformation improved or worsened the adequacy of savings for retirement? How have replacement rates (the ratio of retirement income to prior income) been affected? This part of the chapter examines previous estimates of retirement adequacy and replacement rates. How have elderly households in general fared recently and in the past? The last two sections review the literature on the economic status of the elderly and consider the impact of the recent recession on pension holdings.

DID PENSION COVERAGE RISE?

How has the great transformation affected actual pension coverage? This is a topic that will occupy a large portion of Chapter 4. Has the replacement of DB plans with DC plans improved or worsened pension coverage among U.S. workers?

Several previous studies have documented changes in pension coverage in the United States, particularly the decline in DB pension coverage and the corresponding rise of DC coverage among workers since the early 1980s. Before this, Laurence Kotlikoff and Daniel Smith (1983) provide one of the most comprehensive treatments of pension coverage and show that the proportion of U.S. private-wage and salary workers covered by (traditional DB) pensions more than doubled between 1950 and 1979. However, David Bloom and Richard Freeman (1992), using the CPS for 1979 and 1988, were among the first to call attention to the decline in DB pension coverage. They report that the percentage of all workers aged 25–64 covered by these plans fell from 63 to 57 percent over this period. Among male workers in this age group, the share covered dropped from 70 to 61 percent, while among females the share remained almost constant, at 53 percent.

Alan Gustman and Thomas Steinmeier (1992) were among the first to document the changeover from DB plans to DC plans between 1977 and 1985 on the basis of IRS 5500 filings. They decompose the switch from DB to DC plans into two effects: the first from the decline in DB coverage associated with (that is, conditional on) industry, size, and union status, and the second from shifts in the employment mix away from firms with industry, size, and union status historically associated with high DB coverage rates and toward those with low DB coverage. They estimate that each effect contributed about half to the replacement of DB plans by DC plans. Other studies include those by William Even and David Macpherson (1994a,b,c,d). The 1994c study in particular shows a pronounced drop in DB pension coverage among workers with low levels of education, and Even and Macpherson (1994d) show a convergence in pension coverage rates among female and male workers between 1979 and 1998.

A U.S. Department of Labor (2000) report finds that a large proportion of workers, especially low-wage, part-time, and minority workers, were not covered by private pensions. The coverage rate of all private sector wage and salary workers was 44 percent in 1997. Coverage of part-time, temporary, and low-wage workers was especially low. This appears to be ascribable to the proliferation of 401(k) plans and the frequent requirement of employee contributions to such plans. It also finds important ethnic differences: 47 percent of white workers participated, but only 27 percent of Hispanics. Another important finding is that 70 percent of unionized workers were covered by a pension plan, compared to only 41 percent of nonunionized workers. Pension participation was found to be highly correlated with wages: while only 6 percent of workers earning less than $200 per week had a pension plan, 76 percent of workers earning $1,000 per week participated.

Using CPS data, Munnell and Perun (2006) report a sharp drop-off in pension coverage between 1980 and 2004. In fact, participation dropped between 1979 and 1988, rebounded from 1988 to 1999, and then fell off again between 1999 and 2004. In 1979, 51 percent of non-agricultural wage and salary workers in the private sector aged 25–64 participated in a pension plan. By 2004, that figure was down to 46 percent. The authors also find that the decline in pension coverage occurred for all five earnings quintiles, though it was particularly pronounced for the middle quintile.[1]

In general, these studies report an overall increase in pension coverage during the 1980s and 1990s despite the collapse of DB plans because of an offsetting rise in DC plans. However, they also indicate a drop-off in pension coverage during the 2000s. I look at this issue again in Chapter 4 and find a rise in overall pension coverage among households from 1989 to 2001, but this was followed by a modest decline from 2001 to 2007.

DID PENSION AND RETIREMENT WEALTH INCREASE?

Did the transformation of the pension system out of DB plans and into DC plans improve or worsen the level of pension wealth and retirement wealth in general? Was the great transformation beneficial or hurtful in terms of actual dollar amounts? This topic will be a major focus of Chapters 4 and 5.

In one of the most important studies on this topic, Poterba et al. (2007) consider whether the switchover from DB to DC plans helped or hurt workers in terms of expected retirement wealth. As they note, the American private pension system was once dominated by DB plans and is now currently divided between DC and DB plans. Wealth accumulation in DC plans depends on participants' contribution behavior and on financial market returns, while accumulation in DB plans is dependent on participants' labor market experiences and on plan parameters. Using data from the Health and Retirement Study (HRS), Poterba et al. simulate the distribution of retirement wealth under representative DB and DC plans. In particular, they investigate how asset returns, earnings histories, and retirement plan characteristics contribute to the variation in retirement wealth outcomes. For DC plans they randomly assign individuals a share of wages that they and their employers contribute to the plan. Asset returns are drawn from the historical return distribution. The DB plan simulations draw earnings histories from the HRS and randomly assign each individual a pension plan drawn from a sample of large private and public DB plans. The simulations yield distributions of both DC and DB wealth at retirement. They find that average retirement wealth accruals under current DC plans exceeded those under private sector DB plans, although DC plans were also more likely to generate very low retirement wealth outcomes. The comparison of current DC plans with public sector DB plans was less definitive, because public sector DB plans were more generous on average than their private sector DB counterparts.

What is the effect of pension and retirement wealth in general on the inequality of wealth? The seminal paper on this subject is one by Feldstein (1974), whose main interest was in the Social Security system rather than the private pension system. In it, Feldstein introduces the concept of Social Security wealth and develops its methodology. His main interest in this paper is in the aggregate level of Social Security wealth and its effect on aggregate savings and retirement patterns. However, in a follow-up paper, Feldstein (1976) considers the effects of Social Security wealth on the overall distribution of wealth. He uses the 1962 Survey of Financial Characteristics of Consumers (SFCC), a survey performed by the Federal Reserve Board of Washington and a precursor of the SCF. The paper finds that the inclusion of Social Security wealth had a major effect on lowering the inequality of total household wealth (including Social Security wealth). The Gini coefficient for the sum of net worth and Social Security wealth among families aged 35–64 was 0.51, compared to a Gini coefficient of 0.72 for net worth.

I followed up this study by examining the distributional implications of both Social Security and private pension wealth. Wolff (1987b) uses the 1969 Measurement of Economic and Social Performance (MESP) database, and is the first to add estimates of private pension wealth to Social Security wealth and to examine their joint effects on the overall distribution of wealth. The paper shows that while Social Security wealth had a pronounced equalizing effect on the distribution of augmented wealth (the sum of marketable wealth and retirement wealth), as Feldstein (1976) finds, pension wealth had a *disequalizing* effect on augmented wealth. In particular, the addition of Social Security wealth to net worth reduced the overall Gini coefficient from 0.73 to 0.48 in 1969, but the addition of pension wealth to the sum of net worth and Social Security wealth raised the Gini coefficient back to 0.66. The sum of Social Security and pension wealth had, on net, an equalizing effect on the distribution of augmented wealth but substantially less than that of Social Security wealth alone.[2]

Relatively similar effects are reported in later papers. McGarry and Davenport (1997) use the 1992 wave of the HRS to estimate private pension wealth. They find that pension wealth is only slightly more equally distributed than net worth, and that adding pension wealth to net worth had a modest effect on reducing inequality (the wealth share of the top decile declined from 53 to 45 percent with the addition of pension wealth). Kennickell and Sundén (1999) use the 1989 and 1992 SCF to analyze the effects of Social Security and pension wealth on the overall distribution of wealth. They also find a large net equalizing effect from the inclusion of these two forms of retirement wealth. In particular, the inclusion of pension and net Social Security wealth reduced the share of total wealth held by the top 1 percent of nonelderly households in 1992 from 31 percent to 16 percent.[3]

Brown, Coronado, and Fullerton (2009) examine the redistributional effects of Social Security using the Panel Study of Income Dynamics (PSID) data for the period 1968–1993. They focus on whether the poor benefited from Social Security benefits relative to the middle class and rich. Their main finding is that the degree of redistribution of Social Security fell as the measure of resources used for a basis of comparison became more expansive. In particular, as they expand the definition from current annual income, the measure used in most studies, to lifetime income, the measured effect of the Social Security system became less progressive. In fact, when they use potential labor earnings at the household level as the basis of comparison rather than actual earnings at the individual level, they find that Social Security had virtually no effect on overall inequality.

Brown, Coronado, and Fullerton (2009) also find that even though there were some small positive net transfers to those at the bottom of the lifetime income distribution, this result was driven largely by the lack of redistribution across the middle and upper part of the income distribution. Moreover, in situations where redistribution did occur, they find that many high-income households received positive net transfers, while many low-income households paid net taxes.

In Chapters 4 and 5, I elaborate on how pension wealth and Social Security wealth affect measured wealth inequality. Moreover, I will also consider how the redistributional effects of these two forms of retirement wealth have changed over time, from 1983 to 2007.[4] I also find, as do many of these studies, that Social Security wealth is distributed much more equally than conventional net worth, and its addition to household wealth substantially lowers measured wealth inequality. Private pension wealth, on the other hand, is distributed less equally than Social Security wealth but more equally than net worth, and its addition to net worth leads to only a modest reduction in measured wealth inequality. Moreover, the "equalizing" effect of pension wealth dissipated between 1983 and 2007 as the more equally distributed DB pension wealth was replaced by the less equally distributed DC pension wealth.

A related topic is the makeup or composition of total (augmented) household wealth; in particular, how much of it is composed of pension wealth, Social Security wealth, and standard net worth? Gustman et al. (1997), for example, using the 1992 HRS, estimate that, collectively, pensions, Social Security, and health insurance accounted for about half of the wealth held by all households aged 51–61. However, the proportion varied by wealth level. They find that these three components made up 60 percent of total wealth of wealth percentiles 45–55, but only 48 percent of wealth percentiles 90–95. They conclude that pension wealth and Social Security wealth (as well as health insurance) were more important for middle-class households than the rich. I shall report very similar results in Chapter 6.

In a follow-up study, Gustman and Steinmeier (1998), using the HRS again, focus on the role of pensions in forming retirement wealth. They find that pension coverage was widespread, covering two-thirds of households and accounting for one-quarter of accumulated wealth on average. Social Security benefits accounted for another quarter of total wealth. The remainder consisted of traditional net worth. Here, again, my findings in Chapter 6 are quite similar.

DO PENSIONS REDUCE OTHER FORMS OF SAVINGS?

One ongoing controversy is whether DC pension plans like 401(k) plans have, on net, added to total household savings or whether they have simply substituted for other forms of savings. Some circumstantial evidence on this score was presented in Chapter 2, where we saw a clear displacement of liquid assets by DC pension accounts (see Table 2.3, for example).

On one side of the issue is a series of papers by Poterba, Venti, and Wise. In their 1992, 1993, and 1995 papers, using SIPP data for 1984 and 1991; in their 1998 paper, using HRS data for 1993; and in their 2001 paper, using both macro national accounting data and micro HRS data, Poterba, Venti, and Wise conclude that the growth of IRAs and 401(k) plans did not substitute for other forms of household wealth, and in fact raised household net worth relative to what it would have been without these plans. They find no substitution of DC wealth for either DB wealth or other components of household wealth.

On the other side of the issue is the work of Gale, who, in a series of papers both by himself and with colleagues, finds very little net savings emanating from DC plans. Gale (1995) concludes that when biases in estimation procedures in the previous literature on the subject are corrected, the offset of pension wealth on other forms of wealth can be very high. Gale and Scholz (1994) use the 1983 and the 1986 SCF, the latter of which contains a reinterview of 2,822 households out of the 4,262 households that were first interviewed in the 1983 SCF. Their main finding is that raising the annual IRA contribution limit between

1983 and 1986 would have resulted in little, if any, increase in national savings. These results, they maintain, are consistent with new evidence they present, indicating considerable potential among IRA holders to shift substitutable forms of savings into IRAs.

Using data from the 1984, 1987, and 1991 SIPP, Engen and Gale (1997) estimate that, at best, only a small proportion of 401(k) contributions represented net increments to household savings. In later work, Engen and Gale (2000) refine their analysis to look at the substitution effect by earnings groups. Using data from the 1987 and 1991 SIPP, they find that 401(k)s held by low earners are more likely to represent additions to net worth than 401(k)s held by high earners, who hold the bulk of this asset. Overall, only between 0 and 30 percent of the value of 401(k)s represented net additions to private savings.

Kennickell and Sundén (1999) also find a significant negative effect of both DB plan coverage and Social Security wealth on nonpension net worth but conclude that the effects of DC plans, such as 401(k) plans, on other forms of wealth were statistically insignificant. In contrast, Chernozhukov and Hansen (2004), using data from the 1990 SIPP, find a positive and statistically significant effect of 401(k) plan participation on net financial assets over the entire range of the asset distribution. Moreover, the increase in the lower tail of the distribution of 401(k) wealth translated almost completely into an increase in net wealth. Thus, the authors conclude that 401(k) accumulations added to the net worth of households in general and particularly those in the lower wealth groups. However, there was significant evidence of substitution of 401(k) accumulations for other asset types in the upper tail of the distribution.

In later work, Poterba, Venti, and Wise (2007b) document the transition from the DB to the DC system that occurred in the United States from the early 1980s on. They report, first, that the total value of assets in retirement accounts has increased substantially since 1980. As a percentage of National Income and Product Accounts wage and salary earnings, it rose from 71 percent in 1980 to 261 percent in 2006. Second, the share of employees covered by at least one pension plan remained about constant from 1980 to 2005, but the share covered by more than one plan rose substantially. Third, Poterba, Venti, and Wise project that 401(k) assets will increase "enormously" over time and that by 2040, assets of retirees will be at least twice as large in real dollars as in 2000. Moreover, the increase in retirement assets will occur along the whole distribution of Social Security wealth.

Engelhardt and Kumar (2007) use data from the 1991 wave of the HRS. They are particularly interested in how employer matching of employee 401(k) contributions affects retirement savings. Using detailed administrative contribution, earnings, and pension-plan data from the HRS, they estimate that an increase in the match rate (that is, the percentage of employee contributions to these plans that were met by a similar contribution from the employer) by 25 cents per dollar of employee contribution raised 401(k) participation by five percentage points. They also estimate that an increase in the match rate by 25 cents per dollar of employee contribution raised 401(k) savings by $365 (in 1991 dollars). Overall, they conclude that employer matching did increase 401(k) savings, but the effect was not very large.

Overall, previous studies that consider whether accumulations in DC pension plans add to net household wealth or merely substitute for other forms of household savings have been inconclusive. Reported results on this issue have been quite mixed, with some finding a strong displacement effect and others little or none. Though this is an important issue to address, it is beyond the scope of the present work.

HAS RETIREMENT ADEQUACY IMPROVED OVER TIME?

Retirement adequacy is a very important issue. It addresses the question of whether working individuals have saved enough (or will save enough) to meet their needs during retirement. Pension accumulations, Social Security wealth, and savings in nonretirement assets all play a role in determining whether accumulated wealth at retirement is (or will be) sufficient to meet retirement needs.

Measuring retirement adequacy is usually done by comparing predicted income at time of retirement with previous income (the so-called replacement rate). It should be noted that estimates of the replacement rate are quite sensitive to the choice of denominator. Some studies use family income at the time of the survey, others use a measure of permanent income, and still others use actual (or predicted) income as of the age just before retirement.

Measurement of adequacy also depends on the standard used for adequacy. Calculations of retirement income adequacy typically relate retirement consumption to preretirement consumption in three possible ways. First, a household may be considered adequately prepared for retirement if it can maintain a similar real level of consumption as during its working years. Usually, 80 percent of preretirement income is thus considered adequate since the income needs of retirees are likely to be lower than those of workers (Aon Consulting 2001). Households no longer need to save for retirement, taxes are lower, work-related expenses disappear, the family size of retirees is smaller than that of workers, and households eventually pay off their debt (McGill et al. 1996). Second, retirement income adequacy may be defined as a constant nominal level of consumption during retirement as during working years. This means that consumption needs are expected to decline during retirement over time, but in a somewhat arbitrary fashion. Third, real consumption may decline if the marginal utility of consumption is held constant and uncertainty about income and life expectancy is introduced (Engen, Gale, and Uccello 1999). As households must consider an uncertain future, their marginal utility of certain consumption today is higher than the marginal utility of uncertain consumption in the future.

Several studies have documented that household consumption generally falls after retirement compared to the time when the household is working. Banks, Blundell, and Tanner (1998) use data from the British Family Expenditure Survey covering the years 1968–1992. They first document a significant decline in consumption among British households right after retirement. Moreover, they also find that this drop in consumption could not be fully explained by a forward-looking consumption-smoothing model, such as the life-cycle model, that takes into account expected demographic changes and mortality risk. Fisher et al. (2005) use data from the U.S. Consumer Expenditure Survey covering the years 1984–2003. They first show that as the definition of consumption is expanded from food expenditures only to more comprehensive definitions, the recorded decline of consumption at retirement decreases by more than half. However, even with the most comprehensive definition, they find that consumption expenditures fall by 2.5 percent when individuals retire and continue to decline at about a rate of 1 percent per year after that.

The decline in spending after retirement for the average household is sometimes called the "retirement consumption puzzle." The reason is that in a standard life cycle model of savings, it is typically shown that household welfare is maximized when consumption remains constant over the person's lifetime (see Modigliani [1954] for the classic work on this topic). Thus, the drop in consumption just after retirement is viewed as a puzzle.

Hurst (2008), after summarizing the recent literature on consumption behavior during retirement, argues that collectively there is no puzzle with respect to the spending patterns of most households as they transition into retirement. In particular, the literature shows that there is substantial heterogeneity in spending changes at retirement across consumption categories. The declines in spending after retirement for the average household were limited to the categories of food and work-related expenses. Spending in nearly all other categories of nondurable expenditure remained constant or even rose. Moreover, even though expenditures on food went down after retirement, actual food intake (including food prepared in the home) tended to remain more or less constant. The literature also shows that there was substantial heterogeneity across households in the change in expenditure associated with retirement. However, much of the research on this subject shows that this heterogeneity can be fairly well explained by households involuntarily retiring due to deteriorating health. Overall, the literature shows that the standard life-cycle model of consumption augmented with home production and uncertain health shocks has done an adequate job in explaining the consumption patterns of the average household after retirement.

Scholz and Seshadri (2009) argue that the choice of replacement rates should be theory-based—not the common advice of financial planners, who typically call for a 70 percent replacement rate of average preretirement income. They use an augmented life-cycle model of household behavior to examine optimal replacement rates for a representative set of retired U.S. households and related optimal replacement rates for observable household characteristics. They first note that target replacement rates are usually thought to be less than 100 percent for three main reasons. First, upon retirement, households typically face lower taxes than they face during their working years, if for no other reason than Social Security is more lightly taxed than wages and salaries. Second, households typically save less in retirement than they do during their working years, so saving is a smaller claim on available income. Third, work-related expenses generally fall in retirement.

Scholz and Seshadri (2009) also note that low-income households are thought to need higher replacement rates than high-income households. Prior to retirement, tax rates are lower for low-income households than they are for high-income households. As a result, low-income households' reduction in taxes in retirement is smaller than the reduction experienced by high-income households. Moreover, low-income households save less than high-income households, so the reduction in saving in retirement will be smaller for low-income households. The fact that taxes and saving fall less in retirement for low-income households than for high-income households suggests that their target replacement rate should be higher.

Scholz and Seshadri (2009) suggest that there are different choices of the preretirement income that can be used to compute replacement rates. The usual choice is average income over preretirement years, but replacement rates are sometimes defined using average income over the last five (or fewer) years of the preretirement period, with the idea that living standards may ratchet upward as people age. The authors argue that a natural alternative to replacement rates can be drawn from the life-cycle model, augmented to account for fundamental factors affecting most households, such as demographic changes and uncertainty about future earnings, medical expenses, and longevity.

Using HRS data, Scholz and Seshadri (2009) compute an average optimal replacement rate of 0.68 for the population as a whole on the basis of income averaged over the lifetime as the point of comparison and 0.57 on the basis of income averaged over the top five earnings years. Optimal replacement rates exhibited a U-shaped relation with respect to the lifetime income decile—highest at the top and the bottom and lowest in the middle. They also compute that optimal replacement rates were highest for those who graduated college and lowest for those with less than a high school degree.

As in the literature on the effects of DC accumulations on other forms of household savings, which I review in the last section of this chapter, the studies on retirement savings adequacy have produced differing results. Using the HRS, Gustman and Steinmeier (1998) find that the average household could replace 60 percent of preretirement income in real terms and 86 percent of preretirement income in nominal terms. The finding for the nominal replacement ratio led the authors to conclude that households on average were adequately prepared for retirement. Engen, Gale, and Uccello (1999), using the SIPP and the SCF, estimate that about half of households fell short of what they needed for adequate retirement income but the other half could be expected to meet the target retirement savings. Despite this, they calculate an average replacement ratio for the median income household of 72 percent, a result that led the authors to conclude that households were close to being adequately prepared for retirement.

In a later study, Engen, Gale, and Uccello (2005) find that the upswing in stock prices from 1995 to 1998 did not substantially alter their earlier findings on retirement income. This suggests that much of the increase in retirement wealth was concentrated among households that were already adequately prepared for retirement. Further, Haveman et al. (2003), using Social Security's New Beneficiary Data System, find that retired beneficiaries had a median replacement ratio of about 80 percent, and that only 30 percent of households had a replacement ratio of less than 70 percent in 1982. These four studies all appear to indicate that households in the main had saved enough to be adequately prepared for retirement.

In contrast, several studies conclude that households were inadequately prepared for retirement. Moore and Mitchell (2000) find, using the 1992 HRS, that the median wealth household would have to save an additional 16 percent annually of earnings if it were to retire at age 62, and an additional 7 percent annually for retirement at age 65, to finance an adequate real replacement ratio. Their estimate of a savings rate of 7.3 percent for households wishing to retire at age 65 was three times as much as what households actually saved (Mitchell and Moore 1998). This meant that households had on average between 75 and 88 percent—depending on marital status—of what they needed when retiring at age 65 in 1992.

Similarly, Bernheim (1997) calculates that on average baby boomer households were saving only at 34 percent of what their target savings rate should be. In addition, Gustman and Steinmeier's (1998) figures show that, based on real replacement ratios, the average household had 28 percent less than what it needed for adequate retirement savings. Last, Wolff (2002b) concludes that 61 percent of households could not replace 75 percent of their preretirement income in retirement, based on data from the 1998 SCF, and this figure was up from 56 percent of households in 1989.

One issue to consider, though, is what a shortfall relative to adequate savings means. In some cases, a shortfall will still allow households to finance most of their expected consumption. Engen, Gale, and Uccello (1999) point out that the households used in Mitchell and Moore (1998) could still finance more than 90 percent of the consumption prescribed by their model with no additional savings. Similarly, Haveman et al.'s (2003) study shows that about 20 percent of households had a replacement ratio of between 70 and 80 percent. In other words, one-fifth of households had more than 90 percent, but less than 100 percent, of what is generally assumed to be necessary for retirement income adequacy—80 percent of preretirement earnings.

As wealth is unequally distributed, there may be a large share of households for which the shortfalls are larger. Engen, Gale, and Uccello (1999) calculate that households in the 75th percentile—the closest income percentile for *average* (not median) income—had 121 to 172 percent of what they needed for retirement. For the median household, the same ratios ranged from 47 to 124 percent. Thus, the median household reached only 62 percent of the preparedness of the average household in 1992. Moreover, Wolff (2002b) documents that the gap between average wealth and median wealth to income ratios increased further by 1998. Because of the unequal distribution of wealth, a large share of households was likely to experience retirement consumption shortfalls.

Gustman and Steinmeier (1999) find that households in the bottom quartile had nominal replacement ratios of 50 percent and real replacement rates of 33 percent, compared to nominal replacements of 121 percent and real replacement rates of 81 percent for the top quartile. Also, Wolff (2002b) finds that 16 percent of households could replace less than 25 percent of their preretirement income and that 43 percent of households could replace less than half of their preretirement income during retirement in 1998.

Shortfalls in retirement savings vary with household demographics. Mitchell, Moore, and Phillips (2000) and Engen and Uccello (1999) find that black and Hispanic married households experienced a larger shortfall in retirement income adequacy than whites, and that less educated households had lower retirement income adequacy. Mitchell and

Moore (1998) also find that single households were less adequately prepared than married ones. Haveman et al. (2003) find that single men were more likely be inadequately prepared than single women, who were in turn less likely than married couples to be adequately prepared for retirement.

In comparing these figures with findings of other studies, it needs to be kept in mind that, for instance, Haveman et al. (2003) consider only Social Security earnings for their replacement ratio calculations, thus understating the level of household income. Also, Wolff (2002b) considers the wealth of households nearing retirement, whereas Haveman et al. consider wealth for those who were already retired. Obviously households can increase their savings before entering retirement and occasionally while in retirement.

To make ends meet in retirement, when facing an income shortfall, households will have to curtail their retirement consumption. In fact, one of the distinguishing features between studies that conclude that households are adequately prepared for retirement and those that do not is the hypothesized consumption pattern in retirement. For instance, Engen, Gale, and Uccello (1999) and Gustman and Steinmeier (1999) conclude that households were adequately prepared for retirement on the basis of the assumption that real retirement consumption declines with age. Similarly, Haveman et al. (2003) base their conclusions on the assumption of declining consumption in retirement, albeit at a slower pace than Gustman and Steinmeier.

A number of studies have also looked at the changes in retirement income adequacy over time. Wolff (2002b) finds that the share of households between the ages of 47 and 64 that could replace less than 75 percent of their current income in retirement rose from 56 percent in 1989 to 61 percent in 1998. In comparison, Engen, Gale, and Uccello (2005) find that retirement income adequacy changed little from 1995 to 1998. James Smith (2003), using data from the PSID and the CPS, finds that median after-tax income replacement ratios in retirement have been increasing, particularly since the early 1990s. Sorokina, Webb, and Muldoon (2008), using data from the HRS for age group 51–56, calculate that both pension wealth and replacement rates fell between 1992 and 2004.

An alternative approach to measuring retirement adequacy comes from Munnell, Webb, and Delorme (2006) of the Center for Retirement

Research, who developed what they call a new national retirement risk index (NRRI). The construction of this new NRRI involves two steps. The first is to project replacement rates for each household and to determine a target replacement rate. The second step is to compare the projected replacement rates to the targets to determine the NRRI results. The index covers all working-age U.S. households. The original study used the 2004 SCF. Projected retirement income was based on income from financial assets, including those in DC plans, net of nonmortgage financial debt, housing net of mortgage debt, DB pension plans, and Social Security. The index did not include earnings from work.

Because elderly households generally consume less than working-age households, as Munnell, Webb, and Delorme (2006) indicate, a replacement rate of less than 100 percent is used in the calculation of the target replacement rate. However, the report argues that the projected replacement rate should be higher for low-income than high-income households because low-income households save very little before retirement and enjoy less in the way of tax savings (see Scholz and Seshadri [2009] for a similar argument). Munnell, Webb, and Delorme follow this approach. For example, they use a target replacement rate of 81 percent for couples in the bottom third of the income distribution, 72 percent for couples in the middle third, and 67 percent for couples in the top third. By their calculations, 43 percent of households were at risk in 2004 of having inadequate retirement income. In later work, Munnell et al. (2007) find a sizable increase in the share of households at risk according to the NRRI from 1983 to 2004. Among the bottom third of the income distribution, the share at risk increased from 47 to 53 percent, while among the top two-thirds the proportion rose from 24 to 38 percent.[5]

As in the literature on the effects of DC accumulations on other forms of household savings, the studies on retirement savings adequacy have been relatively inconclusive. Several conclude that retirement savings were adequate and expected replacement rates were generally high, whereas others find that expected replacement rates were relatively low and a large number of households near retirement age were at risk of inadequate income at retirement. I shall return to the subject of retirement adequacy among working-age households in Chapter 7. I will look at their indicators of retirement adequacy—projected retirement income, projected replacement rates, and the projected share of retirees above the poverty line. My results show a very large projected gain in retirement income from 1989 to 2001 but much smaller advances from 2001 to 2007. Expected replacement rates showed improvement from 1989 to 2001 and again from 2001 to 2007, though over the later period at least, gains were due more to a reduction in preretirement income than to advances in projected income at retirement. The share of near retirees at risk of falling below the poverty line at retirement declined from 1989 to 2001 but remained unchanged from 2001 to 2007.

ARE THERE ALSO IMPROVEMENTS IN THE ECONOMIC STATUS OF THE ELDERLY?

Though retirement adequacy by itself is extremely important, its focus is typically on the share of preretirement income replaced at retirement. Equally important is how the elderly have fared in absolute terms and how these indicators have changed over time. The literature on the overall economic status of the elderly deals with these issues.

In one of the earlier studies on this topic, Hurd (1994) shows that the mean income of households aged 65 and over increased sharply between 1970 and 1975 but only moderately from 1975 to 1987. As a fraction of the overall mean household income, average elderly income rose from 54 percent in 1970 to 61 percent in 1975 and then to only 63 percent by 1987. Smith (1997), using 1994 HRS data, finds that median financial wealth among white households aged 70 and over was only $15,600; for white households aged 51–61 it was $23,400, and for black and Hispanic households in the two age groups it was zero. Venti and Wise (1998), using HRS data for 1992, estimated a high degree of wealth dispersion among persons aged 51–61, even after controlling for lifetime earnings.

Bernheim, Skinner, and Weinberg (2001) also report a large variation in household wealth at retirement on the basis of data from the PSID and the Consumer Expenditure Survey. In this study, they seek to determine whether the standard life-cycle model could explain this large dispersion. In particular, they test whether differences in time preference rates, risk tolerance, exposure to uncertainty, relative tastes for work and leisure at older ages, and income replacement rates might be responsible for the large inequality observed in the data. In each case, the authors reject these factors as possible explanatory factors.

Purcell (2009c) presents some recent estimates of the income of elderly Americans on the basis of CPS data. In almost all cases, the results show major gains made by the elderly from 1968 to 2008. The mean annual income in 2008 dollars of persons aged 65 and older rose by 84 percent from 1968 to 2000 and by another 9.2 percent from 2000 to 2008. The median annual income in real terms of individuals aged 65 and above showed a similar pattern, rising by 89 percent from 1968 to 2000 and then by 7.3 percent from 2000 to 2008. On the household level, the real median annual income of elderly households (defined as husband or wife aged 65 or older) gained 91 percent from 1968 to 2000 and an additional 4.5 percent from 2000 to 2008. Moreover, the ratio of the median income of elderly households to nonelderly ones progressed from a ratio of 0.38 in 1968 to 0.49 in 2000 and then to 0.54 in 2008. The gains during the 2000s were primarily due to the sharp fall in the median income of the nonelderly, by 6.7 percent. In fact, on the basis of "scaled" or "equivalent" income, the ratio of elderly to nonelderly mean household income advanced from 0.47 in 1968 to 0.57 in 2000 and then to 0.63 in 2008.[6] The poverty rate of people aged 65 and older fell from 25 percent in 1968 to 9.9 percent in 2000 and then declined a bit more to 9.7 percent in 2008.

In a related study, Purcell (2009b) provides a breakdown of the sources of income of households aged 65 and older. For the bottom quartile, Social Security was by far the major source of income, accounting for 84 percent of the total income of households in that quartile. Pensions were a very small portion, only 5 percent of their income, as was income from assets, 3 percent. For households in the second quartile, Social Security was also the overwhelming source of their income, comprising 67 percent. Pensions were larger, at 14 percent, as was asset income, at 6 percent. Among the third quartile, Social Security dropped to 42 percent as a share of total income, pensions were up to 23 percent, and asset income was up to 8 percent. For the top quartile, Social Security plummeted to 17 percent of income, pensions fell a bit to 16 percent, and asset income was up to 16 percent. Their major source of income was labor earnings, which made up 49 percent of their total income. I shall report somewhat similar findings on the composition of augmented wealth by wealth group in Chapter 6.

Wolff and Zacharias (2009) find that the relative well-being of the elderly was even greater than that measured by gross money income. They examine the economic well-being of the elderly using the Levy Institute Measure of Economic Well-Being (LIMEW), which is is a comprehensive measure that incorporates broader definitions of income from wealth, government expenditures, and taxes than standard income, and also includes the value of household production. Wolff and Zacharias find that, according to LIMEW, the elderly were much better off relative to the nonelderly. The main reason is that income from wealth and net government expenditures for the elderly was much higher than for the nonelderly. Both mean and median LIMEW also grew much faster for the elderly than the nonelderly over the 1989–2001 period. In contrast, growth rates of money income were actually greater for the nonelderly than the elderly over this period. Wolff and Zacharias also find that the degree of inequality in LIMEW was substantially higher among the elderly than among the nonelderly. In contrast, inequality in money income was virtually identical between the two groups. Inequality in the LIMEW grew for both the elderly and the nonelderly, while the inequality in standard money income grew only for the latter group.

Butrica, Murphy, and Zedlewski (2008) also use an expanded measure of well-being, as well as alternative definitions of resource availability and poverty thresholds, to measure poverty among the elderly. They use the 2004 wave of the HRS. Their main finding is that alternative poverty measures that account for spending on health produced higher poverty rates than the official poverty measure, even when the value of housing and financial assets were included in the measure of resource availability. They also find that poverty remained concentrated among single women, blacks, Hispanics, and adults aged 85 and older regardless of how poverty was measured, because these populations have relatively little in the way of housing equity or financial assets.

Several studies have also considered whether households have accumulated an adequate amount of wealth for retirement. Gustman and Steinmeier (2000), using the 1992 wave of the HRS, estimate that by 1992, pensions and retiree health insurance represented one-quarter of the wealth of families on the verge of retirement. Their simulations suggested that between 1969 and 1992, after controlling for the effects of changes in wages and years of covered work on pension benefit amounts, changes in pension coverage and changes in pension plan provisions would have raised the total wealth of each household in the HRS by $67,000 in 1992 dollars. This would have increased the wealth from employer-provided pension benefits per household by 150 percent in real terms. Changes in retiree health benefits, which were only about 7 percent of the value of pensions, experienced similar real growth, increasing in value by $3,700 in 1992 dollars. Most of the increase in pension values and in the value of retiree health insurance was due to improvements in real benefits among covered workers. All classes of wealth holders enjoyed increased wealth from employer-provided retirement plans, but those in the top half of the wealth distribution enjoyed increases that were much larger in absolute terms and were also larger in relation to their total wealth than were the gains received by those in the bottom half of the wealth distribution.

Using data from the 1983, 1989, 1992, 1995, 1998, and 2001 SCF, Engen, Gale, and Uccello (2005) examine the relation between fluctuations in the aggregate value of equities (stocks) and the adequacy of households' saving for retirement. They find that many and perhaps most households appeared to be saving adequate amounts for retirement, and that there was almost no link between stock values and the adequacy of retirement saving. Historical variation in equity values and ownership had little correlation with the historical variation in the adequacy of saving. Even a simulated 40 percent decline in stock values had little effect on the adequacy of saving. These results are explained by the fact that equities are highly concentrated among households with significant amounts of other wealth (as was shown in Tables 2.11a and 2.11b in Chapter 2). Middle-class and poorer households, on the other hand, did not accumulate enough stocks in their portfolios to be very exposed to downturns in the stock market. As a result, stock market downturns do not appear to be a cause of an inadequate level of retirement savings for the vast majority of households.

In two related working papers, Poterba, Venti, and Wise (2007a, 2008) argue that over the past two and a half decades there was a fundamental change in retirement saving, with a rapid shift from employer-managed DB pensions to DC saving plans that are largely controlled by employees. To understand how this change will affect the well-being of future retirees, they project the future growth of 401(k) assets at age 65 for cohorts attaining age 65 between years 2000 and 2040. Using data from the HRS and the SIPP, they estimate that cohorts that attain age

65 in future decades will have accumulated much greater retirement savings (in real dollars) than the retirement savings of current retirees. They also consider how the change in the pension system will affect the wealth of future retirees. The personal retirement account system is not yet mature. A person who retired in 2000, for example, could have contributed to a 401(k) for at most 18 years, and the typical 401(k) participant had only contributed for a little over 7 years. Nonetheless, current 401(k) assets are quite large. Poterba, Venti, and Wise consider in this paper the implications of rising 401(k) savings through the year 2040. In particular, they focus on the growth of the sum of Social Security wealth and 401(k) assets for families in each decile of the Social Security wealth distribution. Their projections show a substantial increase between 2000 and 2040 in the sum of these retirement assets in each wealth decile.

Love, Smith, and McNair (2008), using data from the 1998–2006 waves of the HRS, construct two measures of the current wealth adequacy of older (aged 51–61 in 1992) American households. The first is the ratio of what they call comprehensive wealth—defined as net worth plus expected future income streams—that would be needed to generate expected poverty-line income in future years. According to this index, they estimate that the median older American household was reasonably well situated, with a poverty ratio of about 3.9 in 2006. However, they also find that about 18 percent of households had less wealth than would be needed to generate 150 percent of poverty-line income over their expected future lifetime.

Love, Smith, and McNair's (2008) second measure was the ratio of the annuitized value of comprehensive resources to preretirement earnings. On the basis of this index, they estimate a median replacement rate of about 105 percent, with about 13 percent of households experiencing replacement rates of less than 50 percent. Comparing the leading edge of the baby boomers in 2006 to households of the same age in 1998, they also find that the baby boomers showed slightly less wealth in real terms than the corresponding age group in 1998, and single boomers showed a bit higher incidence of inadequacy than did their elders. Nonetheless, the median single boomer appeared to have adequate resources. Finally, they found a rising age profile of annualized wealth within households over time even after controlling for other factors, suggesting that older households were not spending their wealth as quickly as their survival probabilities were falling.

Smith, Soto, and Penner (2009) use the 1998–2006 waves of the HRS to investigate how U.S. households changed their asset holdings at older ages. They find a sizable increase in the net worth of older households between 1998 and 2006, with most of the growth due to increases in the value of housing. They also find that, at least through 2006, older households did not consume the total amount of their capital gains. This asset accumulation provided older households with a financial cushion for the turbulence experienced after 2007. The wealth distribution was also highly skewed, and the age patterns of asset accumulation and deaccumulation varied considerably by income group. High-income elderly households increased their assets at older ages. Middle-income elderly households reduced their assets in retirement, but at a rate that for most seniors will not deplete assets within their expected life. Many low-income elderly households accumulated fewer assets and spent their financial assets at a rate that will mostly deplete them at older ages, leaving low-income seniors with only Social Security and DB pension income at older ages.

Although there is some variance in reported results on this topic as well, the general upshot is that the economic status of elderly households improved over the last few decades. This finding held in terms of income, wealth, and the poverty status of these households. We have already seen some evidence of this in Chapter 2 in terms of the wealth holdings of elderly households. In Chapter 4 and particularly in Chapter 5, we shall see further evidence of this in the improvement of senior households in terms of augmented wealth (standard net worth plus retirement wealth) over the years 1983–2007.

WHAT WERE THE EFFECTS OF THE 2007–2009 RECESSION ON PENSION WEALTH?

In Chapter 2 we saw evidence that the collapse of the housing and stock prices in 2007–2009 lowered both average and median household wealth. However, different groups of households had different degrees of vulnerability to these price shocks, depending on their asset holdings.

The sharp decline in the stock market in 2007–2009 put many Americans nearing retirement in a difficult financial situation. Although the market had almost fully rebounded as of November 2010 after hitting a low point in March 2009, important losses did occur. The Urban Institute and the Center for Retirement Research at Boston College were both involved in trying to predict the effects of the stock market crash on the retirement readiness of older Americans. As we shall see, the elderly were particularly hard hit by the stock market downturn.

Butrica and Issa (2010) of the Urban Institute analyze the impact of the recession on DC retirement accounts and IRAs. They use data from the Federal Reserve Board's Flow of Funds to do the updating. From the third quarter of 2007 to the first quarter of 2009, retirement accounts declined from a peak of $8.6 trillion to $5.9 trillion, for a loss of $2.8 trillion, or 31 percent of their value in nominal terms. In real terms, the loss was even greater, at 34 percent. However, the value of these accounts did come back, and by the fourth quarter of 2009, their value was $7.6 trillion, though still 15 percent below their peak value (and at the same level as the first quarter of 2006 in real terms).

According to a study done by Sass, Monk, and Haverstick (2010) at the Center for Retirement Research at Boston College, the stock market crash of 2008 significantly dimmed the retirement prospects of many workers who were approaching retirement. These workers are, in general, heavily dependent on 401(k) plans (as opposed to traditional DB pensions) as a source of retirement income. During the economic downturn, these plans lost about one-third of their value. Even before the crash, many older workers lacked the assets needed to enjoy a comfortable retirement. The rational response to a sharp decline in retirement wealth is to "spread the pain" by saving more, working longer, and consuming less in retirement. The extent to which workers are absorbing a portion of the loss by saving more and working longer is thus critical for assessing their economic prospects at retirement.

To address these questions, the Center for Retirement Research in the summer of 2009 surveyed a nationally representative sample of 1,317 workers approaching retirement, aged 45–59, on changes in retirement saving and expected retirement age. The survey also collected data on the financial and employment characteristics, emotional reactions to the downturn, and enhanced financial literacy. The major findings were that two-thirds of working people in this age group said that they now had less retirement savings than they did before the recession, 40 percent expected to retire later than they had planned (by an average of 4 additional years), and many reported experiencing a level of distress equal to or even greater than that caused by the terrorist attacks on September 11, 2001.

However, two-thirds of the workers in the sample reported that they had not changed their saving behavior for their 401(k)s, IRAs, and other retirement accounts. In contrast, 60 percent of the workers reported having changed their spending levels. The main conclusion of the Center for Retirement Research study was that there was a significant increase in expected retirement ages but not much change in retirement saving. The study found no differences in behavior by race or sex. The study also provided some evidence that if credible financial advice were more widely available, we might have seen more alterations in savings behavior to offset the effects of the Great Recession.

Two surveys conducted by Bank of America (2010) in 2008 find similar results regarding unchanged savings behavior. The first survey was conducted in March and the second survey in November by Braun Research via telephone using a random digit dial methodology between the dates of November 5 and 12, 2008. Braun surveyed 750 nationally representative Americans, plus 250 individuals with investable assets of between $100,000 and $3 million. The sample size was about 1,000 in each of the two months.

The survey finds that a growing number of Americans were concerned that the current economic crisis was threatening to leave them further behind on their retirement plans. As a result, 6 in 10 Americans were spending less than they were three months prior. However, even with this decreased spending, 51 percent of the general public and 40 percent of affluent Americans were also saving less than they had been three months earlier, and approximately one in five said that they were saving "much less."

The findings underscore how deeply troubled Americans were about their retirement savings and financial well-being, with 23 percent of respondents indicating that the impact of economic turbulence on their retirement savings was the financial issue that concerned them most. Based on this survey, it appears that many Americans were not fully able to save what was needed to retire as they had planned, and some were tapping into their financial savings to meet more immediate financial needs. Although the majority of respondents (68 percent) with at least one retirement account said that they had not had to withdraw assets from their accounts prematurely, recent economic conditions had caused 18 percent to withdraw assets prematurely. The main reasons for these early withdrawals were near-term financial obligations, such as credit card debt (26 percent) and mortgage payments (22 percent), with an additional 22 percent citing recent job loss. The article argues that if the economy should continue to worsen, these numbers may increase significantly. The possibility of many more Americans dipping into their retirement savings could have profound implications for the country's future economic well-being.

In light of the recent economic turbulence, many Americans (43 percent) believe they now face more years in the workforce than they expected a couple of years ago. This will clearly affect baby boomers the most, or those approaching retirement who may not have time to recover the financial losses incurred during the financial crisis. For this reason, it is not surprising that 36 percent of affluent respondents said current economic conditions had pushed back their expected retirement age.

According to responses to the Bank of America Retirement survey (2010) conducted in March, 53 percent of the general public and 36 percent of affluent Americans were either behind schedule or had not started their retirement planning efforts. Comparatively, according to findings from the later survey conducted in November, 62 percent of the general public and closer to half (44 percent) of affluent Americans were either behind schedule or had not started their retirement planning efforts. Despite the recent market turmoil, 68 percent of respondents had not changed the way they save, invest, or manage their retirement assets in the prior three months. The article notes that this lack of change could be a sign that Americans do not exactly know what to do besides reducing spending and continuing to watch as their retirement assets diminish. This later survey further confirmed that Americans need better guidance and education regarding how best to plan for retirement and manage their retirement assets. In fact, 59 percent of the general public and 52 percent of affluent Americans did not know how much they would need to save in order to maintain their current standard of living in retirement, according to this survey. Nearly half of retired Americans indicated that they do not believe or are unsure whether their retirement assets would cover their financial needs throughout their remaining life-time. According to this survey, 25 percent of the general public and 33 percent of affluent Americans still had at least one 401(k) or 403(b) plan with a former employer. Of those who had a plan with a former employer, close to half (48 percent for the general public, and 46 per-cent for the affluent) intended to keep their assets in the existing plan. The upshot of this survey is that Americans probably do not know how to meet the impending retirement crisis other than to cut their spending.

Rich Morin (2009) of the Pew Research Center reaches similar con-clusions based on a national survey by the center's Social and Demo-graphic Trends Project. During the recession of 2007–2009, which took a heavy toll on household wealth, just over half of all working adults aged 50–64 said that they might delay their retirement, and another 16 percent said that they never expect to stop working. The survey's findings are based on a telephone survey of a nationally representative sample of 2,969 adults conducted from February 23 through March 23, 2009. Overall, 37 percent of full-time employed adults of all ages said that they had thought in the past year about postponing their eventual retirement. This proportion increased to 52 percent among full-time workers aged 50–64 (the so-called threshold generation). They were twice as likely as younger workers to say they never planned to retire (16 percent vs. 8 percent). Moreover, those in the threshold generation who did plan to retire someday said that they planned to keep working, on average, until they were 66 years old, which would make them four years older than the average age at which current retirees 65 or older reported that they had stopped working.

Investment losses appeared to play more of a role in the decision of when to retire. Among the threshold generation as well as among other age groups, higher-income earners were only slightly less likely than lower-income adults to have considered postponing retirement. But regardless of income or age, those who lost 40 percent or more of their retirement account were roughly twice as likely as those who had not lost money in the market meltdown to say that they thought about delaying their eventual retirement from the workforce. The rising inclination to delay retirement was driven in part by the recession of 2007–2009, but it was also in conformity with longer-term labor market trends. Morin reported that the labor force participation rate of those aged 65 and older had already increased from 13 percent in 2000 to 17 percent in 2008.

There were also gender and racial differences in the decision of when to retire. Among all age groups, 46 percent of full-time employed women said that they thought about delaying retirement in the past year, compared with 31 percent of all working men. Also, 40 percent of whites thought about extending their working lives, compared with 32 percent of blacks and 34 percent of Hispanics. Income differences mattered less in the retirement decision. Among those with family incomes of less than $30,000, 44 percent thought about postponing their retirement, compared with 37 percent of those earning $100,000 or more. Similarly, 36 percent of those making $30,000–$50,000 and 38 percent in the $50,000–$100,000 income bracket considered working longer as the recession developed from 2007 to 2009.

Moreover, among adults aged 50–64 who were employed full time, 61 percent of women working full time in this age group said they had reconsidered when they would retire, compared with 45 percent of men. This gender gap is consistent with other research showing that older women approaching retirement have fewer economic resources to draw on than do men. But among this age group, there was little difference in plans to delay retirement by income. Working adults who were closer to age 65 (the traditional retirement age) were even more likely than younger members of the threshold generation (50–64) to have considered delaying their retirement. Over two-thirds of those aged 57–64 said they had thought about delaying retirement, compared with 44 percent of those aged 50–56.

Working members of the threshold generation were the least confident of any age group that they would have enough money to last through their retirement years. Only 21 percent of those aged 50–64 said that they were "very confident" that they had enough income and assets to tide them over, compared with 37 percent of full-time workers younger than age 30 and 40 percent of those aged 65 and older. Most Americans, young or old, said that the recession made it harder to take care of their financial needs in retirement. However, working adults in the threshold generation were more inclined than any other age group to feel this way. Among those aged 50–64 with full-time jobs, 78 percent said that the recession made it more difficult to take care of their financial needs in retirement, compared with 66 percent of those younger than 50. Income differences played little role in fueling the recession-driven financial worries of the threshold generation. Similarly, there was little difference by gender, by level of education, or by race.

It is also the case that among all adults, the threshold generation saw the value of their investments shrink the most, with 76 percent saying that they had lost money in mutual funds, individual stocks, or retirement accounts, compared with 54 percent of those younger than age 50. Working members of this generation who lost money on investments were also more likely than those who did not suffer losses to say that they had considered delaying retirement (54 vs. 45 percent), and they were more likely to have considered taking this step than were adults below the age of 50 who had lost money in the market (54 vs. 34 percent). Investment losses also affected financial confidence, as 82 percent of working members of the threshold generation who lost money in the past year said that the recession would make it harder for them to meet their financial needs in retirement, compared with 66 percent of those aged 18–49. The degree of loss also mattered in this regard: among all adults employed full time, those who had lost 40 percent or more on their investments were twice as likely as those who had lost nothing to say that they thought about delaying their retirement.

Butrica, Smith, and Toder (2009a,b) from the Urban Institute show that delaying retirement even by a year might greatly help offset the effects of the recession. The benefits of delaying retirement would be greatest for the late boomers, less for middle boomers, and least for preboomers, although it would be beneficial to all. Moreover, while people with lower incomes had less to lose in the stock market crash, they would be the ones to benefit the most from an additional year of working life.

Butrica, Smith, and Toder (2009a,b) also show possibilities for the future after the stock market crash. They first note that the sharp decline in the stock market in 2008 placed the retirement security of many Americans at risk (although the market rebounded sharply after its trough in March 2009). They simulate and compare various fast and slow recovery scenarios to a "no-crash" scenario that shows what the long-term trend in retirement assets would have been if the stock market had not collapsed in 2008 but instead had continued to increase at its historical rate from the 2007 level. The three scenarios they consider are 1) a "no recovery" scenario in which the stock market does not rebound but instead resumes its long-term historical rate after 2008; 2) a "repeat 70s" scenario in which real stock prices continue to decline for a number of years after the 2008 crash, as they did between 1974 and 1982; and 3) a "full recovery" scenario in which the stock market fully rebounds after 10 years to the projected no-crash level in 2017.

According to calculations by Butrica, Smith, and Toder (2009a,b), if stocks remain depressed, as after the 1974 crash, 20 percent of pre-boomers born in 1941–1945 and 22 percent of late boomers born in 1961–1965 would see their retirement incomes drop 10 percent or more. Working another year would reduce the share of these big losses to 14 percent for late boomers. Because most preboomers were already retired, their share of big losses would decline slightly to 19 percent. Delaying retirement would disproportionately benefit low-income people because their additional earnings exceed their stock market losses.

Another finding indicates that the effect of the market crash on retirement incomes varied by age, income level, and assumptions about future market performance. About 63 percent of boomers were estimated to have owned stocks in 2008, but those in the higher income quintiles were affected much more than others because they were more likely to have retirement accounts and other financial assets, and to hold larger shares of their financial wealth in stocks. Those farthest from retirement age fared better than older people because they had less wealth when the market crashed because of fewer years of accruals (even though they were more likely to have retirement accounts and invest in equities), and because they had more time to restore their lost wealth through new stock acquisitions and future appreciation before retirement.

Preboomers lost in all scenarios, and all cohorts lost under the no-recovery scenario. Middle boomers and late boomers experienced net income losses under the no-recovery scenario but retirement income gains under the full-recovery scenario. For example, the highest income quintile of middle boomers experienced on average a 14 percent loss in income at age 67 if the market failed to recover, but a 4 percent gain on average if the market fully recovered to its previous path by 2017. Gains and losses also varied depending on the individual's portfolio allocations and the market performance of their investments.

In contrast, Gustman, Steinmeier, and Tabatabai (2009) offer a much more sanguine view of the effects of the stock market crash on retirement preparedness. Their findings indicate that although the consequences of the decline in the stock market were serious for those approaching retirement, the average person approaching retirement age was not likely to suffer a life-changing financial loss from the recession of 2007–2009. Likewise, the probable effects of the stock market downturn on retirement resources have been greatly exaggerated. If there is any postponement of retirement due to stock market losses, on average it will be a matter of a few months rather than years. Counting layoffs, retirements may be accelerated rather than reduced.

Using HRS data, Gustman, Steinmeier, and Tabatabai (2009) calculate trends in pensions among three cohorts: those aged 51–56 in 1992, called the HRS cohort; those 51–56 in 1998, called the war baby cohort; and those 51–56 in 2004, called the early boomer cohort. They find that pension coverage was much more extensive than was usually recognized. Over three-quarters of the households with a person aged 51–56 in 2004 were either currently covered by a pension or had had pension coverage in the past. Pension wealth accounted for 23 percent of the total wealth (including Social Security wealth) of those on the verge of retirement. For those nearing retirement age, DC plans remained small. As a result, 63 percent of pension wealth held by those aged 51–56 in 2004 was in the form of a DB plan.[7] The figures were even higher for the older cohorts. Three-quarters of the pension wealth of the HRS cohort was from DB plans, as was 65 percent of the pension wealth of the war baby cohort. The fact that such a higher share of pension wealth was in the form of DB pension wealth should cushion the drop in overall pension wealth from the stock market crash.

In general, these papers (with the exception of Gustman, Steinmeier, and Tabatabai [2009]) indicate that the 2007–2009 recession wreaked financial havoc on workers close to retirement age. On the basis of direct survey questions, it appears that many of these workers suffered large declines in DC plan pension wealth and on their net worth overall. As a consequence, a large number of them plan to postpone retirement and/or to decrease their future consumption spending. In Chapter 5, I shall also investigate the effects of the crisis of 2007–2009 on the pension wealth holdings of those on the verge of retirement. I also find a large plunge in pension wealth from 2007 to 2009 and, indeed, report that DC pension wealth had remained virtually unchanged from 2001 to 2009. However, I will not investigate the effects of the recession on either retirement behavior or spending plans.

Notes

1. A related topic of interest is whether DC pension plans have substituted for DB-type plans. Popke (1999), using employer data (IRS 5500 filings) for 1992, finds that, indeed, 401(k) and other DC plans substituted for terminated DB plans, and that offering a DC plan raised the chance of a termination in DB coverage.
2. See Wolff (1992) for a discussion of some of the methodological issues involved in estimating both Social Security and pension wealth.
3. Net Social Security wealth is defined as the discounted present value of future Social Security benefits less future taxes paid into the Social Security (OASI) system. Estimates were not provided separately for pension wealth and Social Security wealth.
4. There are a host of studies that examine the *intra-cohort* redistributional effects of Social Security benefits relative to contributions into the Social Security system. They consider which groups are net gainers and which net losers from the Social Security system as a whole. These authors include Wolff (1993a,b), who uses the 1962 SFCC and the 1983 SCF; Coronado, Fullerton, and Glass (2000), who derive their estimates from the PSID; Smith, Toder, and Iams (2001), who base their work on the Survey of Income and Program Participation (SIPP) data matched with Social Security administrative data and the microsimulation MINT model; Liebman (2002), who matches Social Security Administration earnings and benefit records to the 1990 and 1991 panels of the SIPP; and Leimer (2003, 2004), who bases his analyses on Social Security administrative data.
5. Also see Jonathan Skinner (2007) for a review of the literature on savings adequacy.
6. Equivalent or scaled income adjusts household income for household size. The formula used in this study for equivalent income is household income / (number of adults + number of children under 18)$^{0.5}$. The higher ratios of equivalent income in comparison to normal household income are due to the fact that average household size is smaller among elderly households than the nonelderly.
7. These proportions seem a lot larger than the ones I compute from the SCF. For example, DB wealth as a share of total pension wealth among the age group 47–64 was 47 percent in 2001 and only 41 percent in 2007.

4

The Slowdown in Pension
Wealth Growth in the 2000s

As I discuss in Chapter 1, one of the most dramatic changes in
the retirement income system over the last three decades has been the
replacement of many traditional DB pension plans with DC pensions.
Has this transformation been beneficial to most American households?
This is the principal focus of the chapter. Poterba, Venti, and Wise
(1998) find that the transition from DB to DC type plans increased
mean pension wealth dramatically in the 1990s, at least. I find that the
transformation was largely beneficial to American families during the
1980s and 1990s, particularly the latter decade, when the stock market boomed. However, during the period 2001–2007 (and before the
meltdown in the financial markets), pension wealth growth slowed substantially. Moreover, overall pension coverage itself, after rising rapidly
from 1989 to 2001, fell in 2007.

A secondary interest is the effect of pension wealth on overall
wealth inequality. Feldstein (1976), in a seminal paper on this subject,
finds that adding Social Security wealth to marketable net worth led to
a sharp reduction in measured wealth inequality (see Chapter 3). Is this
also true for pension wealth? Does retirement wealth in total (the sum
of Social Security and pension wealth) help to equalize the distribution
of household wealth? This chapter will show that the addition of pension wealth to marketable net worth does reduce overall wealth inequality, but the equalizing effect is much smaller than that of Social Security
wealth (discussed in Chapter 5). Moreover, the evidence of both this
chapter and Chapter 5 will show that the equalizing effect of retirement
wealth dissipated over time, particularly after 2001.

The results of this and the next chapter will also clear up the "puzzle"
discussed in Chapter 2—that (marketable) wealth inequality remained
largely unchanged from 1989 to 2007, while both income inequality
and the ratio of stock prices to housing prices increased. In contrast, I
do find an increase in the inequality of augmented wealth (the sum of

net worth, pension and Social Security wealth) from 1989 to 2007 (see Chapter 5).

The next section of the chapter develops the accounting framework used in the analysis. How has the change in the pension system affected pension coverage for individual workers? In this regard, the section after that presents results on pension coverage for workers both overall and by demographic characteristic for the period 1989–2007.

The chapter then moves on to discuss the change in the pension system and the effects it had on pension coverage and pension values on the household level, and to investigate changes in pension coverage, pension wealth, and private accumulations—i.e., the sum of net worth and (private) pension wealth—on the household level over the more extended time interval, 1983–2007. The final section contains a provisional summary of the results.

A full treatment of the retirement system would not be complete without consideration of the Social Security system. Chapter 5 introduces Social Security wealth and presents results on its movement on the household level from 1983 to 2007. It presents summary measures on total (augmented) household wealth, the sum of net worth, pension wealth, and Social Security wealth. The chapter will show alternative pension wealth calculations and present an update of the pension wealth estimates to 2009 (July 1, 2009, to be exact) on the basis of changes in stock prices.

ACCOUNTING FRAMEWORK

The standard wealth concept is marketable wealth (or net worth), which was defined in Chapter 2. It should be noted that the standard definition of net worth includes the market value of DC pension plans.

Defined contribution plans include a variety of financial instruments. There are two types: individually provided plans and employer-provided plans. Individually provided plans are IRAs and Keogh plans.[1] Standard employer-provided DC plans are 401(k), 403(b), SRA (supplemental retirement account), and 457 plans. Firms also provide a variety of other plans, such as profit-sharing, tax-deferred annuities, portable cash option plans, IRA-SEP (simplified employee pension) or IRA-

SIMPLE (simplified incentive match plan for employers), SARSEP (salary reduction simplified employee pension), TIAA-CREF (Teachers Insurance and Annuity Association/College Retirement Equity Fund), money purchase plans, deferred compensation plans, cash balance plans, stock purchase/ESOP (employee stock option plan), thrift/ savings plans, and the like. I have combined all of these as DC plans.

Defined benefit plans include (but are not limited to) state, local, and federal government plans, PERS (public employees retirement system), employer-provided annuity plans, and traditional DB plans. Some employer-provided plans are a mixture of the two. Following the SCF protocol, I have divided DC plans from DB plans on the basis of whether they are "account-type" plans, with a balance or cash value, or whether they are "formula-type" plans, with no cash balance and the benefit determined by such variables as years of service and earnings history.

My principal data source, as indicated in Chapter 2, is the Survey of Consumer Finances (SCF). While the SCF provides considerable detail on marketable assets and liabilities held by the household, it does not provide estimates of pension or Social Security wealth. These variables have to be estimated by the user.[2]

Before proceeding to the actual empirical results, it is necessary to make imputations of both DB pension wealth and Social Security wealth. The reason for the imputations is that, with the exception of the 1983 SCF, estimates of these two variables are not provided in the SCF data because their estimation requires making assumptions about several parameters, as indicated below.[3] Since researchers may differ in what they believe are the best assumptions to make, the Federal Reserve Board believes it would be inappropriate for them to arbitrarily make specific assumptions.

The imputation of DB pension wealth and Social Security wealth involves a large number of steps, which are summarized below. Greater details are shown in Appendix B.

DB Pension Wealth

For retirees (r) the procedure is straightforward. Let PB be the pension benefit currently being received by the retiree. The SCF questionnaire indicates how many pension plans each spouse is involved in and what the expected (or current) pension benefit is. The SCF question-naire also indicates whether the pension benefits remain fixed in nominal terms over time for a particular beneficiary or are indexed for inflation. In the case of the former, DB pension wealth is given by

$$(4.1a) \quad DB_r = \int_0^{109-A} PB(1-m_t)e^{-\delta t}dt,$$

and in the latter case,

$$(4.1b) \quad DB_r = \int_0^{109-A} PB(1-m_t)e^{-\delta^* t}dt,$$

where A is the current age of the retiree; m_t is the mortality rate at time t conditional on age, gender, and race; δ^* is the real annual discount rate, set to 2 percent; γ is the inflation rate and is assumed to be 3 percent per year; $\delta = \delta^* + \gamma$ is the nominal annual discount rate, equal to 5 percent; and the integration runs from zero to the number of years when the retiree reaches age 109.[4]

Estimates of DC pension wealth (as well as Social Security wealth) are quite sensitive to the choice of inflation rate and discount rate. I choose a 3 percent inflation rate since it is very close to the actual annual change of the CPI-U index from 1983 to 2007 (see Table D.1). Moreover, I choose a 5 percent nominal discount rate because it likewise is close to the actual average annual rate of return on liquid assets over the same period (see Appendix Table D.1). These two choices lead to a 2 percent *real* discount rate (the difference between the two rates). A higher real discount rate will lead to lower estimates of DB pension wealth (and likewise Social Security wealth), and conversely, a lower discount rate will lead to higher estimates of these two variables. I also use a 3 percent real discount rate to estimate both DB pension and Social Security wealth. The general results in this book are not materially altered by the use of this higher discount rate.[5]

Among current workers (w) the procedure is more complex. The SCF provides detailed information on pension coverage among current workers, including the type of plan; the expected benefit at retirement or the formula used to determine the benefit amount (for example, a fixed percentage of the average of the last five years' earnings); the expected retirement age when the benefits are effective; the likely retirement age of the worker; and vesting requirements. Information is provided not only for the current job (or jobs) of each spouse but for up to five previous jobs as well. On the basis of the information provided in the SCF and on projected future earnings (see Appendix B for details), future expected pension benefits (EPB_w) are then projected to the year of retirement or the first year of eligibility for the pension. Then the present value of pension wealth for current workers (w) is given by

$$(4.2) \quad DB_w = \int_{LR}^{109-A} EPB(1 - m_t)e^{-\delta t}dt,$$

where RA is the expected age of retirement and $LR = A - RA$ is the number of years to retirement. The integration runs from the number of years to retirement, LR, to the number of years when the retiree reaches age 109.[6]

It should be noted that the calculations of DB pension wealth for current workers are based on employee response, including his or her stated expected age of retirement (see Appendix B), *not* on employer-provided pension plans.[7]

Social Security Wealth

For current Social Security beneficiaries (r), the procedure is again straightforward. Let SSB be the Social Security benefit currently being received by the retiree. Again, the SCF provides information for both husband and wife. Since Social Security benefits are indexed for inflation, Social Security wealth is given as

$$(4.3) \quad SSW_r = \int_0^{109-A} SSB(1 - m_t)e^{-\delta^* t}dt,$$

where it is assumed that the current Social Security rules remain in effect indefinitely.[8]

The imputation of Social Security wealth among current workers is based on the worker's actual and projected earnings history estimated by regression equation (see Appendix B). The steps are briefly as follows. First, coverage is assigned based on whether the individual expects to receive Social Security benefits and on whether the individual was salaried or self-employed. Second, on the basis of the person's earnings history, the person's average indexed monthly earnings (AIME) is computed. Third, on the basis of the rules current at the time of the survey year, the person's primary insurance amount (*PIA*) is derived from AIME. Then,

$$(4.4) \quad SSW_w = \int_{LR}^{109-A} PIA(1 - m_t)e^{-\delta^* t} dt.$$

As with pension wealth, the integration runs from the number of years to retirement, *LR*, to the number of years when the retiree reaches age 109.[9]

Here, too, it should be noted that estimates of Social Security wealth are based on reported earnings at a single point in time. These estimates are likely to be inferior to those based on longitudinal work histories of individual workers (see, for example, Smith, Toder, and Iams [2001]), whose estimates are based on actual Social Security work histories. In fact, actual work histories do show much more variance in earnings over time than one based on a human capital earnings function projection. Moreover, they also show many periods of work disruption that I cannot completely capture here. In contrast, I do have *retrospective* information on work history provided by the respondent (see "Questions on Work History" in Appendix B for details). In particular, each individual is asked to provide data on the total number of years worked full time since age 18, the number of years worked part time since age 18, and the expected age of retirement (both from full- and part-time work). On the basis of this information, it is possible to approximate the total number of full- and part-time years worked over the individual's lifetime and use these figures in the estimate of the individual's AIME.[10]

I can now define the different accounting measures to be used. Let *NWX* be marketable household wealth excluding *DC* wealth and non-pension wealth. Then

$$(4.5) \quad NW = NWX + DC.$$

Total pension wealth, *PW*, is given by

$$(4.6) \quad PW = DC + DB.$$

Private accumulations, *PA*, is then defined as the sum of *NWX* and total pension wealth:

(4.7) $PA = NWX + PW.$

The term *private accumulations* is used to distinguish contributions to wealth from private savings and employment contracts with both private and government employers from those of social insurance provided by the state, notably, Social Security.

Retirement wealth, *RW*, is then given as the sum of pension and Social Security wealth:

(4.8) $RW = PW + SSW.$

Finally, augmented household wealth, *AW*, is given by

(4.9) $AW = NWX + RW.$

Employer Contributions to DC Pension Plans

To complete the accounting framework, I consider the contributions employers make to DC pension plans. So far I have treated DC and DB pension wealth (as well as Social Security wealth) on a comparable footing, but there is an important difference between them in their definitions. In particular, I define DB wealth as the discounted future stream of DB pension benefits on the assumption that the employee remains at his or her firm of employment until the person's expected retirement date. The computation of Social Security wealth is also based on the assumption that the worker remains at work until the person's expected retirement date. On the other hand, the valuation of DC pension wealth is based solely on the current market value of DC plans. There is no added value in the calculation of DC wealth from the employee remaining at work (until the expected date of retirement).

What if we put DC wealth on an equal footing with DB wealth? To do this, we could add into DC wealth a projection of the future stream of *employer* contributions to DC accounts like 401(k) plans until the expected year of retirement. Luckily, the SCF does provide information on employer contribution to DC plans (see Appendix B). If we assume, as in the case of DB pensions, that workers remain at their company until retirement and that the terms of their DC contract with their employer stay the same, then it is possible to do this. In most cases, the employer contribution is a fixed percentage of the employee's salary. On the basis of the estimated human capital earnings functions for each worker and the "ongoing concern" assumption, it is possible to calculate the annual stream of future employer contributions to the DC plan until retirement, which I call DCEMP.[11] Adding DCEMP to DC would then put DC wealth on the same footing as DB wealth, since both would reflect the available retirement wealth at time of retirement due to employer contributions to retirement plans.[12]

The SCF questionnaire indicates how many DC pension plans each spouse has (up to three per spouse).[13] Information on the employer contribution to DC pension plans is recorded in two ways. First, in some cases, the contribution is given as a flat dollar amount. Though it is not indicated in the survey data whether the dollar contribution is indexed to inflation over time, I assume that it is indexed to the CPI, which seems the more likely arrangement.[14] Let $EMPAMT$ be the dollar amount of the employer contribution to the DC plan. Then, in the case where employer contributions are recorded as a dollar amount, the present value of the stream of future employer contributions, $DCEMP_a$, is given by

$$(4.10) \quad DCEMP_a = \int_0^{LR} EMPAMT\,(1 - m_t)e^{-\delta^* t}dt \,,$$

where m_t is the mortality rate at time t conditional on age, gender, and race; and δ^* is the real annual discount rate, set to 2 percent.[15] The integration runs from the current year to LR, where RA is the expected age of retirement and $LR = A - RA$ is the number of years to retirement.

Second, in most cases the employer contribution is given as a percentage of earnings. If we assume that the proportion, $EMPPER$, is fixed over time, then in the case where the respondent records employer contributions as a percentage of earnings, $DCEMP_b$, is given by

$$(4.11) \quad DCEMP_b = \int_0^{LR} EMPPER \times E^*_t\,(1 - m_t)e^{-\delta^* t}dt,$$

where E^*_t is the predicted earnings of the worker at time t in constant dollars (see Appendix B for details).

The basic accounting framework can then be modified as follows:

$$DCEMP = DCEMP_a + DCEMP_b$$
$$DC* = DC + DCEMP$$
$$PW* = DB + DC*$$
$$PA* = NWX + PW*$$
$$RW* = PW* + SSW$$
$$AW* = NWX + RW*.$$

I shall return to a consideration of DCEMP in Chapter 5.

PENSION COVERAGE ON THE EMPLOYEE LEVEL

Here I address the question of whether the transformation of the pension system increased or lowered pension coverage among individual workers. Though most of the analysis in the book will be conducted on the household level, I first look at pension coverage at the level of the individual worker. In the SCF, almost all of the wealth variables are provided only on the household level. However, one exception is information on pension plans, which is provided for both husband and wife. Both husband and wife list their DC plans separately. Moreover, each is asked about coverage from DB plans. Work history data and earnings are also provided separately for each spouse, so that we can construct estimates of DB pension wealth for each.

The story that will unfold is that DB pension coverage plummeted over time. DC coverage increased sharply and picked up some of the slack from the collapse of DB plans. However, this was true for only certain occupations and industries. For other groups, overall pension coverage diminished.

Table 4.1 begins the statistical portrait by showing pension coverage by type of pension plan for currently employed male and female workers in 1989, 2001, and 2007.[16] I find that while male pension coverage fell over these years, female coverage increased, so that by 2007 virtual parity had been reached between the two genders. In 2007, 62 percent of male workers under the age of 65 had some type of pension coverage.[17] Defined contribution coverage was more prevalent: 28

**Table 4.1 Percentage of Workers with Pension Coverage by Type of
Pension and Gender, 1989, 2001, and 2007**

	1989		2001		2007	
Age group	Male	Female	Male	Female	Male	Female
All workers (under age 65)						
IRA or Keogh accounts	28.2	22.4	29.7	25.6	27.8	25.8
Employer-provided DC accounts	31.3	25.6	44.1	36.0	42.6	38.9
All DC accounts	46.5	40.8	59.6	50.6	56.4	53.9
Current job DB plans	33.5	26.9	19.2	15.4	13.0	13.0
Past job DB plans	4.5	2.5	6.3	3.1	6.8	3.4
Current and past job DB plans	36.3	28.9	24.7	18.2	18.5	15.9
DC and/or DB plans	65.0	54.8	68.1	58.7	61.7	60.4
All workers aged 46 and under						
IRA or Keogh accounts	21.3	17.6	23.2	19.9	21.1	19.5
Employer-provided DC accounts	29.1	26.0	44.6	34.9	38.7	35.6
All DC accounts	40.9	37.2	56.0	45.4	49.5	47.2
Current job DB plans	31.4	23.7	15.5	13.6	10.4	10.4
Past job DB plans	3.3	1.9	2.5	1.0	3.1	1.5
Current and past job DB plans	33.6	25.2	17.3	14.5	12.8	11.8
DC and/or DB plans	59.7	49.8	62.2	52.6	53.1	53.0
All workers aged 47–64						
IRA or Keogh accounts	46.0	34.2	42.2	37.4	38.4	36.0
Employer-provided DC accounts	37.2	24.5	43.0	38.2	48.8	44.2
All DC accounts	61.0	49.8	66.6	61.2	67.3	64.5
Current job DB plans	38.9	34.8	26.5	19.1	17.0	17.3
Past job DB plans	7.4	4.0	13.7	7.3	12.5	6.6
Current and past job DB plans	43.4	38.2	39.1	25.7	27.5	22.4
DC and/or DB plans	78.5	67.1	79.7	71.2	75.2	72.3

NOTE: The table includes only current workers aged 64 and under.
SOURCE: Author's computations from the 1989, 2001, and 2007 SCF.

percent of these workers had an IRA or Keogh account, 43 percent had an employer-provided DC account, and together, 56 percent had some type of DC account. However, only 13 percent were covered by a DB plan from their current job and only 7 percent still had DB entitlements (a "legacy" DB plan) from a past job.[18] Altogether, 19 percent of male workers in 2007 had some form of DB entitlement. Corresponding figures for female workers were only slightly lower than those for men.

Not surprisingly, pension coverage was lower for younger workers than for older ones. Among male workers under the age of 47, 53 percent had some pension coverage, mainly DC plans, while 75 percent of male workers between the ages of 46 and 64 had coverage, again primarily DC plans. Here again, figures for female workers were very similar to those for men.

There were some substantial changes in coverage from 1989 to 2007. From 1989 to 2001, overall coverage rose moderately, by 3.2 percentage points for male workers and 3.9 percentage points for females. However, trends were very different for DC coverage and DB coverage. DC coverage expanded by 13 percentage points for men and 10 percentage points for women, while DB coverage dwindled by 12 and 11 percentage points, respectively. Almost all of the losses in the DB coverage were in current job plans. These were almost exactly offset by increased coverage in employer-provided DC plans. Here, the substitution between DC and DB plans is very evident.

While changes in coverage were very similar for men and women during the 1990s, they were quite different during the 2000s. Male pension coverage dropped substantially from 2001 to 2007, by 6.4 percentage points. There was again a marked decrease in DB coverage, by 6.2 percentage points, but even a loss in DC coverage, by 3.2 percentage points. Losses in coverage were much greater for younger male workers, 9.1 percentage points, than among the older age group, 4.5 percentage points. Younger male workers, in particular, saw a sharp drop in employer-provided DC plans of 6.5 percentage points, as well as in current job DB plans of 5.1 percentage points. (This trend for younger households will reemerge in the next section of the chapter.) Older male workers also saw current job DB plan coverage plummet by 9.5 percentage points but DC plan coverage rise slightly.

In contrast, female workers saw a modest increase in pension coverage from 2001 to 2007, of 1.7 percentage points. This occurred among both younger and older female workers. The main reason was increased access to employer-provided DC plans. As a result, whereas in 1989 and 2001 there was about a 10 percentage point gap in pension coverage between male and female workers, by 2007 almost complete convergence had been achieved.[19]

Pension Coverage by Race and Ethnicity

Table 4.2 shows coverage by race and ethnicity, as well as by educational attainment.[20] The results will show sizable gaps in pension coverage between whites, blacks, and Hispanics. In 2007, 61 percent of white male workers reported some kind of DC account, in contrast to 46 percent of African American workers and only 32 percent of Hispanic workers. Differences in the share with DB entitlements were much smaller between black and white male workers in 2007—virtually zero—while there was a 13 percentage point gap between white male and Hispanic male workers in favor of the former. Altogether, 66 percent of white male workers had some form of pension wealth in 2007, compared to 54 percent of black male workers and only 36 percent of Hispanic male workers. Differences in pension coverage by race and ethnicity were very similar among female workers.

The share of male workers with a DC account advanced more for blacks than whites from 1989 to 2001 but then fell more for the former than the latter from 2001 to 2007. Declines in DB coverage were similar for the two racial groups. As a result, the gap in pension coverage between white and African American male workers declined noticeably between 1989 and 2001, from 11 to 7 percentage points, and then spiked upward between 2001 and 2007 to 12 percentage points, higher than in 1989.

The time trends were different for female workers. In 1989, DB pension coverage was much greater among black female workers than among white female workers, 41 versus 28 percent. However, DB coverage declined much more among black females than among white females from 1989 to 2007, so that by 2007 the DB coverage rate was greater for white than black females. The share reporting a DC account rose about the same for white females and black females from 1989 to 2007. As a result, the share of white female workers with pension coverage advanced from 57 percent in 1989 to 65 percent in 2007, while

Table 4.2 Percentage of Workers with Pension Coverage by Race, Education, and Gender, 1989, 2001, and 2007

	1989		2001		2007	
	Male	Female	Male	Female	Male	Female
By race[a]						
Non-Hispanic whites						
All DC accounts	51.3	45.3	63.4	54.2	61.0	58.9
All DB plans	38.2	27.9	26.0	19.3	20.6	17.1
DC and/or DB plans	69.5	57.2	71.6	62.3	66.3	65.3
(Non-Hispanic) African Americans						
All DC accounts	34.9	28.6	49.9	47.1	45.6	41.8
All DB plans	36.9	40.6	25.9	16.8	20.5	14.0
DC and/or DB plans	58.8	53.3	65.0	55.6	54.2	48.5
Hispanics						
All DC accounts	20.0	18.8	32.9	27.3	32.3	29.9
All DB plans	24.5	25.9	14.7	14.2	7.8	9.3
DC and/or DB plans	37.8	38.7	38.6	36.3	36.2	36.3
By educational attainment						
No high school diploma (or GED)						
All DC accounts	26.6	24.2	25.5	20.4	19.8	22.3
All DB plans	27.0	23.6	17.3	6.4	3.2	2.9
DC and/or DB plans	46.0	42.6	37.5	26.8	22.4	24.2
High school diploma (or GED)						
All DC accounts	40.6	33.0	51.8	40.6	43.4	42.8
All DB plans	34.2	26.3	20.4	13.2	17.6	13.7
DC and/or DB plans	60.9	49.0	60.4	49.0	50.6	49.7
Some college						
All DC accounts	47.9	40.8	53.6	46.9	57.2	50.6
All DB plans	36.7	27.6	23.4	14.2	17.9	13.3
DC and/or DB plans	67.1	52.7	63.5	52.2	62.1	56.4
College degree						
All DC accounts	59.3	57.3	76.2	66.5	74.5	67.2
All DB plans	41.9	35.2	30.3	26.5	23.2	20.4
DC and/or DB plans	75.6	68.2	83.2	76.1	79.2	74.7

NOTE: The table includes all current workers aged 64 and under.

[a] Asians and other races are excluded from the table because of their small sample size.

SOURCE: Author's computations from the 1989, 2001, and 2007 SCF.

the coverage rate for black females fell from 53 to 49 percent, and the racial gap in coverage grew from 4 to 17 percentage points.

The gap in pension coverage remained very high between non-Hispanic white and Hispanic white male workers from 1989 to 2007—a little over 30 percentage points. Among female workers, the difference widened from 19 percentage points in 1989 to 29 percentage points in 2007, mainly due to the greater reduction in the DB coverage rate among Hispanic female workers. In fact, the pension coverage rate among Hispanic females actually fell by 2.4 percentage points from 1989 to 2007.[21]

Pension Coverage by Educational Attainment

The principal finding here is that the gap in pension coverage between college graduates and the other educational groups expanded substantially over the period 1989–2007 (see Table 4.2). The main reason is not that pension coverage advanced dramatically among college graduates but rather that it dwindled among the other educational groups.

In 2007, a mere 22 percent of male workers without a high school degree had some form of pension coverage, compared to 51 percent of those with a high school degree (or GED), 62 percent of those with some college, and 79 percent of those who were college graduates.[22] As a result, there were considerable gaps in pension coverage between college graduates and the other groups. These differences were largely a reflection of the gap in the proportion with a DC account, though there was also a considerable difference in DB coverage between those without a high school degree and college graduates. The pattern of results is very similar for female workers.

Pension coverage showed an absolute decline among the three less-educated groups of workers. For male workers without a high school degree (or GED), DC coverage declined from 27 percent in 1989 to 20 percent in 2007, DB coverage plummeted from 27 to 3 percent, and overall pension coverage from 46 to 22 percent. For male high school graduates, DC coverage rose slightly, from 41 to 43 percent, DB coverage contracted from 34 to 18 percent, and overall coverage fell from 61 to 51 percent. Among those with some college, DC coverage grew by 9 percentage points, DB coverage fell, and overall coverage dipped from

67 to 62 percent. Among college graduates, the overall coverage rate rose moderately, from 76 to 79 percent.

As a result, the gaps in pension coverage considerably widened over time. The difference in the overall pension coverage rate between the lowest educational group and college graduates mushroomed from 30 to 57 percentage points, the difference between high school and college graduates expanded from 15 to 29 percentage points, and the difference in overall pension coverage between those with some college and college graduates climbed from 8 to 17 percent. Here, too, results are similar among female workers.

Pension Coverage by Industry, Occupation, and Employment Status

There are also marked differences in pension coverage by industry, occupation, and employment status (see Table 4.3). Of particular note are the sizable losses in pension coverage among male blue-collar workers. In 2007, the highest pension coverage among male workers was found in public administration, 87 percent, followed by nongovernmental services, 69 percent, wholesale and retail trade, 55 percent, and goods-producing industries, 50 percent.[23] Among female workers, the highest pension coverage was also found in public administration, 89 percent, also followed by nongovernmental services, 63 percent, but then followed by goods-producing industries, 61 percent, and finally wholesale and retail trade, 44 percent. The share of workers reporting a DC account was roughly similar to the proportion with any pension coverage, and the rank order was almost identical. By far, the highest proportion of workers with DB coverage was found in public administration—57 percent for men and 55 percent for women. Defined benefit coverage was quite low in goods-producing industries, 13 and 7 percent, respectively—surprising since this sector includes such heavily unionized industries as autos.

There were also some notable gender differences in coverage. In the goods-producing sector, overall pension coverage was 61 percent for women and only 50 percent for men. These differentials reflect the relatively large concentration of white-collar jobs among the women and of blue-collar jobs among the men employed in this sector. In contrast, overall pension coverage was higher for men than for women in trade

Table 4.3 Percentage of Workers with Pension Coverage by Industry, Occupation, and Employment Status, 1989, 2001, and 2007

	1989		2001		2007	
	Male	Female	Male	Female	Male	Female
By industry of employment[a]						
Goods-producing industries						
All DC accounts	45.5	39.8	55.2	53.5	45.8	58.2
All DB plans	33.6	24.7	23.3	15.1	12.7	7.4
DC and/or DB plans	62.1	52.7	64.7	57.9	50.3	60.5
Wholesale and retail trade						
All DC accounts	39.8	28.5	49.8	39.1	53.1	38.6
All DB plans	15.4	14.8	12.6	7.4	9.4	6.4
DC and/or DB plans	49.0	37.6	54.1	42.5	55.0	41.1
Nongovernmental services						
All DC accounts	49.9	44.2	64.9	52.1	63.4	56.1
All DB plans	42.7	31.0	26.1	19.9	19.5	16.7
DC and/or DB plans	70.4	58.4	72.7	61.5	68.8	63.1
Public administration						
All DC accounts	49.7	47.0	75.5	58.6	72.6	66.1
All DB plans	73.9	62.0	59.0	41.9	56.8	54.5
DC and/or DB plans	96.3	74.9	95.9	75.8	87.4	88.8
By occupation of employment						
Professional and managerial						
All DC accounts	63.3	57.9	72.8	61.8	73.0	61.5
All DB plans	45.1	35.6	26.9	24.4	21.9	20.0
DC and/or DB plans	80.1	70.0	79.2	71.4	77.6	69.3
Technical and clerical						
All DC accounts	46.5	41.3	63.5	50.4	59.1	56.7
All DB plans	24.1	29.4	20.0	14.9	15.3	12.9
DC and/or DB plans	59.7	56.4	68.3	56.9	62.7	61.9
Service workers						
All DC accounts	30.2	19.4	41.3	26.8	43.6	26.4
All DB plans	44.3	20.3	33.5	11.3	31.4	11.5
DC and/or DB plans	63.2	33.6	57.7	34.3	55.4	32.4
Craft, operative, and agricultural						
All DC accounts	36.2	26.0	48.6	41.5	42.0	41.9
All DB plans	33.6	22.4	22.8	13.4	12.8	8.8
DC and/or DB plans	56.0	39.4	59.2	49.6	46.9	47.0

Table 4.3 (continued)

	1989		2001		2007	
	Male	Female	Male	Female	Male	Female
By employment status[b]						
Part-time, full-year						
All DC accounts	30.7	26.1	36.3	37.1	47.1	39.4
All DB plans	24.6	13.2	20.2	11.2	9.3	8.9
DC and/or DB plans	46.6	34.7	45.6	42.9	48.8	42.8
Full-time, part-year						
All DC accounts	46.0	46.9	55.9	51.7	41.7	58.1
All DB plans	30.2	52.5	22.9	38.5	16.8	25.7
DC and/or DB plans	59.6	73.6	64.2	73.2	47.5	70.4
Part-time, part-year						
All DC accounts	34.0	41.0	47.7	42.5	51.8	43.4
All DB plans	11.7	11.5	26.7	12.5	21.0	13.0
DC and/or DB plans	37.8	47.3	54.1	47.5	59.7	47.6
Full-time, full-year						
All DC accounts	47.7	44.5	61.8	54.4	58.3	57.7
All DB plans	38.1	33.4	25.1	17.8	19.1	16.6
DC and/or DB plans	67.1	59.7	70.3	61.6	63.6	64.6
Self-employed workers						
All DC accounts	41.5	49.0	52.3	48.0	43.2	42.9
All DB plans	10.8	20.5	13.7	16.8	6.4	16.4
DC and/or DB plans	45.4	57.1	57.4	56.2	45.5	46.6

NOTE: The table includes all current workers aged 64 and under.

[a] Industries are grouped into four classifications: 1) Agriculture, mining, and manufacturing; 2) wholesale and retail trade; 3) communications, information services, finance, insurance, real estate, repair services, transportation, utilities, professional services, and personal services; and 4) public administration.

[b] Part-time is less than 35 hours per week; part-year is less than 50 weeks per year. Self-employment may be part-time or full-time.

SOURCE: Author's computations from the 1989, 2001, and 2007 SCF.

and in nongovernmental services. The overall coverage rate was about the same for men and women in public administration.

Over time, pension coverage fell off sharply for male workers in goods-producing industries, from 62 percent in 1989 to 50 percent in 2007. This change is traceable to a huge drop in DB coverage, from 34 to 13 percent. On the other hand, overall pension coverage climbed for women, from 53 to 61 percent, as DC coverage expanded. In the trade sector, pension coverage rose from both men and women, because of a rise in coverage from DC plans. There was a precipitous drop in DB coverage in nongovernmental services over this period, from 43 to 20 percent among male employees and from 31 to 17 percent among female employees. Despite this, overall pension coverage remained largely unchanged for men and increased moderately for women over the period because of the sharp rise in DC coverage. In 1989, an astounding 74 percent of male employees in public administration had a DB plan, as did 62 percent of female employees. Overall coverage rates were (an equally astounding) 96 percent for men and 75 percent for women. Defined benefit coverage fell off for both, but DC coverage rose so that while overall pension coverage declined from 96 to 87 percent for male employees, it increased from 75 to 89 percent for female employees, resulting in women having a slightly higher percentage of coverage than did men.

By occupation of employment, pension coverage in 2007 was highest among professional and managerial workers, 78 percent for males and 69 percent for females, and second highest among technical and clerical workers, 63 and 62 percent, respectively. Among male workers, service workers ranked third at 55 percent, while blue-collar jobs (craft, operative, and agricultural) ranked last, at 47 percent. Among women, the rank order was reversed, with a 47 percent coverage rate among blue-collar workers and a 32 percent rate among service workers. As with industry of employment, DC coverage rates were almost as high as overall pension coverage rates, and the rank order was identical to that of the overall coverage rate. Defined benefit coverage rates were relatively small among technical and clerical workers and, surprisingly, among blue-collar workers as well. However, the DB coverage rate was 31 percent among male service workers and 22 and 20 percent among male and female professional and managerial workers, respectively.

The latter result reflects the large proportion of workers in this occupational group who are employed by the government sector.

Pension coverage rates were almost identical for male and female workers in technical and clerical jobs, as well as in blue-collar work. They were slightly higher for men than for women in professional and managerial jobs because of the higher share of men with a DC plan. Among service workers, 55 percent of male employees reported pension coverage compared to only 32 percent of female employees because of the higher rate of both DC and DB plan coverage.

There was little change in the overall pension coverage rate among professional and managerial workers between 1989 and 2007. Defined benefit coverage declined and DC coverage increased to offset the decline in DB coverage. Over the period, overall pension coverage fell from 80 to 78 percent for male employees but stayed the same for female employees at about 70 percent. Among technical and clerical workers, there was a slight increase in overall coverage for both men and women because of the rise in DC coverage rates. In contrast, among service workers, the overall pension coverage rate for male employees tailed off from 63 to 55 percent, mainly because of the decline of DB coverage, while it remained largely unchanged for female employees. Likewise, overall pension coverage slid from 56 to 47 percent among male workers because of the shrinkage of DB coverage, while it increased among female workers from 39 to 47 percent because of the expansion of DC coverage.

The third panel of Table 4.3 shows pension coverage by employment status. I have divided workers into four groups based on hours and weeks worked in the preceding year: part-time, full-year; full-time, part-year; part-time, part-year; and full-time, full-year.[24] I have also separated out self-employed workers. The results do not show dramatic differences by work status. In 2007, the pension coverage rate among male workers was highest among full-time, full-year employees, 64 percent; surprisingly, it was second highest among part-time, part-year employees, 60 percent;[25] next highest among part-time, full-year employees, 49 percent; and lowest among full-time, part-year workers, 48 percent. Among female workers, the rank order was first for full-time, part-year workers; second among full-time, full-year employees; third among part-time, part-year employees; and last among part-time, full-year employees. Self-employed workers ranked lower than any of these groups for male workers and second lowest for female workers.

Despite a drop in DB coverage, part-time, full-year workers saw a modest increase in their overall pension coverage rate between 1989 and 2007 because of an increasing share with a DC account. Full-time, part-year workers saw a modest drop in overall pension coverage because of a sharp decline in DB coverage. Pension coverage climbed among part-time, part-year male workers because of a large jump in DC plan coverage but remained the same among female workers. Defined benefit plan coverage plummeted among both male and female full-time, full-year workers from 1989 to 2007. However, the proportion with a DC plan expanded, and as a result overall pension coverage fell modestly among men but increased modestly among women so that women, though with a lower coverage rate than men in 1989, had a slightly higher coverage rate in 2007 than men. The pension coverage rate remained about the same for self-employed men in 2007 as in 1989, but fell among self-employed women because of a decline in the share with DC accounts.

Pension Coverage by Earnings Quintile

I next divide workers (excluding the self-employed) into earnings quintiles on the basis of their annual earnings to see how pension coverage varies by earnings level (see Table 4.4).[26] As expected, the pension coverage rate was much higher for higher-income workers. I also find that the gap in coverage spread out over time, particularly among male workers, as pension coverage slipped sharply among lower-earning workers.

In 2007, among men, the pension coverage rate varied directly by earnings quintile, from a high of 94 percent for the top quintile to a low of 39 percent for the bottom quintile. Among female workers, there was very little variation in pension coverage among the top three earnings quintiles: it was somewhat lower for the second quintile, and, again, quite a bit lower for the bottom quintile. Pension coverage rates were higher for female employees than for male employees among the bottom three quintiles, particularly the middle one, but were lower for the top two quintiles.

Over time, from 1989 to 2007, pension coverage fell off markedly among the bottom three quintiles for male workers and declined slightly

Table 4.4 Percentage of Workers with Pension Coverage by Earnings Quintile, 1989, 2001, and 2007

	1989		2001		2007	
	Male	Female	Male	Female	Male	Female
Bottom earnings quintile						
All DC accounts	37.6	38.1	43.4	41.6	34.2	40.1
All DB plans	30.9	26.8	16.2	14.1	9.9	10.5
DC and/or DB plans	56.7	52.3	51.6	49.2	38.9	46.0
Second earnings quintile						
All DC accounts	74.9	74.8	67.9	71.7	62.1	67.4
All DB plans	52.1	65.7	28.1	28.1	21.8	24.7
DC and/or DB plans	92.7	89.2	77.4	81.5	69.3	78.1
Third earnings quintile						
All DC accounts	73.8	98.1	76.6	80.8	73.1	85.6
All DB plans	62.7	46.6	40.7	35.4	25.0	24.6
DC and/or DB plans	92.5	99.8	89.6	90.1	79.0	90.5
Fourth earnings quintile						
All DC accounts	91.5	100.0	89.8	95.0	84.9	83.6
All DB plans	41.3	13.3	34.0	15.2	31.9	26.7
DC and/or DB plans	91.5	100.0	90.8	95.0	89.4	86.5
Top earnings quintile						
All DC accounts	72.7	99.5	90.9	58.2	94.0	86.0
All DB plans	66.1	96.5	27.1	28.8	20.3	8.3
DC and/or DB plans	97.0	100.0	92.8	78.4	94.3	86.0

NOTE: The table includes all current workers aged 64 and under. Self-employed are excluded from this table. Earnings quintiles are based on the combined distribution of annual earnings for men and women.
SOURCE: Author's computations from the 1989, 2001, and 2007 SCF.

for the top two quintiles. Among female employees, there was a falloff of pension coverage in each earnings quintile. In the bottom earnings quintile, the overall pension coverage rate diminished by 18 percentage points for men and 6 percentage points for women. In the second earnings quintile, the DB coverage rate collapsed for both male and female workers and the DC coverage rate also fell, but more modestly. Overall, the pension coverage rate lessened by 23 percentage points for men and by 11 percentage points for women.

In the middle quintile, DB coverage again plummeted for male and female workers, the share with DC plans remained almost unchanged for men but slipped for women, and, as a result, the overall pension coverage rate slid by 14 percentage points for men and by 9 percentage points for women. Among the top two earnings quintiles, overall pension coverage rate slipped a bit for men and went down by about 14 percentage points for women.[27]

Among male employees, there was a growing cleavage in pension coverage between the top of the earnings distribution and the bottom three earnings quintiles. This was, in turn, mainly due to a growing gap in the proportion with DC plans. Among female workers, the differentials in pension coverage between the top quintile and the bottom three actually lessened over the period 1989–2007.[28]

Pension Wealth on the Household Level

We now turn our attention to household level wealth. Table 4.5 highlights trends in pension coverage over the 1983–2007 period. In this and the subsequent tables, it should be noted that the unit of observation is the household, not the individual worker. Moreover, I have divided households into three age groups: under 47, 47–64, and 65 and older. The valuation of DB pension rights among younger workers has to be interpreted cautiously. In fact, data for the youngest group are the most problematic, since estimates of DB pension wealth are based on projected benefits in 20–40 years and depend on projecting future work life and future job tenure with the same employer. In the case of the 1983 SCF, the data needed to calculate DB pension wealth are available only for individuals 40 years and older, so I cannot make corresponding estimates of DB wealth for the 46 and under group. Data for retirees are the most secure, since both pension and Social Security benefit levels are already determined. Estimates of both DB and Social Security wealth for the middle-aged group lie in between in terms of reliability. Individuals close to retirement have a fairly good idea of their expected pension benefits and their expected age of retirement and have a high likelihood of remaining with their current employer (see Farber [2001] for some evidence).

The picture that unfolds is a precipitous drop in DB coverage largely compensated for by a sizable increase in DC coverage. Moreover, while

Table 4.5 Percentage of Households with Pension Wealth, 1983–2007

	1983	1989	2001	2007
All households				
DC accounts	11.1	24.0	52.2	52.6
DB plans	—	45.6	34.4	34.0
Pension wealth	—	56.0	65.6	64.1
Aged 46 and under				
DC accounts	13.7	31.2	53.8	49.9
DB plans	—	37.9	22.8	22.6
Pension wealth	—	52.2	60.7	54.7
Aged 47–64				
DC accounts	12.3	28.3	62.0	63.8
DB plans	68.5	56.8	45.3	38.8
Pension wealth	70.3	67.5	75.9	74.1
Aged 65 and over				
DC accounts	2.0	1.3	35.0	40.8
DB plans	67.0	51.3	46.5	50.6
Pension wealth	67.8	51.8	62.6	68.5

NOTE: Households are classified into age groups by the age of the head of household.
   Pension wealth = DB + DC.
SOURCE: Author's computations from the 1983, 1989, 2001, and 2007 SCF.

mean pension wealth gained rapidly in the 1990s, its growth slowed down considerably in the 2000s. Among young households in particular, pension coverage dropped sharply in the 2000s and mean pension wealth stagnated.

The share of all households with DC pension accounts skyrocketed during the 1983–2001 period, from 11 to 52 percent, or by 41 percentage points. The story is very similar for the three different age groups shown in Table 4.5, even among the elderly. The proportion holding pension accounts advanced by 40 percentage points in age group 46 and under, by 50 percentage points among households in age group 47–64, and by 33 percentage points among elderly households. In 2001, 62 percent of households in the age range of 47–64 held some form of DC account, compared to 35 percent of elderly households and 54 percent of younger households. Most of the gains occurred after 1989.

The picture changes during the 2000s. Among all households, there is virtually no change in the DC coverage rate. For the younger age group, the share actually dropped by 4 percentage points. For the middle age group, there was a slight increase of 2 percentage points, and among elderly households an increase of 6 percentage points.

Trends are also different for DB pension wealth. The share of all households with DB pension wealth fell by 11 percentage points between 1989 and 2001. Among households in age group 47–64, the decline was about the same, 12 percentage points from 1989 to 2001. However, the fall was even more precipitous—by 24 percentage points—from 1983 to 2001. Among elderly households the proportion fell by 5 percentage points from 1989 to 2001 and by 20 percentage points from 1983 to 2001, while among young households the share was down by 15 percentage points from 1989 to 2001. In 2001, while 47 percent of elderly households held some form of DB pension wealth, 45 percent of households in age group 47–64 and only 23 percent of young households recorded DB entitlements. Most of the loss in coverage again occurred after 1989.

The trend moderated after 2001. Among households under age 47, the share with DB coverage remained unchanged. For middle-aged households, the share was down another 6.5 percentage points in 2007. Elderly households bucked the trend, as the share with DB coverage rose by 4.1 percentage points.

The percentage of all households covered by either a DC or a DB plan increased from 56 to 66 percent between 1989 and 2001. Among the 47–64 age group, the proportion rose by 8 percentage points, and among the elderly, the share increased by 11 percentage points. However, comparing 2001 to 1983 shows a smaller rise in pension coverage among the 47–64 age group (6 percentage points) and an actual decline among elderly households (5 percentage points). Among younger households the proportion rose by 10 percentage points from 1989 to 2001. The share of households covered by some form of pension in 2001 was 76 percent among the middle-aged, compared to 63 percent among the elderly and 61 percent among the youngest age group.

The story once again changes from 2001 to 2007. The share of households with some form of pension coverage actually declined by 1.4 percentage points. The decline was particularly precipitous among younger households, whose coverage rate fell by 6.1 percentage points. Among the middle-aged, the fall was 1.8 percentage points, whereas among the elderly pension coverage rose by 5.9 percentage points. As shown in Table 4.6, there were huge increases in the average holdings of DC pension accounts. Among all households, the average value of these accounts increased almost fourteenfold between 1983 and 2001, to $52,800 (all dollar figures are in 2007 dollars, unless otherwise noted). Among age group 46 and under the increase was by a factor of 11, and among age group 47–64 the gain was by a factor of 12. Among elderly households, the rise was by a factor of 31. In 2001, mean DC pension wealth was greatest among age group 47–64, at $113,000, second highest among elderly households, at $63,000, and lowest among the youngest age group, at $33,000.

The rise in DC wealth slowed down from 2001 to 2007. Among all households, mean DC wealth increased by (only) 22 percent. Middle-aged households saw their mean DC wealth increase by 18 percent and

Table 4.6 Mean Household Pension Wealth, 1983–2007 (in thousands, 2007$)

	1983	1989	2001	2007
All households				
DC pension wealth	4.6	10.6	62.8	76.8
DB pension wealth	—	56.5	58.0	61.2
Pension wealth	—	67.1	120.8	138.0
Aged 46 and under				
DC pension wealth	3.0	9.2	33.1	30.7
DB pension wealth	—	25.1	20.3	24.6
Pension wealth	—	34.3	53.4	55.3
Aged 47–64				
DC pension wealth	9.7	20.4	113.1	133.8
DB pension wealth	90.1	100.3	98.9	91.4
Pension wealth	99.7	120.7	211.9	225.3
Aged 65 and over				
DC pension wealth	2.1	2.3	62.7	84.5
DB pension wealth	73.6	82.4	89.2	91.2
Pension wealth	75.7	84.7	151.9	175.8

NOTE: Households are classified into age groups by the age of the head of household. Pension wealth = DB + DC.
SOURCE: Author's computations from the 1983, 1989, 2001, and 2007 SCF.

elderly households by 35 percent. On the other hand, younger households actually experienced a decline in DC wealth, by 7 percent, to $31,000 in 2007.

Opposite trends are again evident for DB pension wealth. Among all households, the mean value rose by only 3 percent between 1989 and 2001. Losses occurred for younger households, down by 19 percent, and for age group 47–64, down by 1.4 percent. However, the average value of DB plans among the elderly rose by 8 percent over the period—a reflection of their legacy status with respect to DB plans.

The years 2001–2007 saw continued slow growth in DB pension wealth; among all households, it rose by 5.5 percent. A 21 percent gain was recorded among young households, though the actual level was still quite low, but among middle-aged households mean DB fell by 7.5 percent. Elderly households saw a moderate gain of 2.3 percent. By 2007, mean DB wealth was about the same among elderly and middle-aged households ($91,000), but only $24,600 among younger households.

I can now consider one of the issues raised in the beginning of this chapter: Has the spread of DC-type pension plans adequately compensated for the decline in traditional DB pension coverage? The answer is a resounding "yes" for the period from 1989 to 2001 (and 1983 to 2001), but a "perhaps" for the period 2001–2007. Average pension wealth (the sum of DC and DB pensions) increased for all age groups between 1989 and 2001. Among all households, the mean value of total pension wealth climbed by 80 percent. Among those in age groups 46 and under and 47–64, the mean value increased by 56 and 76 percent, respectively, while among elderly households the mean value jumped by 79 percent.

However, the growth in pension wealth slowed down markedly from 2001 to 2007. Mean pension wealth among all households rose by 14 percent, compared to an 80 percent gain during the 1980s. It inched up by only 4 percent among young households and by 6 percent among middle-aged ones, though it did gain 16 percent among the elderly. By 2007 mean pension wealth was $225,300 among age group 47–64, $175,800 among the elderly, and only $55,300 for young households.

With the transition in the pension system, has the inequality of pension wealth increased or declined? We will see that pension inequality among DC plan holders is considerably greater than that among DB plan holders. As a result, the transition to DC plans raised overall pension inequality. This was true despite a decline in inequality in both DC wealth and DB wealth by themselves.

Table 4.7 records the inequality of pension wealth among *pension holders only* within age group. The inequality of holdings of DC accounts generally declined over the years from 1989 (or 1983) and 2007. This was true among all DC pension holders, young households who held DC plans, and middle-aged ones as well. The drop in the Gini coefficient from 1989 to 2007 was 0.022 among all households, 0.038 among those under age 47, and 0.045 among middle-aged ones. In contrast, the inequality of DC holdings spiked upward among elderly households, with the Gini coefficient rising by 0.101 points from 1989 to 2007. This change reflected the entry into the ranks of the elderly of newer and newer cohorts of elderly households with large holdings of DC wealth.

Table 4.7 Inequality of Pension Wealth among Pension Holders, 1983–2007 (Gini coefficients)

	1983	1989	2001	2007
All pension holders				
DC accounts	—	0.750	0.741	0.728
DB plans	—	0.606	0.582	0.549
Pension wealth	—	0.641	0.676	0.661
Pension holders: aged 46 and under				
DC accounts	—	0.731	0.719	0.693
DB plans	—	0.576	0.552	0.511
Pension wealth	—	0.635	0.672	0.653
Pension holders: aged 47–64				
DC accounts	0.732	0.726	0.714	0.681
DB plans	0.507	0.537	0.571	0.519
Pension wealth	0.524	0.577	0.637	0.617
Pension holders: aged 65+				
DC accounts	0.687	0.635	0.703	0.736
DB plans	0.458	0.605	0.541	0.556
Pension wealth	0.466	0.607	0.607	0.642

NOTE: Households are classified into age groups by the age of the head of household. Pension wealth = DB + DC.
SOURCE: Author's computations from the 1983, 1989, 2001, and 2007 SCF.

Despite the reduction of inequality in DC wealth, the level of inequality in DC pension wealth was still very high in 2007. The Gini coefficient among all DC pension account holders was 0.728 in 2007. This compares to a Gini coefficient for net worth of 0.834. Inequality among DC account holders within age group was almost as great as among all DC account holders.[29]

The inequality of DB wealth also fell over these years. The Gini coefficient for DB wealth among all households who held DB plans fell by 0.058 points from 1989 to 2007. It declined by 0.065 points among young households, 0.018 among middle-aged ones, and by 0.048 points among elderly ones.

However, when we consider total pension wealth, we find just the opposite story, despite the declines in both DC and DB wealth inequality. Pension wealth inequality overall increased by 0.020 Gini points among all pension holders from 1989 to 2007, by 0.018 Gini points among young households, by 0.039 Gini points among middle-aged ones, and by 0.036 Gini points among elderly ones. On the surface, these results may appear rather paradoxical. However, the explanation emanates from the fact that DC wealth inequality is considerably higher than DB wealth inequality. In 2007, for example, the Gini coefficient for DC wealth among all households with DC plans was 0.728, compared to only 0.549 for DB plan holders. Similar differences exist for the individual age groups.

Not surprisingly, the switchover from DB pension plans to DC pension plans resulted in a rise in overall pension wealth inequality. The reason is that the Gini coefficient for the sum of DB and DC wealth is equal to a weighted sum of the Gini coefficients for DC and DC individually (plus an interaction term), where the weight is equal to the share of each component in total pension wealth. The rising share of DC wealth in total pension wealth over time, from 1989 to 2007, thus led to a rise in the Gini coefficient in overall pension wealth, despite the fact that the Gini coefficient for both DC wealth and DB wealth declined over time individually.[30]

Figure 4.1a gives dramatic evidence of how differently DC and DB wealth are distributed and about how much more unequal DC wealth is than DB wealth. In this case, I divide pension wealth into its DB and DC components and show the distribution of each among account holders *only* by their corresponding percentile level in 2007. Here it is clear that DB dominates DC values at least up to the 95th percentile, and then at the very upper reaches of the respective distributions the reverse is true. This pattern reflects the small accumulations of DC plans like IRAs and some 401(k) plans and the more substantial values of most DB plans. For example, at the 25th percentile the value of DC plans was $11,000 versus $44,000 for DB plans. However, at the 95th percentile the value of the former was $1.5 million while that of the latter was $1.0 million. The contrasting distributions also illustrate why DC inequality is higher than DB inequality, since there is a larger share of DC holders with both small and large amounts of pension wealth than DB holders.

The percentage difference declined with percentile level, from 88 percent at the 5th percentile to 15 percent at the 90th. At the 99th percentile, DC exceeded DB by 43 percent, a reflection of the fact that the DC system has particularly benefited the high end of the pension (and wealth) distribution. A similar pattern is evident for age group 47–64 (see Figure 4.1b). However, here the crossover point was between the 90th and 95th percentiles. At the 95th percentile and above, DC exceeded DB. Indeed, at the 99th percentile, DC exceeded DB by a sizable 54 percent.

Figures 4.2a and 4.2b provide a slightly different perspective on the distribution of pension wealth by considering its distribution among *all households* (not just pension holders). The story that emerges is different from when we consider only pension holders. In fact, the inequality of pension wealth among all households remained fairly unchanged over the years 1989–2007. The reason is that the disequalizing effect of rising pension wealth inequality among pension holders alone was offset by the equalizing effect of a rising share of households holding pension wealth.

As shown in Figure 4.2a, there were large gains in pension wealth over the 1989–2001 period at all percentiles, reflecting the increase in the share of households with a pension plan and the rising value of pension wealth. However, the overall pattern is U-shaped. The percentage gain declined from 214 percent at the 50th percentile to 72 percent at the 75th percentile, and then increased to 86 percent at the 99th percentile. These results illustrate that the largest growth of pension wealth occurred at both the bottom and the top of the pension wealth distribution. As a result, overall pension wealth inequality remained almost unchanged over these years.

110   Wolff

Figure 4.1a Percentage Difference between DC and DB Pension Wealth among Account Holders by Pension Percentile, All Households, 2007

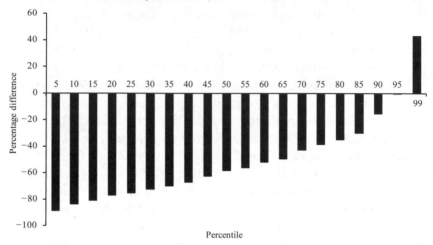

Figure 4.1b Percentage Difference between DC and DB Pension Wealth among Account Holders by Pension Percentile, Aged 47–64, 2007

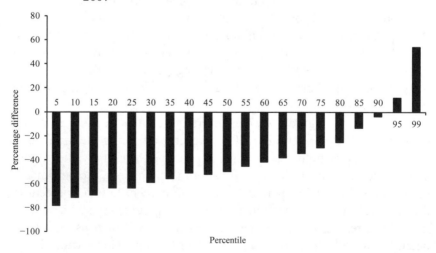

SOURCE: Author's computations from the 2007 SCF.

Figure 4.2a Percentage Change in Pension Wealth by Percentile, All Households, 1989, 2001, and 2007

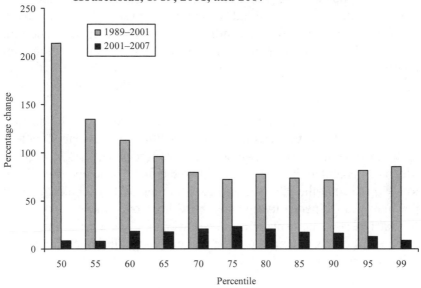

Figure 4.2b Percentage Change in Pension Wealth by Percentile, Aged 47–64, 1989, 2001, and 2007

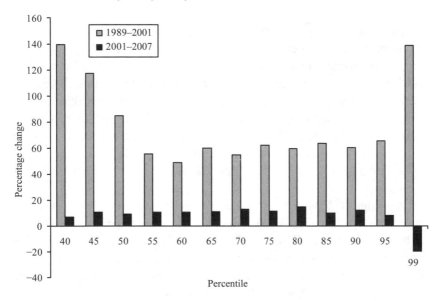

SOURCE: Author's computations from the 1989, 2001, and 2007 SCF.

From 2001 to 2007, pension wealth showed much more modest gains at all percentiles. Moreover, the largest gains were in the middle part of the pension wealth distribution (averaging about 20 percent from the 60th to the 90th percentile) and much smaller at the bottom and top. This result too is in accordance with the finding that the Gini coefficient for pension wealth changed very little over this period, since the largest increase in pension wealth occurred in the middle of the pension wealth distribution.

Results were quite similar among middle-aged households (see Figure 4.2b). Relative gains in pension wealth had a U-shaped pattern between 1989 and 2001, declining from 139 percent at the 40th percentile to 49 percent at the 70th percentile in the first period and then rising to 139 percent at the 99th percentile. As among all households, overall pension wealth inequality changed very little over these years. Over the later period, percentage advances were fairly uniform and small (around 10 percent) across percentiles, and inequality again remained relatively unchanged.[31]

TRENDS IN PRIVATE ACCUMULATIONS

How has the radical makeover of the retirement system affected trends in both the level and the inequality of private accumulations? Recall that private accumulations are defined as the sum of net worth and DB. It thus represents the resources available to households for retirement from private sources—their own wealth accumulations and private (as opposed to public) pension funds. The results indicate that with the dismantling of the DB pension system, private accumulations generally grew slower than household net worth. Moreover, inequality in the distribution of private accumulations increased more than that of net worth.

As noted in Chapter 2, there was very strong growth in net worth during the 1990s and 2000s. Mean net worth rose 73 percent from 1983 to 2007, while the median rose 38 percent (see Table 4.8).[32] When DB wealth is added to net worth to obtain private accumulations, I find that its mean value was up by 63 percent between 1989 and 2007, lower than that of net worth, while its median value increased by 25 percent,

Table 4.8 Mean and Median Net Worth and Private Accumulations, 1983–2007 (in thousands, 2007$)

	1983	1989	2001	2007
All households				
Mean net worth	270.4	309.8	445.1	536.1
Mean private accumulations	—	366.1	503.2	597.5
Median net worth	69.5	74.3	86.1	102.5
Median private accumulations	—	114.0	118.3	142.8
Aged 46 and under				
Mean net worth	126.6	171.2	205.0	209.9
Mean private accumulations	—	196.3	225.3	234.5
Median net worth	30.4	27.8	24.2	21.8
Median private accumulations	—	40.5	38.5	35.0
Aged 47–64				
Mean net worth	437.5	477.0	700.5	803.2
Mean private accumulations	526.3	577.3	799.4	894.7
Median net worth	126.8	156.0	161.1	206.5
Median private accumulations	215.3	226.9	249.4	283.8
Aged 65+				
Mean net worth	434.2	454.1	652.8	809.1
Mean private accumulations	505.9	536.5	742.0	900.4
Median net worth	122.5	128.1	176.5	211.1
Median private accumulations	191.9	187.7	258.5	277.1

NOTE: Households are classified into age groups by the age of the head of household. Private accumulations = nonpension wealth + pension wealth.
SOURCE: Author's computations from the 1983, 1989, 2001, and 2007 SCF.

again slower than that of net worth. The differences reflect the much slower growth (and for households under age 65, the absolute decline) in the value of DB plans over these years.

The pattern is repeated among middle-aged and elderly households. Mean private accumulations among the former rose by 55 percent from 1989 to 2007, compared to a 68 percent increase in net worth, whereas median private accumulations were up by 25 percent, compared to a 32 percent gain in median net worth. Among elderly households, mean private accumulations advanced 68 percent, less than the 78 percent gain in new worth, and median private accumulations grew by 48 percent, again less than the 72 percent increase in median net worth. Among households under age 47, the story is somewhat different: Mean private accumulations were up by 19 percent, compared to a 23 percent growth in net worth. This result is similar to the other age groups. However, median private accumulations actually dropped by 14 percent in absolute terms, compared to a 22 percent decline in median net worth. This finding that the fortunes of young households deteriorated during the 1990s and 2000s will be a recurrent theme in this book.

Generally speaking, households fared worse in terms of private accumulations than in terms of conventional net worth between 1989 and 2007 (except for young households, for whom median private accumulations declined in absolute terms less than did median net worth). This finding indicates that the explosive growth of DC plans after 1989 did not fully compensate for the collapse of DB plans, at least in terms of the growth of household wealth.

I also find that the attrition of DB plans led to a rise in wealth inequality (see Table 4.9). The reason is that DB wealth is fairly equalizing, as discussed earlier, and its disappearance helped fuel a rise in wealth inequality. In 2007, the Gini coefficient for net worth among all households was 0.834, while that for private accumulations was 0.805. The higher level of inequality in the distribution of net worth than in private accumulations reflects the fact that DB pension wealth is distributed much more equally than net worth.

It was also the case that the equalizing effect of DB pension wealth lessened with the passage of time. Whereas the Gini coefficient for net worth among all households increased by a very modest 0.002 points over the years from 1989 to 2007, the Gini coefficient for private accumulations advanced even more, by 0.012 points. Alternatively, adding DB wealth to net worth resulted in a 0.039 decline in the Gini coefficient in 1989 but only a 0.029 decrease in 2007.

The results are even stronger for middle-aged households and over the longer time span, 1983–2007. For this group, the Gini coefficient for net worth increased by 0.033 points between 1983 and 2007, while the Gini coefficient for private accumulations ballooned by 0.070 points. Here we see even stronger evidence that the equalizing effect of DB pension wealth wore off over time. Adding DB wealth to net worth caused the Gini coefficient to decline by 0.073 in 1983, 0.053 in 1989, 0.043 in 2001, and 0.036 in 2007. These results help solve the puzzle discussed in Chapter 2 of why traditional wealth inequality remained

Table 4.9 Inequality of Net Worth and Private Accumulations, 1983–2007 (Gini coefficients)

	1983	1989	2001	2007
All households				
Net worth	0.799	0.832	0.826	0.834
Private accumulations	—	0.793	0.796	0.805
Aged 46 and under				
Net worth	0.797	0.887	0.859	0.880
Private accumulations	—	0.851	0.830	0.850
Aged 47–64				
Net worth	0.761	0.775	0.798	0.795
Private accumulations	0.688	0.721	0.756	0.758
Aged 65+				
Net worth	0.778	0.778	0.762	0.784
Private accumulations	0.708	0.738	0.724	0.748

NOTE: Households are classified into age groups by the age of the head of household. Private accumulations = nonpension wealth + pension wealth.
SOURCE: Author's computations from the 1983, 1989, 2001, and 2007 SCF.

relatively static from 1989 to 2007, while both income inequality and the ratio of stock prices to housing prices rose. The reason is that traditional wealth fails to include DB wealth. Once this is included, the results show a much sharper increase in wealth inequality from 1989 to 2007. In Chapter 5 we will see whether this pattern of results holds up when Social Security wealth is also included in total household wealth.

Results are similar for elderly households. Among the elderly, private accumulations inequality increased by 0.040 points from 1983 to 2007, whereas net worth inequality remained virtually unchanged. However, the pattern is different for younger households. Among them, the Gini coefficient for private accumulations changed by −0.001 from 1989 to 2007, slightly more than the −0.007 change in the Gini coefficient for net worth.[33]

Figure 4.3a provides an alternative picture of the change in the size distribution of private accumulations, among all households between 1989–2001 and 2001–2007. Over the earlier period, the major gains were made by households at the high end of the private accumulations distribution, while households at the bottom of the distribution experienced an absolute decline. Between these two extremes, relative gains

Figure 4.3a Percentage Change in Private Accumulations by Percentile, All Households, 1989, 2001, and 2007

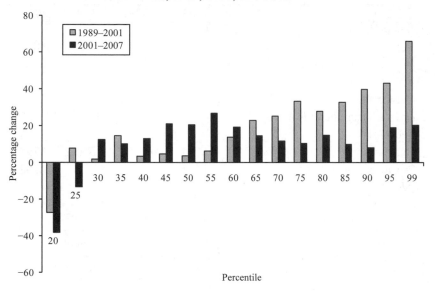

Figure 4.3b Percentage Change in Private Accumulations by Percentile, Aged 46 and Under, 1989, 2001, and 2007

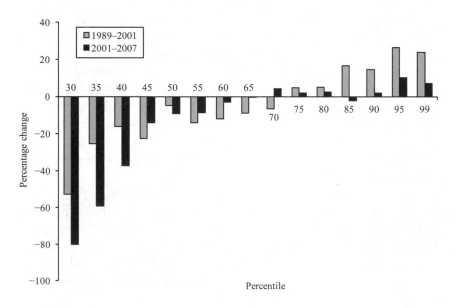

Figure 4.3c Percentage Change in Private Accumulations by Percentile, Aged 47–64, 1989, 2001, and 2007

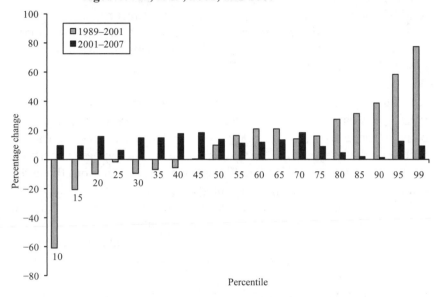

Figure 4.3d Percentage Change in Private Accumulations by Percentile, Aged 65 and Over, 1989, 2001, and 2007

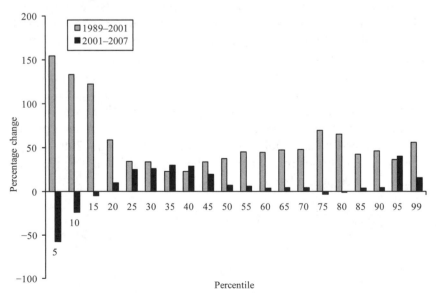

SOURCE: Author's computations from the 1989, 2001, and 2007 SCF.

showed no discernible pattern, which is consistent with the finding of a slight increase in the Gini coefficient over these years. From 2001 to 2007, the highest growth in private accumulations occurred roughly in the middle of the private accumulations distribution, with sharp declines at the bottom end. This pattern also seems consistent with the modest increase in the Gini coefficient for private accumulations over these years.

Among young households (Figure 4.3b), percentage changes in private accumulations were negative up to the 75th percentile and then positive above this during the earlier period. The pattern was very similar during the later period. The results for the later period are consistent with an increase in the Gini coefficient over these years, but those for the earlier period seem inconsistent with a decline in the Gini coefficient. However, further investigation shows that the reason for the decline in inequality in the earlier period is that private accumulations for households in the bottom 20 percent of the private accumulations distribution became more negative over the period (this also happened from 2001 to 2007).

Among middle-aged households, the percentage change in private accumulations was negative up at the 45th percentile and then positive after that over the earlier period (see Figure 4.3c). Over the second period, the percentage growth in private accumulations was positive at all percentiles but with no discernible pattern. These results are consistent with the finding of a rising Gini coefficient over the earlier period and little change over the second. In contrast, among elderly households (Figure 4.3d), private accumulations showed positive growth at all percentile levels in the earlier period, though percentage gains were greater at the bottom than the top, and as a result there was a modest decline in private accumulations inequality. During the later period, changes in private accumulations were negative up to the 20th percentile and generally positive above that, leading to a rise in the inequality of private accumulations.

DC EMPLOYER CONTRIBUTIONS (DCEMP) TO DEFINED CONTRIBUTION PENSION PLANS

To complete the picture of pension wealth, I look at trends in DCEMP. Recall that DCEMP is defined as the present discounted value of future employer contributions to DC plans. I will reserve a discussion of the effects of DCEMP on private accumulations (and augmented wealth) until the next chapter.

The share of all households reporting an employer contribution rose swiftly in the 1980s and 1990s, from 5 percent in 1983 to 28 percent in 2001, and then stayed at this level in 2007 (see Table 4.10). In contrast, the share of DC plan holders reporting an employer contribution climbed from 45 percent in 1983 to 63 percent in 1989, and then in 2001 fell to 54 percent, where it remained in 2007. The results indicate that employer matching contributions to DC pension plans (the employer "take-up rate") fell off over the last 20 years or so. This retrenchment likely reflects general cutbacks in employee compensation.

Likewise, the mean value of DCEMP, the present discounted value of future employer contributions to DC plans, among all households rose from virtually zero in 1983 to $34,300 (in 2007$) in 2001 but then fell off by 13 percent to $29,900 in 2007. Among those reporting employer contributions, the median value of DCEMP climbed from $18,900 in 1983 to $68,900 in 2001 but then fell by 16 percent to $57,900 in 2007. By all four measures, employer contributions to DC plans peaked in the early 2000s and then retreated in the mid- and late 2000s.

Younger workers were hit particularly hard during the 2000s. The share of all households in this age group reporting employer contributions grew rapidly, from 9 percent in 1983 to 24 percent in 1989 and then 38 percent in 2001. However, employers pulled back in the 2000s and their share fell to 34 percent. Likewise, the mean value of DCEMP mushroomed from $3,100 in 1983 to $47,900 in 2001 before slipping 22 percent to $37,400 in 2007. The share of DC plan holders who reported an employer contribution climbed from 63 percent in 1983 to 77 percent in 1989 and then fell off to 70 percent in 2001 and 67 percent in 2007. In a slightly different pattern, the median value of DCEMP among recipients only rose rather steadily, from $20,400 in 1983 to $78,000 in 2001, and then plunged by 14 percent to $66,800.

**Table 4.10 Employer Contributions to DC Plans (DCEMP), 1983–2007
(in thousands, 2007$)**

	1983	1989	2001	2007
All households				
Percent of households with DCEMP	4.9	15.0	28.4	28.4
Percent of DC plan holders with DCEMP	45.0	62.7	54.3	53.9
Mean DCEMP	1.9	14.3	34.3	29.9
Median DCEMP (recipients only)	18.9	41.1	68.9	57.9
Aged 46 and under				
Percent of households with DCEMP	8.6	24.1	37.8	33.6
Percent of DC plan holders with DCEMP	62.9	77.1	70.3	67.4
Mean DCEMP	3.1	22.2	47.9	37.4
Median DCEMP (recipients only)	20.4	41.7	78.0	66.8
Aged 47–64				
Percent of households with DCEMP	1.4	9.1	32.3	36.0
Percent of DC plan holders with DCEMP	11.4	32.0	52.1	56.5
Mean DCEMP	0.5	10.2	36.0	37.7
Median DCEMP (recipients only)	13.2	37.8	53.0	51.8

NOTE: Households are classified into age groups by the age of the head of household.
SOURCE: Author's computations from the 1983, 1989, 2001, and 2007 SCF.

Middle-aged households fared better during the 2000s. The share of all households in this age group reporting an employer contribution rose steadily, from virtually zero in 1983 to 36 percent in 2007. The percent of DC plan holders with DCEMP also increased more or less steadily, from 11 percent in 1983 to 57 percent in 2007. Mean DCEMP surged upward from virtually zero in 1983 to $36,000 in 2001 and then inched up by 4.7 percent to $37,700 in 2007. Median DCEMP among plan holders also gained rapidly from 1983 to 2001, from $13,200 to $53,000, but then slipped to $51,800 in 2007. All in all, there appeared to be much smaller gains in employer contributions to DC plans among middle-aged households after 2001.

SUMMARY OF FINDINGS

The 1980s and 1990s witnessed the unraveling of the traditional DB pension system in favor of DC pension coverage. Have U.S. households in general gained from this transformation? Have particular groups been hurt? Has the devolution of the DB system lowered or raised over-all inequality? In general, there was a marked turnaround in the fortunes of U.S. households in the 2000s as compared to the 1980s and 1990s.

The analysis in this book began with pension coverage rates among workers currently employed. So far I have looked at both changes over time and differences in coverage rates by gender, age group, race, edu-cational attainment, and employment status. In 2007, 56 percent of male workers under the age of 65 had some type of DC account, 19 percent had some form of DB entitlement, and altogether, 62 percent had some type of pension coverage. Not surprisingly, pension coverage was lower for younger workers (under age 47) than older ones (aged 47–64): 53 versus 75 percent.

Over time, DB coverage dropped considerably while DC coverage expanded. This systemic change benefited female workers but hurt male workers. From 1989 to 2001, expanded DC coverage more than com-pensated for dwindling DB coverage, and overall coverage rose by 3 percentage points for male workers and 4 percentage points for female workers. However, from 2001 to 2007, male pension coverage actu-ally dropped substantially, by 6 percentage points, and there was even a decrease in DC coverage. In contrast, female workers saw a modest increase of 2 percentage points in pension coverage from 2001 to 2007. As a result, the male coverage rate declined from 65 percent in 1989 to 62 percent in 2007, while the female coverage rate advanced from 55 to 60 percent. Moreover, whereas in 1989 and 2001 there was about a 10 percentage point gap in pension coverage between male and female workers, by 2007 almost complete convergence had been achieved.

The pension transformation also harmed younger male workers more than older ones. The coverage rate for younger male workers fell by 7 percentage points from 1989 to 2007, while that for older ones declined by only 3 percentage points.

Black workers were more adversely affected by the pension make-over than white workers. In 2007, there was a large gap in pension coverage (12 percentage points) between black male workers and (non-Hispanic) white male workers, and a huge gap (30 percentage points) between Hispanic male workers and non-Hispanic white male workers. Between 1989 and 2007, the pension coverage rate fell more for black male workers (4.6 percentage points) than for white male workers (3.2 percentage points). The decline for Hispanic male workers was less (1.6 percentage points) but was much lower than for whites or blacks. Black female workers saw their pension coverage rates plummet by 4.8 percentage points, while that for white female workers climbed by 8.1 percentage points (there was also a small decline among Hispanic female workers), and the gap in pension coverage between white females and black females advanced from 4 to 17 percentage points.

Pension coverage among the college-educated was helped by the pension transformation, but that among less-educated male workers was damaged. In 2007, only 22 percent of male workers without a high school degree had some form of pension coverage, compared to 51 percent of those with a high school degree, 62 percent of those with some college, and 79 percent of college graduates. Pension coverage showed an absolute decline among the three less-educated groups of male workers between 1989 and 2007, while among male college graduates the overall coverage rate rose moderately. As a result, the gap in pension coverage between college graduates and the other three educational groups expanded substantially over the 1989–2007 period.

Male blue-collar workers were also adversely affected by the changeover in the pension system. The pension coverage rate among male workers plummeted 12 percentage points in goods-producing industries in 1989–2007, while it fell considerably less in nongovernmental services and public administration and even expanded somewhat in the trade sector. Likewise, pension coverage fell 9 percentage points among craft, operative, and agricultural male workers, and 8 percentage points among male service workers. It contracted much less among male professional and managerial workers, and even gained a bit among technical and clerical male workers.

Similarly, lower-paid workers were hurt more by the pension makeover than higher-paid ones. In 2007, pension coverage among male workers was highest for the top quintile, 94 percent; second highest for the fourth quintile, 89 percent; third for the middle quintile, 79 percent; fourth for the second quintile, 69 percent; and markedly lower for the bottom quintile, 39 percent. Over time, pension coverage fell off markedly among the bottom three quintiles for male workers while declining only slightly among the top two quintiles between 1989 and 2007. Indeed, among male employees in 1989, overall pension coverage rates were over 90 percent among the top four earnings quintiles. This, in turn, was due to the concentration of DB plans in the middle of the earnings distribution. During the 1980s, the DB pension system helped shore up the middle class. However, with the unraveling of DB pensions, the overall pension coverage rate plunged among the bottom three earnings quintiles.

What did the pension transformation mean for pension coverage and pension wealth at the household level? I find that after phenomenal growth in the share of all households covered by DC plans from 1983 to 2001, the coverage rate leveled off from 2001 to 2007. In contrast, the DB coverage rate plummeted from 1989 to 2001, and though it leveled off during the new century, the overall pension coverage rate slipped by 1.4 percentage points from 2001 to 2007.

Mean DB pension wealth remained steady from 1989 to 2007. Buoyed by the stock market boom and rising DC coverage, average DC pension wealth skyrocketed from 1989 to 2001. It continued to rise from 2001 to 2007 but at a much slower pace. As a result, mean pension wealth climbed by 80 percent from 1989 to 2001 but then rose by only 14 percent from 2001 to 2007. Gains were particularly low among nonelderly households during the 2000s.

Younger households experienced smaller gains in both pension coverage and pension wealth as a result of the transition from the DB to the DC system. Many middle-aged people were still protected under the older DB system. Moreover, the elderly were by and large fully protected from the transition of the pension system since those with DB pensions were almost fully protected because of "grandfather" provisions. As a result, among households aged 46 and under, overall pension coverage advanced by only 2 percentage points from 1989 to 2007, compared to a 7 percentage point gain for middle-aged households and a 17 percentage point gain for elderly ones. Average pension wealth grew by 61 percent over this period, compared to an 87 percent gain for middle-aged ones and a 108 percent gain for the elderly.

In general, as was discussed in Chapter 2, U.S. households saw marked improvements in both mean and median marketable net worth over the period 1989–2007. However, mean private accumulations among all households grew slower than mean net worth, as did median private accumulations in comparison to median net worth. This pattern also held for middle-aged and elderly households. Among young households, mean private accumulations also grew slower than mean net worth. However, both median net worth and median private accumulations actually declined in absolute terms over these years.

How did the transformation of the pension system affect overall wealth inequality? Even though inequality in the distribution of both DC wealth and DB wealth fell among households that held that form of pension wealth, overall pension wealth inequality among pension holders actually rose from 1989 to 2007. The switchover from DB to DC plans was the main reason behind the rise in pension wealth inequality. Despite the decline in both DC and DB wealth inequality, the higher *level* of DC pension inequality coupled with its rising share in total pension wealth was the main factor accounting for the rise in pension wealth inequality.

Correspondingly, the pension transformation led to the increased inequality of private accumulations. First, it is of note that the Gini coefficient for private accumulations is lower than that for net worth (a 0.030-point difference among all households in 2001, for example). This difference is due to the smaller level of inequality in DB pensions than in net worth. Moreover, while the Gini coefficient for net worth among all households increased by 0.002 from 1989 to 2007, that for private accumulations increased more, by 0.012. In other words, the "inequality-reducing" effect of DB pensions declined from 0.039 in 1989 to 0.029 in 2007, largely because of the declining share of DB wealth in total private accumulations. This effect is most notable among middle-aged households, the group that was most subject to the transition of the pension system. Among them, the Gini coefficient for net worth rose by 0.033 from 1983 to 2007, while that for private accumulations surged by 0.070. Correspondingly, the difference in Gini coefficients between net worth and private accumulations tumbled from 0.073 in 1983 to 0.036 in 2007. Thus, the inequality of private accumulations rose much more than that of traditional net worth.

These results also help unravel the "puzzle" noted at the end of Chapter 2 and at the beginning of this chapter, namely that while income inequality surged in the 1990s and 2000s, (traditional) net worth inequality remained largely unchanged. We can see that if we expand the definition of net worth to include DB pension wealth, then there is a rise in wealth inequality during the 1990s and the 2000s.

Notes

1. This group also includes Roth IRAs and rollovers from pension accounts.
2. An alternative data source often used in these studies is the Health and Retirement Survey (HRS). This data source has an advantage over the SCF in that it has relatively complete data on earnings histories and has employer-provided information on individual DB pension plans of each employee covered by these plans. However, the SCF has three advantages over the HRS. First, the SCF provides much better data on the assets and liabilities that constitute marketable net worth. Second, the SCF data date from 1983, whereas the HRS data start in 1992. Since the transformation of the pension system dates from the late 1980s, the SCF data allow us to better track this change over the transition period. Third, the age coverage of the HRS is limited, whereas the SCF covers the whole population. This is important since young households were particularly hurt by the pension transformation, and these households are not covered in the HRS.
3. As I discuss in Appendix B, even though estimates of both DB pension and Social Security wealth are provided in the 1983 SCF, I reestimate the values of both to be consistent with later years.
4. I use age 109 somewhat arbitrarily as the last possible year of living. Moreover, the difference between the two formulas is that in the first the nominal discount rate δ is used whereas in the latter the real discount rate δ^* is used.
5. The results using the 3 percent real discount rate are not shown in this volume because reporting these results would vastly increase the number of tables in the book. Another crucial choice is the selection of which mortality rates to use in the calculation of DB and Social Security wealth. I have used here the standard ones from the *Statistical Abstract of the United States* based on age, gender, and race. However, there are also available unofficial life expectancy estimates for individuals by age, gender, and income class (and even by educational attainment). As is well known, higher-income (and more-educated) individuals live longer on average than lower-income (or less-educated) ones. The use of mortality rates conditional on income (or education) will have the effect of increasing estimates of DB pension wealth and Social Security wealth of higher-income (and better-educated) individuals relative to lower-income (and less-educated) individuals.
6. Technically speaking, the mortality rate m_t associated with the year of retirement is the probability of surviving from the current age to the age of retirement.
7. A couple of studies have looked at the reliability of employee-provided estimates of pension wealth by comparing self-reported pension benefits with estimates based on provider data. Using data from the 1992 wave of the HRS, Gustman and Steinmeier (1999) and Johnson, Sambamoorthi, and Crystal (2000) find that

individual reports of pension benefits tend to differ from those based on provider information. However, the latter also calculate that the median values of DB plans from the two sources were quite close (about a 6 percent difference). As a result, for *average* values of pension wealth, employee-provided estimates of expected pension wealth seem to be fairly reliable.

It should also be noted that my definition of DB wealth is based on a so-called ongoing concern treatment. It is assumed in this that employees continue to work at their place of employment until their expected date of retirement (this is also true for Social Security wealth). The alternative is to use the accrual value in which DB wealth (and Social Security wealth) is valued as of the current year on the basis of work experience *up to that date only*. I elect the ongoing concern method because it is consistent with my calculations of retirement adequacy in Chapter 7. The accrual method will produce lower values of both DB and Social Security wealth. Indeed, the accrual method and the ongoing concern treatment represent two extremes in the valuation of both DB and Social Security wealth. The latter treatment in particular relies on the assumptions that the firm or organization remains in existence over time and the employee continues working at the enterprise.

8. Separate imputations are performed for husband and wife and an adjustment in the Social Security benefit is made for the surviving spouse. See Appendix B for details.

9. As with pension wealth, the mortality rate m_t associated with the year of retirement is the probability of surviving from the current age to the age of retirement.

10. Though I can approximate the *number* of years of full- and part-time work for a given worker, I cannot determine when in his or her work history periods of nonemployment occurred.

11. As explained in Note 5, I have opted for the ongoing concern method rather than the accrual method. In the latter method, it is assumed that the worker stops working as of the year of the survey—say, 2007. One can then compute the expected DB pension entitlements as of 2007. One can also make such a calculation for Social Security wealth. I choose the ongoing concern method because this approach is consistent with my later estimates of retirement adequacy (see Chapter 7).

12. I do not include future *employee* contributions to DC plans (which I will later call DCEMPW) here, since this represents additional savings by the employee in the same vein as investments in other assets like housing, stocks, and bonds. In Chapter 7, however, when I treat retirement adequacy, I include the value of DCEMPW in projections of future retirement income. Likewise, I do not provide for a full projection of total wealth accumulation over time. This process would require a household microsimulation model, such as the MINT model, which the Urban Institute and the Social Security Administration use (see, for example, Smith, Toder, and Iams [2001]). However, in Chapter 7 I do provide for a simple projection of nonpension wealth to date of retirement.

This approach also avoids the difficulty of determining whether or not DC contributions add to net savings over time. As discussed in Chapter 3, the evidence is rather mixed, with Poterba, Venti, and Wise (2001) concluding that the growth of IRAs and 401(k) plans do not substitute for other forms of household wealth, and Engen and Gale (2000) finding that DC plans do not add to net savings but rather substitute for other forms of savings. Moreover, it is also possible that participation in a DB plan might reduce future savings (see, for example, Munnell [1996] and Kennickell and Sundén [1999]).

Although the addition of DCEMP to DC wealth makes DC wealth more comparable to DB wealth, some differences still remain between the two. In particular, there is greater risk associated with DC wealth. The benefit levels in DB plans are already set by the terms of the plans—that is why these are called *defined benefits*. Defined benefit wealth depends only on future labor force participation in the company and future earnings. The establishment of the Pension Benefit Guaranty Corporation in 1974 does, at least, insure the pension benefits (up to a fixed amount) in the event of the bankruptcy of a company. In comparison, DC wealth depends not only on future labor force participation and future earnings but also on future employee contributions, future employer contributions, and future rates of return. Indeed, the stock market experience of the 2000–2003 and 2007–2009 periods shows how difficult it would have been to project the future value of DC wealth even over these short periods. The benefits from DB plans are more certain than DC benefits. Indeed, the shifting of the risk from employer to employee is one of the reasons behind the rise of DC plans (see Wolff [2007c] for a discussion of this issue).

13. The SCF records DC plans only for the main job of each respondent. No information on DC plans is provided for secondary employment. This does not appear to be a significant problem because in 2001, 99.4 percent of the total labor earnings of the head and 98.8 percent of that of the spouse came from the person's primary job.

14. This will, if anything, bias upward the estimated employer contribution to the DC pension plan.

15. It should be noted that past employer contributions to DC plans are already included in the current market value of DC wealth.

16. Because of differences in methodology, it is not possible to include 1983 in this and the next three tables.

17. Part-time, temporary, and teenage workers are included in this tabulation. DC coverage is defined to include only workers with a positive balance in a DC plan and therefore excludes workers who are covered by a 401(k) plan but do not participate in such a plan, as well as people who have a pension account but do not contribute to that account. The 62 percent figure for men might seem high compared to previous estimates (see Chapter 3, for example, as well as Note 19, below) but this seemingly high estimate is explained by the fact that my figure includes individuals with an IRA or Keogh plan and individuals with a DB plan from a past job.

18. This means that the employee had worked long enough to become vested. By law, such entitlements remain in effect even after the employee leaves a company.

19. Munnell and Quinby (2009) also find a decline in the share of workers who participated in pension plans. They use the CPS as their data source, and the years covered were 1979 and 2008. Their sample consisted of workers aged 25–64. They report that in 2008, 42 percent of male workers and 39 percent of female workers participated in a pension plan. These figures are quite a bit lower than my calcula-

tions for 2007 (62 and 60 percent for male and female workers, respectively). The differences in results are attributable to different definitions of pension coverage. Munnell and Quinby include in their pension coverage estimates only workers who are covered in a plan by their current employers, while my figures include DB pension entitlements from past jobs, as well as IRA and Keogh holdings. They find that the coverage rate for male workers declined from 56 percent in 1979 to 42 percent in 2008, while for female workers the rate actually increased from 36 to 39 percent. These results are consistent with my findings reported here. As a consequence, Munnell and Quinby find that the coverage gap between male and female workers fell from 20 percentage points in 1979 to only 3 percentage points in 2008, results also similar to mine. They note that among full-time, full-year workers in 2008, women actually had a slightly higher level of pension coverage than men.

Also, see Sanzenbacher (2006) for an illuminating comparison of different estimates of pension coverage from the CPS, SCF, SIPP, and the Panel Study of Income Dynamics.

Purcell (2009a), also using CPS data, finds a slight decline in the overall share of workers who participated in employer-sponsored retirement plans between 2007 and 2009, from 52.0 to 51.1 percent. He also reports that the share of workers whose employer sponsored a retirement plan also fell slightly, from 59.9 to 59.0 percent. Purcell found that year-round, full-time female workers had reached virtual parity with their male counterparts, with pension coverage rates of 51.0 and 51.2 percent, respectively. This is very similar to my results on gender differences.

20. I combine the two age groups since differences between younger and older workers are very similar within each demographic grouping, as they are among all workers (see Appendix Tables B.1–B.3 for details by age group).

A breakdown of pension wealth by demographic characteristic is also shown for households in Chapter 6.

21. Several studies have examined racial differences in pension coverage. Mok and Siddique (2009) also report a substantial gap in pension coverage between African Americans and whites on the basis of data from the CPS and the National Longitudinal Survey of Youth (NLSY) over the period 1997–2008. On average they find that 75 percent of white male workers had a pension plan compared to 68 percent of black male workers. However, the racial gap was reversed among females, as 77 percent of black female workers had a pension plan compared to 75 percent of white female workers.

Munnell and Sullivan (2009) also find racial and ethnic gaps in the share of workers with a 401(k) plan. Using the 2001, 2004, and 2007 SCF, they calculate that 57 percent of white workers were eligible for a 401(k) plan on average over these years, compared to 55 percent of black workers and only 37 percent of Hispanic workers. The take-up rate was also higher among white workers. On average, 78 percent of white workers eligible for a 401(k) plan elected to participate, compared to 70 percent of black workers and 70 percent of Hispanic workers. However, because of differences in definitions of pension coverage, it is not possible to provide a direct comparison between these two sets of results and mine.

Purcell (2009a) also finds that white workers had higher coverage rates than minority workers. In 2008, the pension coverage rate for employer-sponsored retirement plans was 57 percent for non-Hispanic whites, 46 percent for non-Hispanic blacks, and 30 percent for Hispanic workers. These results are similar to mine.

22. GED refers to the General Educational Development test, given in lieu of a high school degree.

23. The industries are grouped into four categories: 1) agriculture, mining, and manufacturing; 2) wholesale and retail trade; 3) communications, information services, finance, insurance, real estate, repair services, transportation, utilities, professional services, and personal services; and 4) public administration. The classification scheme is dictated by the industry groupings provided in the SCF data.

24. The question of hours worked in the 2007 SCF is: How many hours (do you/does [he/she]) work on (your/her/his) main job in a normal week?

25. This can be traced to the high share of part-time workers with an IRA or Keogh account.

26. In the case of married couples, the husband's and wife's earnings are treated as separate earnings.

27. The very high DB coverage rate for women in the top quintile in 1989 can be traced to the high concentration of government employees in this group.

28. One similar analysis was conducted by Karamcheva and Sanzenbacher (2010) on the basis of CPS data over the period 1979–2008. They divide the earnings distribution into three equal tiers for private sector male workers in the age group 25–64. They find that on average over this period only about one-third of workers in the bottom third worked for an employer that sponsored a pension plan, in comparison with over 70 percent of the top third. Moreover, while the pension participation rate of the top third was near 100 percent and constant over time, that of the middle third fell from 94 to 86 percent over this period and that of the bottom third from 85 to 69 percent. As a result, the overall share of workers in the top third who participated in a pension plan averaged about 70 percent over the period and remained fairly constant, while the overall share in the middle third averaged about 60 percent and fell by 22 percent over the period, and that of the bottom third averaged about 30 percent and fell 29 percent. Purcell (2009a) likewise reports on the basis of CPS data that only 28 percent of workers in the lowest quartile in terms of annual earnings in 2008 participated in a retirement plan at work, compared to 69 percent of workers in the top quartile.

I also report large differentials in pension coverage between the bottom, middle, and top earnings quintile of male workers under the age of 65. Moreover, I find that pension coverage had slipped among the bottom and middle earnings quintiles from 1989 to 2007 but had remained roughly constant for the top quintile. However, it is not possible to directly compare actual estimates between my work and the two studies cited above, since the definition of pension coverage differs between the three studies. For example, I include past DB pension in my definition of coverage, whereas Karamcheva and Sanzenbacher do not. This makes my estimate of DB coverage rates higher than those of Karamcheva and Sanzenbacher.

29. This result is in accordance with media accounts of a large divide in the value of 401(k) plans between executives and staff workers in large corporations (see, for example, Leonhardt [2002]).

30. This relationship can perhaps be seen most clearly by a decomposition of the coefficient of variation. As derived in Wolff (1987b), for any variable $X = X_1 + X_2$,

$$CV^2(X) = p_1^2 CV^2(X_1) + p_2^2 CV^2(X_2) + 2CC(X_1, X_2),$$

where CV is the coefficient of variation (the ratio of the standard deviation to the mean), CC is the coefficient of covariation, defined as the ratio of the covariance to X^2, $p_1 = X_1/X$, and $p_2 = X_2/X$. The interaction term principally reflects the correlation coefficient between DC and DB wealth. The correlation coefficient also rose over time (from 0.07 in 1989 to 0.24 in 2007 among all households). The rising interaction term as a result also made a positive contribution to the growth in overall pension wealth inequality.

31. The Gini coefficient for PW among all households was 0.799 in 1989 and 0.783 in 2007, while that for PW among middle-aged households was about 0.715 in the two years.

32. When I exclude DC wealth to obtain nonpension net worth, I find that mean nonpension wealth rose by a lesser amount from 1989 to 2007, 54 percent, while median nonpension net worth was up by only 6 percent. It is at once clear how important DC plans were to the growth of net worth. This is not to say, of course, that households would not have accumulated wealth in alternative instruments in the absence of the existence of DC plans. However, the accumulations were likely to have been less for two reasons. First, savings in DC plans are tax-sheltered, which means that they accumulate at a higher rate in DC plans, ceteris paribus, than in taxable investments. Second, the value of employer-provided DC plans, like the 401(k), also incorporates the contributions made by employers. Employer contributions would not likely have occurred in alternative investments. A comparison of trends in net worth with those in NWX suggests that households substituted savings in 401(k) and other DC plans for other forms of private savings. This result is more in accord with the arguments of Gale (1995) and Engen and Gale (2000) than Poterba, Venti, and Wise (2001). (See Chapter 3 for a review of the pertinent literature).

33. The use of a higher (lower) discount rate in the calculation of DB pension wealth would have lowered (raised) the value of DB pension wealth and consequently increased (decreased) the measured inequality of private accumulations. Correspondingly, the use of a higher (lower) discount rate would have led to a lower (higher) increase in the Gini coefficient for private accumulations between 1989 (or 1983) and 2007.

5

Stagnation of Retirement
Wealth in the 2000s

One of the main topics to be addressed in this book is retirement adequacy. A full picture of retirement resources would not be complete without a consideration of expected Social Security benefits and Social Security wealth (SSW). This chapter fills in that gap.

We pick up the story from Chapter 4 by focusing on SSW, retirement wealth in general, and augmented wealth. As discussed in Chapter 1, over the last three decades traditional DB pension plans were largely replaced with DC pensions. We focused on two major issues in the previous chapter. First, has this transformation been beneficial to most U.S. households? Second, has it led to a rise or a decline in inequality?

I find that mean augmented wealth (the sum of net worth, pension and SSW), after rising dramatically during the 1990s, showed much smaller gains in the new century. Moreover, median augmented wealth by age group was generally stagnant over the years 2001 to 2007. Furthermore, the inequality of augmented wealth showed an increase from 1989 to 2007, while the inequality of net worth remained unchanged.

The next section of the chapter looks at time trends in SSW on the household level from 1983 to 2007. I then present summary measures on total (augmented) household wealth. After that, alternative pension wealth calculations are treated, followed by an update on pension wealth and augmented wealth to July 1, 2009, on the basis of changes in the stock market. The final section provides a summary and concluding remarks.

SOCIAL SECURITY AND TOTAL RETIREMENT WEALTH

I first look at how SSW compares to pension wealth. Is it greater or smaller than pension wealth—and, correspondingly, is it a more or less important source of retirement income than pension wealth? Has SSW grown faster or slower than pension wealth?

Social Security wealth among all households averaged $165,300 in 2001 (see Table 5.1); this compared to an average pension wealth of $138,000. Thus, even as of 2007, SSW was a more important retirement asset than pension wealth. Median SSW in 2007 was $139,300—close to that of mean SSW—and eight times greater than median pension wealth.[1] The fact that mean and median SSW were so close was due to a normal or nearly normal distribution of SSW. Mean SSW among middle-aged households was 26 percent greater than that among elderly households, and median SSW 39 percent larger. The greater SSW among middle-aged relative to elderly households largely reflected the higher lifetime earnings of the former. Mean and median SSW among young households was about 40 percent lower than among age group 47–64. This discrepancy was mainly due to the greater discount factor applied to future Social Security benefits among young earners (from the larger number of years left before retirement).

During the 1980s, SSW gained less than pension wealth. Mean SSW among all households rose by 46 percent between 1989 and 2001, in comparison to an 80 percent gain in mean pension wealth, the sum of DB and DC wealth. Mean SSW gained 56 percent among middle-aged households, 38 percent among young households, and 35 percent among elderly households. The increase in median SSW was very close to that of mean SSW—a reflection of both the low degree of inequality in SSW and the relative constancy in SSW inequality over time.[2] The rise in SSW over these years reflected primarily increasing real wages, particularly in the late 1990s, and rising longevity. This was offset, in part, by the increase in the age (65 to 67) at which full Social Security benefits were received for persons born after 1938 and the rising share of minorities in the labor force, whose life expectancy is shorter than that of whites.

In contrast to the 1990s, the years 2001–2007 witnessed almost no growth in SSW. Indeed, mean and median SSW fell slightly among young, middle-aged, and elderly households. This turnaround was largely attributable to the wage stagnation of this decade, as well as to the increasing age at which full Social Security benefits were received. Another factor was the increasing share of minorities in the workforce. Additional factors were the higher unemployment rates of the 2000s

Table 5.1 Mean and Median Retirement Wealth, 1983–2007 (in thousands, 2007$)

	1983	1989	2001	2007
All households				
Mean pension wealth	—	67.1	120.8	138.0
Mean Social Security wealth	—	111.9	163.3	165.3
Mean retirement wealth	—	179.0	284.1	303.3
Median pension wealth	—	5.6	17.6	19.0
Median Social Security wealth	—	100.5	141.3	139.1
Median retirement wealth	—	126.0	184.5	187.6
Aged 46 and under				
Mean pension wealth	—	34.3	53.4	55.3
Mean Social Security wealth	—	92.9	128.5	125.7
Mean retirement wealth	—	127.2	181.9	181.0
Median pension wealth	—	0.8	4.7	1.8
Median Social Security wealth	—	87.7	119.9	112.5
Median retirement wealth	—	100.4	136.4	130.5
Aged 47–64				
Mean pension wealth	99.8	120.7	211.9	225.3
Mean Social Security wealth	158.5	138.4	216.0	215.7
Mean retirement wealth	257.8	259.1	427.9	440.9
Median pension wealth	46.8	37.4	69.1	75.4
Median Social Security wealth	149.1	138.1	206.4	195.8
Median retirement wealth	205.7	189.5	298.3	301.9
Aged 65 and over				
Mean pension wealth	75.7	84.7	151.9	175.8
Mean Social Security wealth	140.0	127.6	171.7	169.6
Mean retirement wealth	215.6	212.3	323.6	345.4
Median pension wealth	43.0	5.7	35.1	47.4
Median Social Security wealth	129.1	105.9	148.6	132.6
Median retirement wealth	184.4	153.6	218.8	211.8

NOTE: Households are classified into age groups by the age of the head of household. Computations are for all households in the group. Key: Pension wealth = defined contribution + defined benefit. Retirement wealth = pension wealth + Social Security wealth.

SOURCE: Author's computations from the 1983, 1989, 2001, and 2007 SCF.

compared to the 1990s and the drop in the median retirement age compared to the 1990s. Both of these led to fewer years of employed work life. Moreover, though longevity increased over this period, the rate of increase slowed down relative to the 1990s. Pension wealth also grew slowly during the 2000s but faster than SSW.

The inequality of SSW was much lower than that of pension wealth (or even net worth). As shown in Table 5.2, in 2007, the Gini coefficient for SSW among all households was 0.36, compared to 0.78 for pension wealth (and 0.83 for net worth).[3] The inequality of SSW among all households fell slightly, by 0.007 Gini points, over the 1989–2007 period. The inequality of SSW also fell slightly among middle-aged households but rose modestly among young households. Among the elderly, there was a substantial drop in the inequality of SSW, reflecting primarily an increase in Social Security coverage over these years.[4]

Table 5.2 Inequality of Retirement Wealth, 1983–2007 (Gini coefficients)

	1983	1989	2001	2007
All households				
Pension wealth	—	0.799	0.788	0.783
Social Security wealth	—	0.370	0.344	0.363
Retirement wealth	—	0.485	0.493	0.514
Aged 46 and under				
Pension wealth	—	0.810	0.801	0.810
Social Security wealth	—	0.306	0.320	0.327
Retirement wealth	—	0.405	0.430	0.440
Aged 47–64				
Pension wealth	0.666	0.715	0.724	0.716
Social Security wealth	0.297	0.314	0.297	0.305
Retirement wealth	0.378	0.454	0.464	0.470
Aged 65+				
Pension wealth	0.638	0.796	0.754	0.755
Social Security wealth	0.412	0.463	0.356	0.415
Retirement wealth	0.378	0.529	0.486	0.535

NOTE: Households are classified into age groups by the age of the head of household. Key: Pension wealth = defined contribution + defined benefit wealth. Retirement wealth = pension wealth + Social Security wealth. — = data not available.
SOURCE: Author's computations from the 1983, 1989, 2001, and 2007 SCF.

Another look at the change in the distribution of SSW is provided in Figures 5.1a–5.1d. Among all households there was strong growth in SSW at all percentiles over the 1989–2001 period (see Figure 5.1a). Moreover, in contrast to the U-shaped pattern of pension wealth growth, the largest gains were made by the lowest percentiles, resulting in a decline in the Gini coefficient. The pattern was different over the 2001–2007 period, during which percentage gains in SSW were negative at lower percentiles and positive at higher percentiles, and the Gini coefficient rose as well.

Among younger households, the percentage gains in SSW were all positive but U-shaped over the 1989–2001 period, corresponding to a slight rise in SSW inequality (Figure 5.1b). Over the 2001–2007 period, there were generally small losses in SSW across the board and a very slight rise in inequality. The pattern among middle-aged households was very similar to that among all households (Figure 5.1c). Over the 1989–2001 period, percentage gains were positive at all percentiles but higher at the lower ones, and the Gini coefficient declined. Over the years 2001–2007, the pattern was one of very small changes, both positive and negative, over the percentiles, and inequality remained fairly constant. In contrast, among elderly households (Figure 5.1d), changes in SSW were all positive but much greater at the bottom end, and inequality fell as well. During the second period, changes in SSW were negative at the bottom and positive at the top, and the Gini coefficient for SSW rose as well.

When we put together DC pensions, DB pension wealth, and SSW, how has total retirement wealth changed over time? Among all households, mean retirement wealth grew by 59 percent from 1989 to 2001 (see Table 5.1). The percentage gain was, not surprisingly, lower than that of pension wealth but higher than that of SSW. Moreover, mean retirement wealth was up strongly among each of the three age groups over these years—43 percent among young households, 65 percent among middle-aged ones, and 52 percent among the elderly. Median retirement wealth also climbed sharply—46 percent among all households, 36 percent among young households, 58 percent among middle-aged ones, and 43 percent among the elderly.

In contrast, from 2001 to 2007 mean retirement wealth was up by only 7 percent among all households. This figure was once again about midway between the growth in pension wealth and that of SSW. By age

Figure 5.1a Percentage Change in Social Security Wealth in 2007$ by Percentile, All Households, 1989, 2001, and 2007

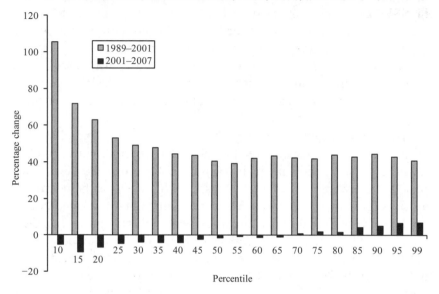

Figure 5.1b Percentage Change in Social Security Wealth in 2007$ by Percentile, Aged 46 and under, 1989, 2001, and 2007

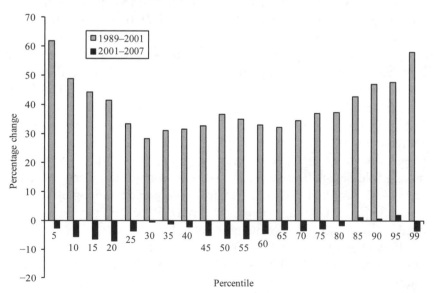

Figure 5.1c Percentage Change in Social Security Wealth in 2007$ by Percentile, Aged 47–64, 1989, 2001, and 2007

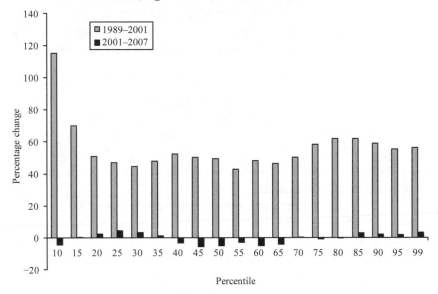

Figure 5.1d Percentage Change in Social Security Wealth in 2007$ by Percentile, Aged 65 and over, 1989, 2001, and 2007

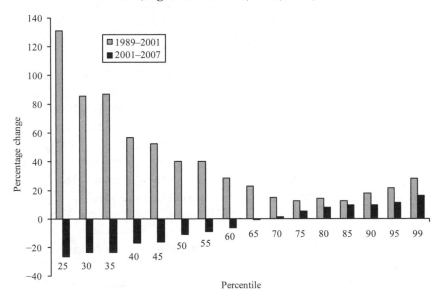

SOURCE: Author's computations from the 1989, 2001, and 2007 SCF.

group, mean retirement wealth was down by 1 percent among young households, up by a very modest 3 percent among middle-aged ones, and up 7 percent for the elderly. Median retirement wealth was basically unchanged among all households, down 4 percent among young ones, unchanged among middle-aged ones, and down 3 percent among the elderly.

In the last chapter we saw a very high level of pension wealth inequality. However, SSW exerted a moderating influence so that the inequality of retirement wealth was substantially lower. In fact, the inequality of retirement wealth, not surprisingly, lay between that of pension and SSW (Table 5.2). In 2007, the Gini coefficient for retirement wealth among all households was 0.51, compared to 0.36 for SSW and 0.78 for pension wealth.

The inequality of retirement wealth increased by 0.029 Gini points from 1989 to 2007 among all households, despite a reduction in the inequality of both pension wealth and SSW. There are two reasons. First, the share of pension wealth in total retirement wealth rose over the period (from 37 to 45 percent). Since pension wealth was more unequally distributed than SSW, this change had the effect of raising the inequality of retirement wealth (the sum of the two components). Second, the correlation between the two rose substantially over these years (from 0.26 to 0.38). In other words, households with large pension wealth holdings tended to have increasing levels of SSW over time, thus leading to greater skewness in the distribution of retirement wealth.[5]

Among young households, the Gini coefficient for retirement wealth rose by 0.034 Gini points, largely because of the rising inequality of SSW. Among middle-aged households, the Gini coefficient was up by 0.017 points, despite little change in the inequality of both pension and SSW. In this case, the main reason is the rising share of pension wealth in total retirement wealth over the period. Among the elderly, the inequality of retirement wealth remained virtually unchanged, despite drops in the inequality of both pension wealth and SSW. The explanation in this case is a sharp rise in the correlation between these two components.

Figures 5.2a–5.2d give a clearer picture of changes in the distribution of retirement wealth by subperiod, covering 1989–2001 and 2001–2007. Among all households (Figure 5.2a), percentage gains in retirement wealth were all positive over the 1989–2001 period and formed a U-shaped pattern. The strong growth in retirement wealth among the lowest percentiles reflected the large increases in SSW at the bottom, while the sharp gains among the top percentiles were due to the substantial gains of pension wealth at the top (primarily DC wealth). The decline in the middle was a reflection of the losses in pension wealth in this part of the distribution. There was a modest gain in inequality over these years as well. However, from 2001 to 2007, changes in retirement wealth were much smaller. They were also negative up to the 40th percentile or so and then generally positive above that. These changes reflected declines in SSW in the bottom percentiles and increases of pension wealth in the middle and upper percentiles. This period, not surprisingly, was characterized by an increase in the Gini coefficient for retirement wealth.

Similar patterns are evident among the younger, middle-aged, and elderly age groups. Among the former (Figure 5.2b), the gains in retirement wealth were all positive over the 1989–2001 period, and the pattern of gains was again U-shaped, bottoming out at the 60th percentile. Over the later period, changes in retirement wealth were again negative at the bottom (up to the 70th percentile) and then positive. The pattern of percentage gains was also U-shaped among middle-aged households over the first period (Figure 5.2c). Over the second period, retirement wealth recorded losses in the bottom percentiles (up to the 40th) and then generally positive gains after that. Among the elderly (Figure 5.2d), the percentage changes in retirement wealth were once again all positive and formed a U-shaped pattern for the 1989–2001 period, bottoming out at the 65th percentile. In contrast, from 2001 to 2007, retirement wealth declined at the lower percentiles (up through the 55th percentile) and rose at the upper ones. Percentage gains were almost directly related to percentile level, rising from −17 percent at the 10th percentile to 22 percent at the 99th percentile. This pattern almost directly mirrored changes in SSW among the elderly over the period.

Another perspective is afforded by Figure 5.3, which shows changes in retirement wealth by nonpension net worth percentile among all households in 1989, 2001, and 2007. It is apparent that there is a strong correlation between nonpension net worth and retirement wealth. In 2007, retirement wealth ranged from a low of $184,000 for the bottom vintile (the bottom 5 percent) to $940,000 for the top vintile—a

**Figure 5.2a Percentage Change in Retirement Wealth in 2007$ by
Percentile, All Households, 1989, 2001, and 2007 (2007$)**

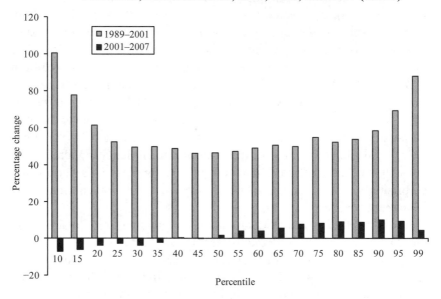

**Figure 5.2b Percentage Change in Retirement Wealth in 2007$ by
Percentile, Aged 46 and Under, 1989, 2001, and 2007**

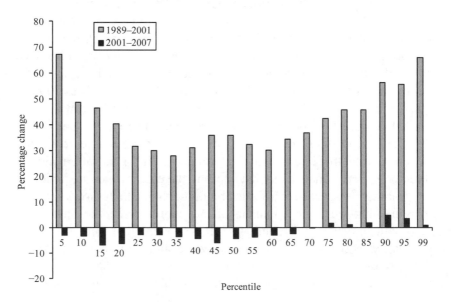

**Figure 5.2c Percentage Change in Retirement Wealth in 2007$ by
Percentile, Aged 47–64, 1989, 2001, and 2007**

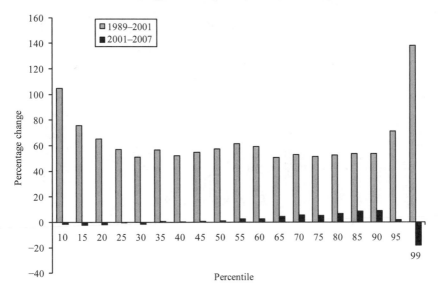

**Figure 5.2d Percentage Change in Retirement Wealth in 2007$ by
Percentile, Aged 65 and Over, 1989, 2001, and 2007**

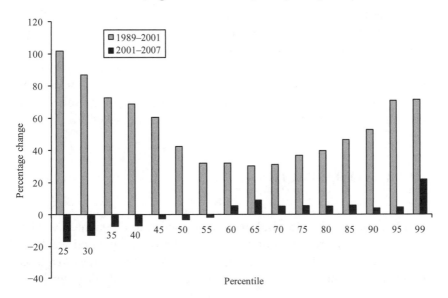

SOURCE: Author's computation from the 1989, 2001, and 2007 SCF.

**Figure 5.3 Percentage Growth of Retirement Wealth in 2007$, All
Households, by Nonpension Wealth Vintile, 1989, 2001,
and 2007**

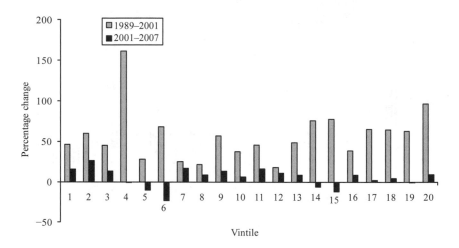

SOURCE: Author's computation from the 1989, 2001, and 2007 SCF.

fivefold difference. It also appears that the correlation became stronger
over time between 1989 and 2001 and then weakened from 2001 to
2007. And, it is evident that between 1989 and 2001 retirement wealth
displayed positive gains for all vintiles, though the pattern was a bit
uneven. From 2001 to 2007, there was a mixture of positive and negative changes in retirement wealth by nonpension net worth vintile, and
once again no clear pattern emerged. These results will be useful when
we consider changes in the inequality of augmented wealth.

AUGMENTED WEALTH

I now turn to an appraisal of what happened to augmented wealth,
the sum of net worth, pension wealth, and SSW. Augmented wealth is
the most comprehensive measure of the full set of resources available
for retirement, and so its change over time is of interest when consider-

ing trends in retirement adequacy. I find that whereas there was rapid growth in augmented wealth during the 1990s, a marked slowdown occurred during the 2000s. Indeed, median augmented wealth barely moved at all for the older age groups and actually fell in absolute terms among young households.

I noted above that mean net worth among all households rose by 44 percent between 1989 and 2001, while median net worth increased by 16 percent (see Table 5.3 as well). If DB pension wealth is now added in, then the mean value of private accumulations was up by 37 percent and its median value by 4 percent. Finally, if SSW is now included, then the mean value of augmented wealth rose by 39 percent and its median

Table 5.3 Augmented Wealth, 1983–2007 (in thousands, 2007$)

	1983	1989	2001	2007
All households				
Mean net worth	270.4	309.8	445.1	536.1
Mean augmented wealth	—	478.0	666.5	762.8
Median net worth	69.5	74.3	86.1	102.5
Median augmented wealth	—	225.0	277.5	309.2
Aged 46 and under				
Mean net worth	128.1	171.2	205.0	209.9
Mean augmented wealth	—	289.2	353.8	360.2
Median net worth	30.8	27.8	24.2	21.8
Median augmented wealth	—	140.5	165.3	155.8
Aged 47–64				
Mean net worth	436.8	477.0	700.5	803.2
Mean augmented wealth	684.3	715.7	1,015.3	1,110.3
Median net worth	126.8	156.0	161.1	206.5
Median augmented wealth	364.6	373.2	475.4	485.4
Aged 65+				
Mean net worth	436.3	454.1	652.8	809.1
Mean augmented wealth	645.9	664.0	913.7	1,070.0
Median net worth	119.3	128.1	176.5	211.1
Median augmented wealth	342.3	310.7	426.5	435.5

NOTE: Households are classified into age groups by the age of the head of household.
  Key: Augmented wealth = nonpension wealth + pension wealth + Social Security wealth.
SOURCE: Author's computations from the 1983, 1989, 2001, and 2007 SCF.

value by 23 percent. The rapid growth of SSW over the 1990s made up, in part, for the slower growth of pension wealth in the middle of the distribution, thus explaining the more rapid increase in augmented wealth than in private accumulations.

Patterns vary by age group. Among young households, mean augmented wealth increased by 22 percent, compared to a 20 percent rise in net worth, and median augmented wealth rose by 18 percent, compared to a 13 percent drop in net worth. Among middle-aged households, mean augmented wealth grew by 42 percent, compared to a 47 percent increase in net worth, and median augmented wealth gained 27 percent, compared to a 3 percent rise in net worth. The elderly experienced a 38 percent gain in mean augmented wealth, compared to a 44 percent growth in mean net worth, and median augmented wealth advanced by 37 percent, about the same as the 38 percent gain in median net worth.

The years 2001–2007 again look different. The growth in mean augmented wealth slowed down, registering a 14 percent gain among all households compared to a 39 percent increase in 1989–2001. Median augmented wealth advanced by only 11 percent, in comparison to a 23 percent rise in 1989–2001. Evidence of the slowdown in the growth of augmented wealth is evident for each of the three age groups as well. Mean augmented wealth remained virtually unchanged, and median augmented wealth declined in absolute terms for young households in the 2001–2007 period, whereas both rose at about 20 percent during the 1990s. Mean augmented wealth grew by only 9 percent for middle-aged households in the later period, whereas it increased by 42 percent in the 1989–2001 period, and median augmented wealth showed almost no change in the 2000s, compared to a 27 percent growth in the 1990s. For the elderly, mean augmented wealth advanced by 17 percent in the 2000s, compared to 38 percent in the 1990s, and median augmented wealth remained virtually unchanged in the later period, though it gained 37 percent in the earlier period.

We saw in the last chapter that adding DB wealth to net worth to create private accumulations resulted in a modest reduction in measured inequality. Here, it will become apparent that also including SSW results in a fairly sizable decrease in measured inequality.

In 2007 the Gini coefficient for net worth among all households was 0.834. Adding DB wealth to net worth to obtain private accumulations resulted in a 0.030 decline of the Gini coefficient to 0.805. This decrease in inequality was due to the relatively small level of inequality in DB wealth. In contrast, adding SSW to nonpension net worth caused an even more sizable reduction in the Gini coefficient of 0.141 points, from 0.834 to 0.693. This drop in inequality reflected both the much lower level of inequality in SSW than in marketable wealth, as well as its relatively low (though positive) correlation with net worth. Finally, adding both DB wealth and SSW to net worth produced only a very modest further diminution of the Gini coefficient, to 0.684. As a consequence, it is apparent that the main equalizing effect of retirement wealth comes from Social Security, not private pensions. Results are very similar for the three individual age groups.

As we saw in the previous chapter, the inequality of net worth among all households was essentially unchanged over the years 1989–2007. In contrast, the inequality of augmented wealth showed a sizable increase over these years, rising by 0.021 Gini points (see Table 5.4). This is tantamount to saying that the equalizing effect of retirement wealth mitigated over the 1989–2007 period. While the addition of retirement wealth to net worth reduced the Gini coefficient by 0.169 points in 1989, the difference was only 0.150 in 2007. Thus, the inequality-reducing effects of adding retirement wealth to net worth fell over the years 1989–2007.[6]

Among young households, the inequality of both net worth and augmented wealth declined slightly from 1989 to 2007. Among middle-aged households the Gini coefficient for net worth increased by 0.020 from 1989 to 2007, whereas that for augmented wealth advanced by 0.031 points. Indeed, over the full 1983–2007 period, while the Gini coefficient of net worth was up by 0.033 points, that for augmented wealth gained 0.076 points. Among the elderly, the inequality of net worth rose by a slight 0.006 Gini points and that of augmented wealth increased a little more, by 0.013 Gini points. In fact, from 1983 to 2007, the Gini coefficient for net worth was almost unchanged, while that for augmented wealth climbed 0.066 points. Thus, for both middle-aged and elderly households, the same pattern ensued as that for all households, namely, that the inequality of augmented wealth rose more than that of net worth.

Why did the inequality of augmented wealth increase while that of net worth remained unchanged from 1989 to 2007? The main reason is that the inequality of retirement wealth increased. This was the

Table 5.4 Inequality of Augmented Wealth, 1983–2007 (Gini coefficients)

	1983	1989	2001	2007
All households				
Net worth	0.799	0.832	0.826	0.834
Private accumulations	—	0.793	0.796	0.805
Nonpension wealth + Social Security wealth	—	0.676	0.665	0.693
Augmented wealth	—	0.663	0.661	0.684
Aged 46 and under				
Net worth	0.797	0.887	0.859	0.880
Private accumulations	—	0.851	0.830	0.850
Nonpension wealth + Social Security wealth	—	0.650	0.612	0.636
Augmented wealth	—	0.642	0.616	0.636
Aged 47–64				
Net worth	0.761	0.775	0.798	0.795
Private accumulations	0.688	0.721	0.756	0.758
Nonpension wealth + Social Security wealth	0.607	0.644	0.655	0.673
Augmented wealth	0.574	0.619	0.637	0.650
Aged 65+				
Net worth	0.778	0.778	0.762	0.784
Private accumulations	0.708	0.738	0.724	0.748
Nonpension wealth + Social Security wealth	0.638	0.670	0.637	0.678
Augmented wealth	0.599	0.652	0.626	0.665

NOTE: Households are classified into age groups by the age of the head of household. Key: Private accumulations = nonpension wealth + pension wealth. Augmented wealth = nonpension wealth + pension wealth + Social Security wealth. — = data not available.
SOURCE: Author's computations from the 1983, 1989, 2001, and 2007 SCF.

case for all households except elderly households. A secondary reason is the increased correlation between nonpension wealth and retirement wealth (see Figure 5.3 and the pertinent discussion above). The correlation coefficient between the two advanced from 0.18 to 0.25 among all households and from 0.16 to 0.22 among middle-aged ones.[7]

Figures 5.4a–5.4d give a graphical depiction of changes in the distribution of augmented wealth in 1989, 2001, and 2007. Among all households (Figure 5.4a), percentage changes in augmented wealth over the 1989–2001 period, like those of retirement wealth, were all positive and formed a U-shaped pattern, bottoming out at the 50th percentile. The pattern seems to mirror rather closely the pattern of percentage gains in retirement wealth. In contrast, from 2001 to 2007, changes in augmented wealth were negative at the bottom of the distribution (up through the 30th percentile) and generally positive above this. More-over, percentage gains are positively correlated with the initial aug-mented wealth level. These results are consistent with the finding of little change in the inequality of augmented wealth from 1989 to 2001 and an increase in inequality from 2001 to 2007.

Among young households (Figure 5.4b), a similar pattern unfolded. Over the first period, augmented wealth rose at all percentiles and there was a U-shaped pattern in percentage gains. Over the later period, changes in augmented wealth were uniformly negative up to the 60th percentile and then generally positive thereafter. The pattern of percent-age gains was largely repeated among middle-aged households (Figure 5.4c) in the earlier period. Over the second period, changes were almost all positive but the pattern was quite uneven. In contrast, among the elderly (Figure 5.4d), the percentage gains in augmented wealth were all positive in the first period but tended to decline with percentile level. Over the second period, changes in augmented wealth were generally negative at the bottom part of the distribution (up to the 15th percentile) and then generally positive above. These results are consistent with the finding that the inequality of augmented wealth fell over the 1989–2001 period and then rose over the 2001–2007 period.

ALTERNATIVE PENSION WEALTH CALCULATIONS

How robust are the findings reported in Chapters 4 and 5 to alterna-tive measures of pension wealth? I consider two modifications to the definition of pension wealth here. First, as discussed in Chapter 4, I include DCEMP, an estimate of future employer contributions to DC pension plans in the definition of pension wealth (the sum of DCEMP

Figure 5.4a Percentage Change in Augmented Wealth in 2007$ by Percentile, All Households, 1989, 2001, and 2007

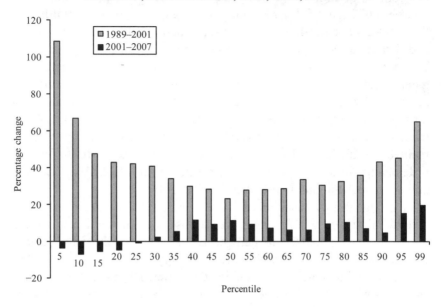

Figure 5.4b Percentage Change in Augmented Wealth in 2007$ by Percentile, Aged 46 and Under, 1989, 2001, and 2007

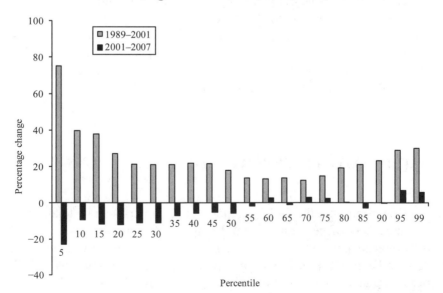

Figure 5.4c Percentage Change in Augmented Wealth in 2007$ by Percentile, Aged 47–64, 1989, 2001, and 2007

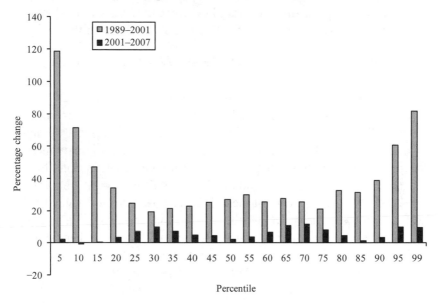

Figure 5.4d Percentage Change in Augmented Wealth in 2007$ by Percentile, Aged 65 and Over, 1989, 2001, and 2007

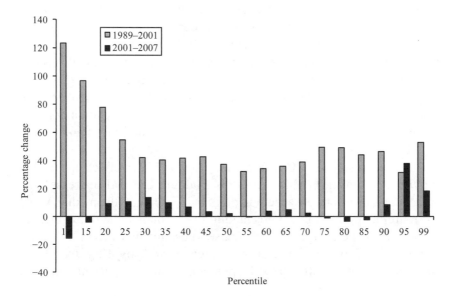

SOURCE: Author's computations from the 1983, 1989, 2001, and 2007 SCF.

with another variable is noted with an asterisk, e.g., DC + DCEMP is shown as DC*). Second, as discussed below, DC accumulations are tax-deferred savings, and I consider how my estimates would change if I use a net (after-tax) measure of defined contribution wealth.

DC Employer Contributions to Defined Contribution Pension Plans

How does the inclusion of employer contributions to DC plans affect time trends in augmented wealth AW* and its other components? I first consider how the inclusion of DCEMP affects the level of measured wealth. Recall from Chapter 4 that DCEMP is defined as the present discounted value of future employer contributions to DC plans. In 2007, the average value of DCEMP among all households was $29,900, or 39 percent of mean DC. This represented a substantial addition to the value of DC wealth and, in earlier years, such as 2001, put total DC wealth at a value far greater than DB wealth. The addition of DCEMP in 2007 increased the mean value of pension wealth by 22 percent, mean private accumulations by 5 percent, the mean value of retirement wealth by 10 percent, and mean augmented wealth by 4 percent (see Table 5.5). Among younger households, the net effect of adding DCEMP was much larger. It raised mean DC wealth by 122 percent (since DC accumulations among young workers are relatively small), mean pension wealth by 68 percent, mean private accumulations by 16 percent, mean retirement wealth by 21 percent, and mean augmented wealth by 10 percent. Among age group 47–64, the effect of adding DCEMP to other components of retirement wealth was smaller, since DC accumulations among older workers were already relatively high. The inclusion of DCEMP enlarged mean DC wealth by 28 percent, mean pension wealth by 17 percent, mean private accumulations by 4 percent, mean retirement wealth by 9 percent, and mean augmented wealth by only 3 percent.

The inclusion of DCEMP actually has a larger effect on median values than on mean values. In 2007, adding DCEMP increased the median value of private accumulations by 17 percent, the median value of retirement wealth by 9 percent, and the median value of augmented wealth by 8 percent among all households; median private accumulations by 65 percent, median retirement wealth by 12 percent, and median augmented wealth by 17 percent among younger households;

Table 5.5 Augmented Wealth, Including Employer Contributions to Defined Contribution Plans, 1983–2007 (in thousands, 2007$)

	1983	1989	2001	2007
All households				
Mean values				
Defined contribution pension wealth*	6.4	29.4	97.1	106.7
Pension wealth*	—	86.0	155.1	167.9
Private accumulations*	—	384.3	537.5	627.4
Retirement wealth*	—	197.8	318.4	333.2
Augmented wealth*	—	496.2	700.8	792.7
Median values				
Pension wealth*	—	12.0	39.5	38.1
Private accumulations*	—	127.3	148.8	166.4
Retirement wealth*	—	133.9	208.5	205.4
Augmented wealth*	—	237.2	311.1	335.2
Aged 46 and under				
Mean values				
Defined contribution pension wealth*	6.0	38.4	80.9	68.1
Pension wealth*	—	63.5	101.2	92.7
Private accumulations*	—	224.0	273.2	271.8
Retirement wealth*	—	156.3	229.8	218.4
Augmented wealth*	—	316.9	401.7	397.6
Median values				
Pension wealth*	—	5.0	21.1	7.0
Private accumulations*	—	63.3	68.4	57.8
Retirement wealth*	—	111.0	155.8	146.0
Augmented wealth*	—	159.3	196.5	182.0
Aged 47–64				
Mean values				
Defined contribution pension wealth*	10.2	33.9	149.1	171.6
Pension wealth*	100.3	134.3	248.0	263.0
Private accumulations*	526.8	590.1	835.4	932.4
Retirement wealth*	258.7	272.5	463.9	478.7
Augmented wealth*	684.8	728.5	1,051.3	1,148.1

(continued)

Table 5.5 (continued)

	1983	1989	2001	2007
Aged 47–64				
Median values				
Pension wealth*	46.8	48.5	91.3	98.2
Private accumulations*	215.3	231.2	274.5	310.0
Retirement wealth*	206.1	194.0	318.4	318.8
Augmented wealth*	365.5	374.7	500.2	510.7

NOTE: Households are classified into age groups by the age of the head of household. Key: Pension wealth* = defined benefit + defined contribution* = defined benefit + defined contribution + employer contributions to defined contribution plans. Private accumulations* = nonpension wealth + pension wealth*. Retirement wealth* = pension wealth* + Social Security wealth. Augmented wealth* = nonpension wealth + pension wealth* + Social Security wealth. — = data not available.
SOURCE: Author's computations from the 1983, 1989, 2001, and 2007 SCF.

and median private accumulations by 9 percent, median retirement wealth by 6 percent, and median augmented wealth by 5 percent among age group 47–64.

How does the inclusion of employer contributions to DC plans affect the measured growth in the various components of wealth? In Chapters 4 and 5, we saw that there was a marked slowdown in the growth of pension wealth, private accumulations, retirement wealth, and augmented wealth between the 1990s (1989 to 2001) and the 2000s (2001 to 2007). This was the case for both mean and median values.

Because the ratio of DCEMP to DC jumped from 0.38 in 1983 to 1.79 in 1989 among all households (reflecting the initiation of many firm-level defined contribution plans), the growth of DC* wealth (the sum of DC wealth and DCEMP) over this period was much higher than that of DC wealth (361 percent versus 129 percent). However, after 1989, DCEMP fell as a share of DC wealth to 0.55 in 2001 and then to 0.39 in 2007, so that relative gains in mean DC* were lower than that of mean DC after 1989. As a consequence, we still find sharp slowdowns in the growth of both mean and median pension wealth, private accumulations, retirement wealth, and augmented wealth between the 1990s and the 2000s. In fact, the slowdowns are even greater when employer contributions to DC plans are included in the definition of wealth. While, for example, median augmented wealth (without employer contributions) gained 11 percent from 2001 to 2007, median AW* advanced by only 8 percent.

The pattern is very similar for age group 47–64, though the differences are somewhat smaller. DCEMP as a share of DC first surged from 0.05 in 1983 to 0.66 in 1989 and then fell off to 0.28 in 2007. As a result, mean DC* grew much faster than mean DC from 1983 to 1989 but the opposite was true after 1989, and the slowdown in percentage increase of both mean and median pension wealth, private accumulations, retirement wealth, and augmented wealth between the 1990s and the 2000s became even greater. In fact, median RW* remained virtually unchanged over the later period and median AW* grew by only 2 percent.[8]

Three findings are particularly noteworthy. First, median AW* among all households had much lower gains in the 2001–2007 period in comparison to the 1989–2001 period. This remained true with or without the inclusion of employer contributions to DC plans. Second, among younger households, both mean and median PA* and AW* declined in absolute terms in the later period. Third, among age group 47–64, median PA* showed almost no change over the 2001–2007 period. Thus, the main results derived in Chapters 4 and 5 without the inclusion of DCEMP remain largely unaltered.

The story is very similar when we consider trends in inequality (see Table 5.6). As we saw above, the inequality of both private accumulations and augmented wealth advanced from 1989 to 2007, while that of traditional net worth remained largely unchanged.

It is first of interest that adding employer contributions, DCEMP, reduces overall pension wealth inequality (from a Gini coefficient of 0.783 to 0.758 among all households in 2007). Results are similar by individual age groups. The reason is that DCEMP was distributed more equally than pension wealth (PW). The equalizing effect of DCEMP on PW* was offset to a modest extent by the fact that the correlation of DCEMP and standard pension wealth was positive though quite low (0.21 among all households in 2007).[9] Thus, the addition of DCEMP to standard pension wealth tended to even out the distribution of PW* among households. Likewise, the inclusion of DCEMP lowered the inequality of private accumulations and augmented wealth. The reasons are similar—a lower level of inequality of DCEMP than either net worth or augmented wealth, despite a positive though low correlation

Table 5.6 Inequality of Augmented Wealth*, Including Employer Contributions to Defined Contribution Plans, 1983–2007 (Gini coefficients)

	1983	1989	2001	2007
All households				
Pension wealth*	—	0.787	0.749	0.758
Private accumulations*	—	0.776	0.773	0.789
Retirement wealth*	—	0.502	0.498	0.521
Augmented wealth*	—	0.658	0.650	0.677
Aged 46 and under				
Pension wealth*	—	0.809	0.748	0.775
Private accumulations*	—	0.818	0.782	0.813
Retirement wealth*	—	0.471	0.470	0.479
Augmented wealth*	—	0.643	0.608	0.631
Aged 47–64				
Pension wealth*	0.666	0.716	0.709	0.706
Private accumulations*	0.688	0.715	0.746	0.750
Retirement wealth*	0.379	0.466	0.473	0.483
Augmented wealth*	0.574	0.618	0.633	0.647

NOTE: Households are classified into age groups by the age of the head of household. Key: Pension wealth* = defined benefit + defined contribution* = defined benefit + defined contribution + employer contributions to defined contribution plans. Private accumulations* = nonpension wealth + pension wealth*. Retirement wealth* = pension wealth* + Social Security wealth. Augmented wealth* = nonpension wealth + pension wealth* + Social Security wealth.
SOURCE: Author's computations from the 1983, 1989, 2001, and 2007 SCF.

of DCEMP with net worth (0.11 in 2007 among all households) and of DCEMP with augmented wealth (0.12 among all households in 2007).

Nonetheless, we still find that the inequality of both PA* and AW* among all households advanced over the years from 1989 (or 1983) to 2007, while that of net worth remained essentially unchanged. Among middle-aged households, we likewise find that the inequality of PA* and AW* increased more than that of net worth.[10]

Future Tax Liability on Pension Wealth

I have so far applied a pretax valuation to pension wealth. However, as many of us are painfully aware, contributions to DC plans are tax sheltered or tax-deferred when they are made but subject to income tax on withdrawal.[11] Because of this, their posttax value is lower (usually quite a bit) than their stated (pretax) market value. In contrast, most other assets in the household portfolio, such as mutual funds, are not subject to income taxes on withdrawal. As a result, when we include the market value of DC plans as a part of net worth, we are adding an asset with an attached tax liability to other assets that do not have this liability.

Thus, in principle, the posttax value of DC plans should be used when computing net worth. Likewise, DB pension benefits (and lump-sum distributions) are taxable on receipt, so that, in principle, the post-tax value of DB pension wealth should also be used instead of its pretax value when computing total pension wealth.[12]

I make a somewhat rough adjustment to the values of DB and DC pension wealth for future taxes on income receipt. In principle, to make a proper calculation we would have to predict future income (and its composition), future tax deductions and exemptions, and the future tax schedule as well at retirement. For the sake of simplicity, I assume that for current workers income at retirement equals 80 percent of the pre-retirement income.[13] In the case of current beneficiaries, I assume that their (postretirement) income remains fixed over their remaining life. I assume that marital status remains unchanged and that couples file joint returns. I assume that the tax schedule remains fixed over the remaining lifetime of the individual.[14] I also treat the taxation of Social Security benefits according to the tax code current at the time of the survey.[15]

How does the use of net (after-tax) DB and DC pension wealth affect trends in the level of and the degree of inequality in augmented wealth and its various components? Do the results reported above still hold up? I find that the slowdown in pension wealth and augmented wealth between the 1990s and the 2000s holds up when net pension wealth is used instead of gross pension wealth. Moreover, I find that augmented wealth becomes more unequal over the period 1989–2007 irrespective of whether net or gross pension wealth is used.

Results for 1983, 1989, 2001, and 2007 are shown in Table 5.7. For 2007, the average tax rate on pension wealth was 11.8 percent among all households, and that on SSW was 9.4 percent. The mean tax rate on pension wealth fell from 15.5 percent in 1983 to 11.8 percent in 1989, rose a bit to 13.4 percent in 2001, and then fell off again to 11.8 percent

Table 5.7 Augmented Wealth, Net of Federal Income Taxes on Receipt, 1983–2007 (in thousands, 2007$)

	1983	1989	2001	2007
All households				
Mean values				
Net pension wealth	—	53.8	93.4	108.5
Net private accumulations	—	352.9	475.8	568.0
Net retirement wealth	—	156.5	235.7	253.4
Net augmented wealth	—	455.5	618.1	712.9
Median values				
Net pension wealth	—	5.0	14.9	16.7
Net private accumulations	—	109.6	113.0	136.4
Net retirement wealth	—	116.1	164.3	168.5
Net augmented wealth	—	213.9	255.7	289.3
Aged 46 and under				
Mean values				
Net pension wealth	—	27.0	40.9	44.2
Net private accumulations	—	189.0	212.8	223.3
Net retirement wealth	—	111.7	152.2	155.0
Net augmented wealth	—	273.7	324.1	334.1
Median values				
Net pension wealth	—	0.6	3.8	1.6
Net private accumulations	—	39.7	36.0	32.3
Net retirement wealth	—	95.5	122.0	119.0
Net augmented wealth	—	133.7	152.7	147.3
Aged 47–64				
Mean values				
Net pension wealth	74.9	96.8	161.6	175.6
Net private accumulations	502.8	553.3	749.0	845.0
Net retirement wealth	233.5	222.0	346.7	361.3
Net augmented wealth	661.3	678.5	934.1	1,030.7
Median values				
Net pension wealth	39.1	31.3	57.1	64.9
Net private accumulations	202.6	211.6	234.0	270.9
Net retirement wealth	196.1	170.7	261.6	260.6
Net augmented wealth	357.6	364.0	430.1	444.4

Table 5.7 (continued)

	1983	1989	2001	2007
Aged 65+				
Mean values				
Net pension wealth	60.1	69.3	121.5	139.3
Net private accumulations	492.3	521.0	711.6	863.9
Net retirement wealth	200.1	189.7	276.9	291.7
Net augmented wealth	632.2	641.5	867.0	1,016.4
Median values				
Net pension wealth	39.9	5.6	31.2	44.7
Net private accumulations	181.9	187.0	255.2	272.5
Net retirement wealth	175.8	145.8	202.5	202.1
Net augmented wealth	338.1	304.0	414.0	423.5

NOTE: Augmented wealth excludes employer contributions to defined contribution pension plans. Households are classified into age groups by the age of the head of household. Key: Private accumulations = nonpension wealth + pension wealth. Retirement wealth = pension wealth + Social Security wealth. Augmented wealth = nonpension wealth + pension wealth + Social Security wealth. — = data not available.
SOURCE: Author's computations from the 1983, 1989, 2001, and 2007 SCF.

in 2007. In contrast, the mean tax rate of SSW rose from zero in 1983 to 6.0 percent in 1989 and then to 9.8 percent in 2001 before falling slightly to 9.4 percent in 2007.

The projected future tax liability on pension wealth took a large chunk out of pension wealth. The average net value of pension wealth (that is, net of expected taxes on receipt and excluding DCEMP) among all households was 80 percent of its gross average value in 1989 and 79 percent in 2007. Future tax liabilities took a smaller bite out of SSW. The average net value of retirement wealth was 87 percent of its gross average value in 1989 and 84 percent in 2007. Federal income taxes took about the same sized bite out of expected retirement benefits in 2007 as in 1989.

As a result, while the mean value of gross retirement wealth (excluding DCEMP) among all households grew by 70 percent between 1989 and 2007, its net value increased by only 62 percent (the corresponding figures are 68 and 62 percent when including DCEMP, as shown in Appendix Table C.1). Likewise, while the median value of gross retirement wealth among all households increased by 49 percent (53 percent for RW*), the median value of net retirement wealth gained only 45 percent (49 percent for RW*).

Future income tax liabilities had less effect on private accumulations and augmented wealth. The mean value of private accumulations was reduced by 4 percent in 1989 and 5 percent in 2007 and that of augmented wealth by 5 percent in 1989 and 7 percent in 2007 (the effect was about the same for PA* and AW*). As a result, the mean value of gross augmented wealth climbed by 60 percent (and by 60 percent for AW* as well) over the period, while the net value gained 57 percent (57 percent also for AW*). Finally, while the median value of gross augmented wealth advanced by 37 percent (41 percent for AW*), the median value of net augmented wealth grew somewhat less, by 35 percent (38 percent for AW*).

As with gross pension wealth, I find a marked slowdown in the growth of pension wealth and augmented wealth over the two subperiods, 1989–2001 and 2001–2007, when net pension wealth is used instead. Mean and median values of both gross and net pension wealth (with and without DCEMP) show strong positive growth during the earlier period but much smaller gains over the later period. Mean values of both gross and net private accumulations (with and without DCEMP) also show strong growth (of the order of 35 to 40 percent) during the first period and slower growth during the second (of the order of 17 to 19 percent). Mean and median values of both gross and net retirement wealth (with and without DCEMP) show strong gains in the first period but tepid growth in the second. Mean and median values of both gross and net augmented wealth (with and without DCEMP) indicate robust growth in the early period and much slower gains in the second. The results are quite similar for age groups 46 and under and 47–64, with net values showing a slightly smaller increase over time due to the moderate increase in future tax liabilities on SSW and pension wealth.

Netting out implicit income taxes on retirement wealth had an equalizing effect, but the effect was rather modest on pension wealth among all households (see Table 5.8). In 2007 the Gini coefficient for pension wealth among all households was reduced by 0.014 (0.016 for PW*). Netting out future income tax liabilities had a larger effect on retirement wealth inequality. The Gini coefficient for retirement wealth was lessened by 0.035 and that for RW* by 0.036. The greater reduction of the Gini coefficient for total retirement wealth than pension wealth

Table 5.8 Inequality of Augmented Wealth, Net of Federal Income Taxes on Receipt, Both Excluding and Including Employer Contribution to Defined Contribution Plans, 1983–2007 (Gini coefficients)

	1983	1989	2001	2007
All households				
Gini coeff. excluding employer contributions to defined contribution plans				
Net pension wealth	—	0.789	0.776	0.769
Net private accumulations	—	0.790	0.798	0.807
Net retirement wealth	—	0.458	0.458	0.479
Net augmented wealth	—	0.663	0.662	0.686
Gini coeff. including employer contributions to defined contribution plans				
Net pension wealth*	—	0.774	0.733	0.742
Net private accumulations*	—	0.779	0.776	0.792
Net retirement wealth*	—	0.472	0.460	0.485
Net augmented wealth*	—	0.657	0.650	0.677
Aged 47–64				
Gini coeff. excluding employer contributions to defined contribution plans				
Net pension wealth	0.641	0.701	0.708	0.698
Net private accumulations	0.692	0.721	0.759	0.762
Net retirement wealth	0.345	0.424	0.423	0.433
Net augmented wealth	0.573	0.618	0.638	0.652
Gini coeff. including employer contributions to defined contribution plans				
Net pension wealth*	0.641	0.699	0.689	0.685
Net private accumulations*	0.692	0.718	0.750	0.753
Net retirement wealth*	0.345	0.433	0.431	0.443
Net augmented wealth*	0.573	0.617	0.634	0.648

NOTE: Households are classified into age groups by the age of the head of household.
SOURCE: Author's computations from the 1983, 1989, 2001, and 2007 SCF. Key: Retirement wealth* = pension wealth* + Social Security wealth. Augmented wealth* = nonpension wealth + pension wealth* + Social Security wealth. — = data not available.

alone reflected the fact that the implicit tax rates on Social Security benefits are notably higher for high earners, and netting out taxes from SSW is strongly redistributive. However, netting out implicit taxes on pension and SSW barely affected the measured inequality of either private accumulations or augmented wealth. As a result, inequality trends in both private accumulations and augmented wealth between 1989 and 2007 remained almost unchanged after subtracting implicit taxes from retirement wealth.

Among middle-aged households, netting out taxes had a somewhat larger effect on the inequality of both pension wealth and retirement wealth than that for all households. The 2007 Gini coefficient for pension wealth declined by 0.018 (0.021 for PW*), and the Gini coefficient for retirement wealth fell by 0.037 (0.040 for RW*). However, once again, netting out taxes did not have much effect on inequality trends for private accumulations and augmented wealth (as well as for PA* and AW*). Thus, the central findings on trends in both private accumulations and augmented wealth remained largely unchanged when after-tax values were used instead of gross values.

UPDATE TO 2009

Following the procedures outlined in Chapter 2, I next update both net worth and pension wealth to July 1, 2009, on the basis of the change in the stock market and housing prices. As discussed in Chapter 2, house prices fell by 23.5 percent in real terms and the S&P 500 index was down by 40.9 percent in real terms. I also report in that chapter that in 2007, 40.2 percent of households held stocks through one or more pension accounts and 31.4 percent of the value of all stocks owned directly or indirectly were held in pension funds. Additionally, 43.6 percent of the value of DC pension plans was invested in stocks in that year.

Not surprisingly, as shown in Table 5.9, DC wealth was decimated by the stock market crash of 2008–2009. The average value of DC plans fell by 17 percent from 2007 to the midpoint of 2009.[16] Younger households (under age 47) had a smaller share of their pensions invested in stocks (40 percent) and consequently took a somewhat smaller hit in the value of their pensions (16 percent), as did middle-aged households (17

Table 5.9 Augmented Wealth, 2007 and Projections to 2009 (in thousands, 2007$)

	2007	Projected 2009
All households		
Mean values		
Defined contribution pension wealth	76.8	63.5
Pension wealth	138.0	124.7
Net worth	536.1	443.8
Private accumulations	597.5	505.0
Retirement wealth	303.3	290.0
Augmented wealth	762.8	670.3
Median values		
Pension wealth	19.0	16.4
Net worth	102.5	65.4
Private accumulations	142.8	104.2
Retirement wealth	187.6	184.1
Augmented wealth	309.2	271.2
Ratio of stocks held in defined contribution plans to value of defined contribution plans	43.6	
Aged 46 and under		
Mean values		
Defined contribution pension wealth	30.7	25.6
Pension wealth	55.3	50.3
Net worth	209.9	162.3
Private accumulations	234.5	186.9
Retirement wealth	181.0	176.0
Augmented wealth	360.2	312.7
Median values		
Pension wealth	1.8	1.6
Net worth	21.8	5.4
Private accumulations	35.0	14.6
Retirement wealth	130.5	128.8
Augmented wealth	155.8	136.7
Ratio of stocks held in defined contribution plans to value of defined contribution plans	39.7	

(continued)

Table 5.9 (continued)

	2007	Projected 2009
Aged 47–64		
Mean values		
Defined contribution pension wealth	133.8	111.6
Pension wealth	225.3	203.0
Net worth	803.2	674.5
Private accumulations	894.7	765.9
Retirement wealth	440.9	418.7
Augmented wealth	1,110.3	981.6
Median values		
Pension wealth	75.4	66.8
Net worth	206.5	147.9
Private accumulations	283.8	225.4
Retirement wealth	301.9	295.6
Augmented wealth	485.4	438.9
Ratio of stocks held in defined contribution plans to value of defined contribution plans	40.8	
Aged 65+		
Mean values		
Defined contribution pension wealth	84.5	68.1
Pension wealth	175.8	159.3
Net worth	809.1	678.1
Private accumulations	900.4	769.3
Retirement wealth	345.4	328.9
Augmented wealth	1,070.0	938.9
Median values		
Pension wealth	47.4	47.1
Net worth	211.1	168.4
Private accumulations	277.1	237.2
Retirement wealth	211.8	209.6
Augmented wealth	435.5	392.9
Ratio of stocks held in defined contribution plans to value of defined contribution plans	47.6	

NOTE: The projections to 2009 assume that housing prices declined by 23.5 percent in real terms and stock prices declined by 40.9 percent in real terms from 2007 to July 1, 2009. Households are classified into age groups by the age of the head of household. Key: Private accumulations = nonpension wealth + pension wealth. Retirement wealth = pension wealth + Social Security wealth. Augmented wealth = nonpension wealth + pension wealth + Social Security wealth.
SOURCE: Author's computations from the 2007 SCF.

percent decline). Elderly households, on the other hand, had 48 percent of their pensions invested in stocks and, as a result, suffered a 20 percent decline. These results, by the way, show the extreme vulnerability of the DC pension system to stock market fluctuations.

Mean pension wealth suffered a 10 percent drop overall. Results were similar by age group. Mean net worth, as discussed in Chapter 2, plunged by 17 percent among all households. Younger households experienced a larger decline, 23 percent, while middle-aged households and elderly households were down by about 16 percent. As a result, mean private accumulations tumbled by 16 percent overall, 20 percent for younger households, and about 14 percent for middle-aged and elderly ones; and mean augmented wealth fell by 12–13 percent across the board. Declines in overall median values were even more acute for pension wealth (14 percent), net worth (36 percent), and private accumulations (27 percent). Similar patterns existed for younger and middle-aged households, but among the elderly median pension wealth fell less than mean pension wealth, and median private accumulations declined about the same as mean private accumulations. However, overall and for each of the three age groups, median augmented wealth shrank about the same as mean augmented wealth. The reason that median augmented wealth declined less than net worth is that median retirement wealth fell only slightly between 2007 and 2009.

However, all in all, the decade of the 2000s (2001–2009) was truly a "lost decade." Mean net worth and augmented wealth were basically unchanged, while median net worth dwindled by 24 percent and median augmented wealth fell by 2.3 percent. For younger households, both mean and median net worth crashed, and mean and median augmented wealth sank by 12 and 17 percent, respectively. Among middle-aged households, mean net worth fell by 4.2 percent and median net worth by 8.2 percent, while mean augmented wealth was down by 3.3 percent and median augmented wealth by 7.7 percent. The elderly fared a little better, with mean net worth up by 3.9 percent and mean augmented wealth up by 2.8 percent, but median net worth declined by 4.6 percent and median augmented wealth slid by 7.9 percent.

In Chapter 2, I estimate a large increase in wealth inequality from 2007 to the middle of 2009, with the Gini coefficient for net worth climbing from 0.834 to 0.865. In contrast, the inequality of pension wealth remained largely unchanged (see Table 5.10). As a result, the dis-

**Table 5.10 Inequality of Augmented Wealth, 2007, and Projections to
              2009 (Gini coefficients)**

	2007	Projected 2009
All households		
Net worth	0.834	0.865
Pension wealth	0.783	0.781
Private accumulations	0.805	0.827
Retirement wealth	0.514	0.501
Augmented wealth	0.684	0.684
Aged 46 and under		
Net worth	0.880	0.959
Pension wealth	0.810	0.812
Private accumulations	0.805	0.912
Retirement wealth	0.440	0.431
Augmented wealth	0.684	0.638
Aged 47–64		
Net worth	0.795	0.820
Pension wealth	0.716	0.715
Private accumulations	0.758	0.776
Retirement wealth	0.470	0.457
Augmented wealth	0.650	0.649
Aged 65+		
Net worth	0.784	0.795
Pension wealth	0.755	0.746
Private accumulations	0.748	0.753
Retirement wealth	0.535	0.521
Augmented wealth	0.665	0.658

NOTE: The projections to 2009 assume that housing prices declined by 23.5 percent in real terms and stock prices declined by 40.9 percent in real terms from 2007 to July 1, 2009. Households are classified into age groups by the age of the head of household. Key: Private accumulations = nonpension wealth + pension wealth. Retirement wealth = pension wealth + Social Security wealth. Augmented wealth = nonpension wealth + pension wealth + Social Security wealth.

SOURCE: Author's computations from the 2007 SCF.

tribution of private accumulations became more unequal because of the rising inequality in net worth. Retirement wealth became less unequal because of the declining share of pension wealth and hence the rising share of SSW in retirement wealth. Its Gini coefficient fell by 0.013 points. As a result, augmented wealth inequality stayed unchanged. There were two reasons for this. First, the declining inequality of retirement wealth offset the rising inequality of net worth. Second, retirement wealth, especially SSW, which was more equally distributed than net worth, assumed a greater share in augmented wealth. As a consequence, retirement wealth had a greater equalizing effect on augmented wealth in 2009 than in 2007, with the difference between the Gini coefficient of net worth and that of augmented wealth expanding from 0.150 to 0.181. Thus, the contraction of pension wealth, which was itself a consequence of the stock market slide, led to a reduction in the inequality of augmented wealth.

Results are roughly similar for the middle-aged group as well as for elderly households. However, for the youngest age group, we observe a huge increase in net worth inequality from 2007 to 2009 (0.079 Gini points), little change in pension wealth inequality, a large jump in the inequality of private accumulations, and a decline in the inequality of retirement wealth. However, unlike the other age groups, the inequality of augmented wealth fell by 0.046 Gini points because of the sharp reduction in pension wealth.

When we consider the whole decade of the 2000s, we find that the inequality of net worth rose substantially (0.039 Gini points), that the inequality of retirement wealth was largely unchanged, and that the inequality of augmented wealth also rose, though by less than that of net worth (0.023 Gini points). The pattern is similar for middle-aged households, among the elderly, the inequality of augmented wealth climbed by about the same extent as that of net worth. In contrast, among young households, the Gini coefficient for net worth mushroomed by a staggering 0.100 Gini points while that of augmented wealth fell by 0.022 Gini points. Thus, one unintended consequence of the stock market crash of the late 2000s and the consequent contraction of pension wealth is that it lessened the inequality of augmented wealth.

SUMMARY AND CONCLUSIONS

The 1980s and 1990s witnessed a marked transformation of the traditional DB pension system in favor of DC pension coverage. Have households gained from this change? Has inequality been affected?

The chapter began with an analysis of SSW. While mean SSW grew by 46 percent from 1989 to 2001 among all households, there was virtually no change from 2001 to 2007. As result, mean and median retirement wealth were up sharply over the 1989–2001 period (by 59 and 46 percent, respectively, for all households), but mean retirement wealth grew very slowly from 2001 to 2007, and median retirement wealth actually fell slightly in absolute terms from 2001 to 2007. Both mean and median augmented wealth advanced strongly from 1989 to 2001. However, the growth in both mean and median augmented wealth fell off in the 2001–2007 period. Indeed, median augmented wealth declined in absolute terms for young households and gained only 2 percent among middle-aged households and the elderly. Thus, in terms of the broadest measure of retirement resources, the years from 2001 to 2007 were particularly unfavorable to American households.

Thus, in contrast to the sharp rise in both mean and median net worth during 2001–2007, we find a notably smaller growth in augmented wealth over these years. This was particularly the case for middle-aged and elderly households, for whom median augmented wealth advanced by only 2 percent, much less than median net worth. Among young households, median net worth showed an absolute decline, and as a consequence, so did augmented wealth. Clearly, by the period 2001–2007, even before the financial meltdown, the DC pension system was not providing the boost to household well-being that it had in the 1990s.

I next considered the effects of adding expected employer contributions to DC plans (DCEMP) to pension wealth. It is first of note that employer contributions to DC plans appear to have peaked in the early 2000s and then retreated in the late 2000s. Younger workers were particularly hard hit during the 2000s in terms of DCEMP. All in all, there appeared to be quite a sizable pullback in employer contributions to DC plans after 2001. When DCEMP is added in to pension wealth, my basic findings remain unchanged. In particular, the slowdown in the growth of augmented wealth between the 1989–2001 and 2001–2007 periods was about the same as when DCEMP is not included in pension wealth.

I also considered what happened when expected future income taxes on receipt of pension benefits were netted out of both pension and SSW. The basic findings are actually strengthened a bit, with a somewhat greater slowdown in the growth of mean and median net augmented wealth between the 1989–2001 and 2001–2007 periods than when gross pension and SSW are used.

Another issue considered in the chapter is whether the equalizing effects of retirement wealth lessened over time. Net worth inequality remained essentially flat from 1989 to 2007 despite a rise in income inequality. Retirement wealth did have a marked effect on inequality. Adding retirement wealth to net worth substantially lowered the Gini coefficient (from 0.834 to 0.684 in 2007, for example). Most of the equalizing effect came from the addition of SSW.

Considering the period 1989–2007, I did find that the equalizing effect of retirement wealth diminished. While the Gini coefficient for net worth remained largely unchanged over these years, the Gini coefficient for augmented wealth rose by 0.021. The differences are most marked for middle-aged households, the group most affected by transformation of the pension system. Among that group, the Gini coefficient for net worth rose by 0.020, while that of augmented wealth advanced by 0.031. Indeed, from 1983 to 2007, the Gini coefficient for augmented wealth among this age group climbed by 0.076, while that for net worth increased by only 0.033. In other words, the addition of retirement wealth to net worth reduced the overall Gini coefficient among all households in 1989 by 0.169 but by only 0.150 in 2007. Among middle-aged households, adding retirement wealth to net worth decreased the Gini coefficient by 0.187 in 1983 but by 0.145 in 2007. When employer contributions to DC pension plans are added in to pension wealth, and when expected future income taxes on receipt of pension benefits are netted out of both pension and SSW, the same pattern holds.

A somewhat rough update to the middle of 2009 shows that DC pension wealth was eviscerated by the stock market plunge of 2008–2009. I estimated that the average value of defined contribution plans fell by 17 percent from 2007 to the midpoint of 2009. Young households were particularly vulnerable. Their mean net worth plummeted by 21 percent and their median net worth by 78 percent; their mean pension wealth was down by 6 percent; and their mean augmented wealth slipped by 12 percent, and their median augmented wealth dipped by 17 percent. The contraction of pension wealth resulting from the stock market plunge did have the beneficial effect of reducing augmented wealth inequality, however.

These results also help to clear up the puzzle noted at the end of Chapter 2, namely that while income inequality surged in the 1990s and 2000s, (traditional) net worth inequality remained largely unchanged. The results show that when the definition of net worth is expanded to include DB pension wealth, then we do see a rise in (augmented) wealth inequality during the 1990s and the 2000s.

Notes

1. The low value for median pension wealth in 2007, $19,000, is mainly a reflection of the relatively large share of households (36 percent) without any pension wealth.
2. A small decline in both mean and median SSW for middle-aged and elderly households can be seen in the data for the period from 1983 to 1989. This seems to be due to the number of individuals reporting Social Security benefits received in 1983 as opposed to 1989. For example, among individuals 65 and over, the percentage of males reporting Social Security benefits increased from 86.0 percent in 1983 to 90.7 percent in 1989, while the share of females 65 and over reporting such benefits declined from 51.6 to 41.5 percent. Average Social Security benefits (in 1989 dollars) rose from $5,685 to $6,306 for elderly males but declined from $2,687 to $1,729 for elderly females. It is not clear whether the change for females is due to reporting problems in the 1989 SCF or represents a real change. For age group 47–64, the decrease in SSW might reflect the decline in average real wages over the period according to the Bureau of Labor Statistics' real hourly wage series.
3. The Gini coefficients of pension wealth reported in Table 5.2 differ from those in Table 4.7 because the former refer to all households, whereas the latter are for pension holders only.
4. The inequality of SSW first fell very substantially from 1989 to 2001, a trend that reflected primarily increasing Social Security coverage, and then rose sharply from 2001 to 2007, though not enough to offset its fall during the 1990s. The change over the 2000s mainly reflected the rising spread in (annual) earnings and, by implication, the rise in lifetime earnings inequality among the elderly.
5. Note that a higher correlation between two components of a variable leads to a higher coefficient of variation of that variable.
6. The use of a higher (lower) discount rate in the calculation of DB pension wealth would have lowered (raised) the value of DB pension wealth and consequently increased (decreased) the measured inequality of augmented wealth. Correspond-

ingly, the use of a higher (lower) discount rate would have led to a lower (higher) increase in the Gini coefficient for augmented wealth between 1989 (or 1983) and 2007. A similar argument holds for the choice of the discount rate for the calculation of SSW.

7. Among elderly households, the primary reason for the rise in augmented wealth inequality was the increasing share of net worth in augmented wealth, which rose from 68 percent in 1989 to 76 percent in 2007. Since the level of inequality of net worth is greater than that of retirement wealth, this shift resulted in higher inequality of augmented wealth in the later year. A secondary reason was the increase in the correlation between nonpension wealth and retirement wealth.

8. The pattern is again quite similar for age group 46 and under. The ratio of DCEMP to DC first ballooned from 1.03 in 1983 to 3.16 in 1989 and then diminished to 1.22 in 2007, and the slowdown in percentage gains of both mean and median pension wealth, private accumulations, retirement wealth, and augmented wealth between the 1990s and the 2000s became even larger. In fact, mean and median retirement wealth RW* (including employer contributions) and augmented wealth AW* (also including employer contributions) all showed absolute declines over the 2001–2007 period.

9. Recall that a larger correlation between two components of a variable leads to a higher coefficient of variation of that variable.

10. The story is different among younger households. In this case, the Gini coefficient for PA* (including employer contributions) and AW* (including employer contributions) showed a small decline from 1989 to 2007, while that for private accumulations (without employer contributions) and augmented wealth (without employer contributions) both showed an increase. For this age group, the addition of DCEMP to pension wealth had a greater equalizing effect in 2007 than in 1989.

11. The exception is Roth IRAs, which are not subject to income taxes on withdrawal.

12. Two other taxes associated with wealth holdings are capital gains tax on the sale of an asset and estate tax liability on inheritances. Neither DC nor DB pension wealth are salable, so a capital gains tax would not apply to these assets. On the other hand, estate tax liability would apply to all asset components of net worth, including DC wealth, though not generally to DB pension wealth. (The exception would be lump-sum distributions from DB plans, which is a relatively small amount— only 2.7 percent of total DB wealth in 2001, for example.) It is beyond the scope of this chapter to adjust wealth holdings for capital gains or estate taxes. See Poterba (2004) for further discussion of the tax treatment of retirement savings.

13. The 80 percent figure is a typical replacement rate (see Chapter 3 for a review of the pertinent literature). I also use adjusted gross income as the income concept, which is provided in the SCF data. The use of a higher replacement rate (say, 90 percent) would increase the marginal tax rate paid by the household and therefore reduce the estimated value of after-tax pension wealth, SSW, retirement wealth, and augmented wealth.

14. I also assume that families take the standard deduction and that the number of exemptions is two for singles and four for married couples (this includes the extra exemption for being 65 years of age or over). Moreover, it is assumed that tax

exemptions and the standard deduction are fixed in value over time. The latter assumption is plausible since both exemptions and the standard deduction are indexed for inflation.

15. In 1989, 2001, and 2007, Social Security benefits were subject to income tax only if AGI, excluding Social Security benefits, was greater than $32,000 for a married couple filing jointly and $25,000 for singles or couples filing separately. Otherwise, 15 percent of Social Security benefits is excluded from taxable income. In 1983, there was no tax on Social Security benefits.

16. This compares with the estimates of Butrica and Issa (2010), using the Federal Reserve Board's Flow of Funds, of a decline of 33.7 percent in the value of retirement accounts in real terms from the third quarter of 2007 to the first quarter of 2009, and of 14.6 percent from the third quarter of 2007 to the fourth quarter of 2009 (see Chapter 2 for more discussion).

6

Differences in Retirement Wealth by Demographic and Household Characteristics

How have different demographic groups fared with the transition in the structure of the pension system? We saw an inkling of this in Chapter 4 when we examined changes in pension coverage for different groups of workers. We find that female workers actually fared very well, while men saw their pension coverage rates decline. The pension make-over also harmed younger male workers more than older ones. Black workers were more adversely affected by the pension transformation than white workers. Pension coverage among the college-educated was aided by the systemic change in pensions, but coverage among less-educated male workers was damaged. The pension transition decimated coverage among blue-collar male workers and those in the bottom three quintiles of the earnings distribution.

In this chapter, we look at the relative income, retirement wealth, and augmented wealth of different demographic groups over the period 1989–2007. Because I am comparing relative gains made by different groups, I will focus on the 1989–2007 period exclusively. The next section presents a summary of aggregate trends in retirement and augmented wealth, and then shows results on the composition of augmented wealth for different population segments. Following that, the chapter considers how different demographic groups have fared with regard to retirement and augmented wealth. I focus on three divisions of the population: 1) race/ethnicity, 2) marital status, and 3) educational attainment. The chapter concludes with summary and concluding remarks. In Chapter 7, I will take up the issue of retirement income adequacy for the same set of population groups.

As will be seen in this chapter, there was a remarkable turnaround in the relative fortunes of minorities, though significant gaps still remained in 2007. Likewise, single females improved their position relative to married couples in terms of total (augmented) wealth. In contrast, differences in wealth by educational groups have, if anything, splayed out over the years, with college graduates in particular increasing their lead over the other educational groups.

TRENDS AND COMPOSITION OF RETIREMENT AND AUGMENTED WEALTH

There are three tiers of retirement savings to consider: Social Security, private pensions, and other forms of savings.[1] Social Security, as we saw in Chapter 5, has evolved into a near-universal program that provides a basic retirement benefit. Private employer-sponsored pensions would presumably supply the bulk of the additional income, and that additional savings would round out retirement income as "icing on the cake." It will be clear from my figures that Social Security fulfills its role as a basic retirement benefit and that its importance has even grown in recent years. However, large holes remain with respect to employer-sponsored pensions. In fact, private savings outside of retirement wealth play more than just a supplemental role, and wealth outside of retirement wealth can be a substantial addition to retirement savings.

Prior to retirement at age 65, median SSW is the largest of the three forms of savings (see Table 6.1). This was true in both 1989 and 2007. In 2007, households between the ages of 47 and 55 had a median SSW of $180,000 (in 2007 dollars), almost three times median private pension wealth. We observe a similar divergence for the age group 56–64, which had a median SSW of $216,100, more than twice as large as median private pension wealth. Among age group 46 and under, the discrepancy is even larger, with median SSW more than 100 times that of median pension wealth. Among elderly households, median SSW was almost three times median pension wealth in 2007.

Households have amassed substantial amounts of wealth outside of retirement savings. Median augmented wealth (the sum of net worth and retirement wealth) for households aged 47–55 was $424,300 in 2007, compared to $270,000 in retirement wealth for the same age group. For households aged 56–64, median retirement wealth amounted to $364,100 in 2007, compared to a median augmented wealth of $568,200. Among elderly households, median augmented wealth was $435,500

Table 6.1 Household Income and Wealth, 1989 and 2007 (in thousands, 2007$)

	1989	2007	% change, 1989–2007
Aged 46 and under			
Mean income	61.6	67.1	8.9
Mean nonpension wealth	162.0	179.2	10.6
Mean pension wealth	34.3	55.3	61.0
Mean Social Security wealth	92.9	125.7	35.4
Mean augmented wealth	289.2	360.2	24.5
Median income	47.2	46.0	−2.4
Median nonpension wealth	24.9	11.6	−53.5
Median pension wealth	0.8	1.8	—
Median Social Security wealth	87.7	112.5	28.2
Median retirement wealth	100.4	130.5	30.0
Median augmented wealth	140.5	155.8	10.9
Aged 47–55			
Mean income	90.9	110.2	21.3
Mean nonpension wealth	446.0	588.9	32.0
Mean pension wealth	103.3	179.4	73.7
Mean Social Security wealth	131.0	198.2	51.2
Mean augmented wealth	680.3	966.4	42.1
Median income	58.5	61.0	4.2
Median nonpension wealth	153.9	114.3	−25.7
Median pension wealth	25.7	61.0	137.3
Median Social Security wealth	139.3	180.0	29.2
Median retirement wealth	181.4	270.0	48.8
Median augmented wealth	364.0	424.3	16.6
Aged 56–64			
Mean income	67.8	111.7	64.7
Mean nonpension wealth	467.7	780.6	66.9
Mean pension wealth	139.3	288.6	107.2
Mean Social Security wealth	146.3	239.9	64.0
Mean augmented wealth	753.3	1309.1	73.8
Median income	41.8	53.0	26.8
Median nonpension wealth	137.6	172.4	25.2

(continued)

Table 6.1 (continued)

	1989	2007	% change, 1989–2007
Aged 56–64			
Median pension wealth	56.7	104.6	84.4
Median Social Security wealth	138.1	216.1	56.5
Median retirement wealth	210.4	364.1	73.0
Median augmented wealth	388.7	568.2	46.2
Aged 65+			
Mean income	43.8	66.9	52.6
Mean nonpension wealth	451.8	724.6	60.4
Mean pension wealth	84.7	175.8	107.6
Mean Social Security wealth	127.6	169.6	32.9
Mean augmented wealth	664.0	1070.0	61.1
Median income	24.1	29.0	20.4
Median nonpension wealth	128.1	191.0	49.1
Median pension wealth	5.7	47.4	738.6
Median Social Security wealth	105.9	132.6	25.2
Median retirement wealth	153.6	211.8	38.0
Median augmented wealth	310.7	435.5	40.2

NOTE: Households are classified by the age of the head of household. Key: Pension wealth = defined contribution + defined benefit wealth. Retirement wealth = pension wealth + Social Security wealth. Augmented wealth = nonpension wealth + retirement wealth.
SOURCE: Author's computations from the 1989 and 2007 SCF.

and median retirement wealth was about half as much, $211,800. Non-retirement wealth was thus substantial among these age groups in 2007. However, among younger households (46 and under), the discrepancy was much smaller, with a median retirement wealth of $130,500 and a median augmented wealth of $155,800.

One important aspect with respect to wealth accumulation that deserves further attention is the distribution of wealth. Typically, all forms of wealth are relatively unequally distributed, with the exception of SSW (see Chapters 4 and 5). For instance, median private pension wealth of households between the ages of 47 and 55 was only 34 percent of the average private pension wealth in that age group in 2007, which indicates that pension wealth was heavily concentrated among those with substantial amounts of private pension wealth (see Chapter 4). In contrast, the SSW of the typical household in this age group was 91 percent of the average SSW of this age group. For households aged 56–64, the ratios were 36 percent and 90 percent, suggesting that private pension wealth was substantially more unequally distributed than SSW in this age group, too.

How has the situation changed over time? Median SSW saw strong gains from 1989 to 2007 for households between the ages of 47 and 64 (Table 6.1). Median pension wealth also saw strong increases from 1989 to 2007. For age group 47–55, the change in median private pension wealth was substantially greater than that in SSW. The same was true for age group 56–64. Among the elderly, both median SSW and pension wealth showed robust growth over this period as well. In contrast, among age group 46 and under, median SSW showed a large gain from 1989 to 2007, but median pension wealth was virtually zero in both years.[2]

For age group 47–55, median household income showed a modest increase in real terms from 1989 to 2007 (by 4 percent) but solid growth for age group 56–64 (by 27 percent).[3] Real median income also showed strong growth among elderly households (20 percent) but a slight decline among young households.

One factor that may put a damper on increases in retirement resources is a rise in income and wealth inequality. For all ages, average incomes and average wealth increased faster than median income and wealth over the 1989–2007 period. The divergence was most pronounced for households aged 47–55, for whom average augmented wealth rose more than twice as fast as median augmented wealth. These results generally accord with the calculations in Chapter 5, which show an increase in the Gini coefficient for augmented wealth among age group 47–64 and among the elderly, but a slight decline among younger households (see Table 5.4).

We next turn to how the composition of augmented wealth varies by age group (Table 6.2). First, for all households, we can see how the shares of the three major components of augmented wealth have changed over the period 1989–2007. Nonpension wealth fell as a share of augmented wealth, from 63 percent in 1989 to 60 percent in 2007. In contrast, the share of pension wealth rose from 14 percent in 1989 to 18

Table 6.2 Composition of Augmented Wealth, 1989 and 2007 (percentage of augmented wealth)

	1989	2007
Aged 46 and under		
Nonpension wealth	56.0	49.7
Pension wealth	11.9	15.4
Defined contribution accounts	3.2	8.5
Defined benefit plans	8.7	6.8
Social Security wealth	32.1	34.9
Total	100.0	100.0
Aged 47–64		
Nonpension wealth	63.8	60.3
Pension wealth	16.9	20.3
Defined contribution accounts	2.9	12.1
Defined benefit plans	14.0	8.2
Social Security wealth	19.3	19.4
Total	100.0	100.0
Aged 65+		
Nonpension wealth	62.1	59.6
Pension wealth	18.5	22.0
Defined contribution accounts	0.3	7.9
Defined benefit plans	18.1	14.1
Social Security wealth	19.4	18.3
Total	100.0	99.9
All households		
Nonpension wealth	62.6	60.2
Pension wealth	14.0	18.1
Defined contribution accounts	2.2	10.1
Defined benefit plans	11.8	8.0
Social Security wealth	23.4	21.7
Total	100.0	100.0

Table 6.2 (continued)	1989	2007
Composition of augmented wealth*: aged 47–64		
Nonpension wealth	62.6	58.3
Pension wealth*	18.4	22.9
Defined contribution accounts	2.8	11.7
Defined benefit plans	13.8	8.0
Employer contributions to defined contribution pension plans	1.8	3.3
Social Security wealth	19.0	18.8
Total	100.0	100.0
Composition of net augmented wealth*: aged 47–64		
Nonpension wealth	66.3	65.6
Net pension wealth*	15.5	16.2
Net Social Security wealth	18.2	18.2
Total	100.0	100.0

NOTE: Households are classified into age groups by the age of the head of household. Key: Augmented wealth = nonpension wealth + retirement wealth. Augmented wealth* = nonpension wealth + retirement wealth*. Totals may not sum to 100.0 due to rounding.
SOURCE: Author's computations from the 1989 and 2007 SCF.

percent in 2007. Of the two parts of pension wealth, DC wealth showed a very strong gain, from 2 percent of augmented wealth in 1989 to 10 percent in 2007, while DB showed a corresponding decline, from 12 to 8 percent. The share of SSW fell slightly, from 23 to 22 percent. The composition of augmented wealth was remarkably similar among age groups 47–64 and 65 and older. However, among young households, age 46 and under, the share of SSW was higher, a third or more, while the shares of nonpension wealth and pension wealth were correspondingly lower.

When employer contributions to DC pension plans (DCEMP) are added in to produce AW*, we see that the share of DCEMP in AW* among middle-aged households was relatively small—between 2 and 3 percent. The inclusion of DCEMP in AW* resulted in a modest rise in the share of PW* in augmented wealth and a corresponding decline in the shares of the other two components. Looking at net (after-tax) AW*, we see, not surprisingly, lower shares of net PW* and net SSW in net

AW* and a correspondingly higher share of nonpension wealth. There was little change over time in the shares of these three components. The share of nonpension wealth in net AW* was about the same in 2007 as in 1989 (66 percent), as were the shares of net PW* (16 percent) and net SSW (18 percent).

In sum, we can now get a good idea of what the sources of retirement income are. On the basis of gross (before-tax) retirement wealth, the share of nonpension wealth was about three-fifths, that of pension wealth about one-fifth, and that of SSW also about one-fifth among all households. These shares should generally correspond to the breakdown of retirement income. The composition of augmented wealth was very similar among middle-aged and elderly households. However, among younger households, the share of SSW was higher, about one-third, that of nonpension wealth about one-half, and that of pension wealth about one-sixth. On a net (after-tax) basis, the importance of nonpension wealth was greater (about two-thirds) and that of pension wealth smaller (about 16 percent), as was that of SSW (about 18 percent). We would also expect the make-up of augmented wealth (and thus the sources of retirement income) to vary both by income level and by demographic characteristic, as we shall see below.

Table 6.3 considers the composition of AW* by income quintile for age group 47–64. I have elected to use here AW* because it gives a more comprehensive measure of pension resources than standard pension wealth. It is clear that SSW is much more important for lower-income households than upper-income ones. In 2007, the share of SSW in AW* was 44 percent for the bottom income quintile, 40 percent for the second quintile, 33 percent for the middle quintile, 29 percent for the fourth quintile, and only 9 percent for the top quintile. In contrast, nonpension wealth was much more important for the top income quintile, comprising 71 percent of AW* in 2007, compared to a range of 38–48 percent for the lower quintiles. PW*, on the other hand, was more important in the middle income quintiles, accounting for 29 percent of AW* for the middle quintile and 32 percent for the fourth quintile, compared to 9 percent for the bottom, 21 percent for the second, and 21 percent for the top. These results indicate that SSW will be a relatively more important source of retirement income among low-income households, nonpension wealth will be relatively more impor-

Table 6.3 Composition of Augmented Wealth by Income Quintile, Aged 47–64, 1989 and 2007 (percentage of augmented wealth*)

	1989	2007
Bottom income quintile		
Net worth minus defined contribution wealth	39.5	47.8
Pension wealth*	11.1	8.6
Social Security wealth	49.5	43.6
Total	100.0	100.0
Second income quintile		
Net worth minus defined contribution wealth	44.7	39.5
Pension wealth*	19.7	21.0
Social Security wealth	35.6	39.5
Total	100.0	100.0
Third income quintile		
Net worth minus defined contribution wealth	46.0	38.2
Pension wealth*	24.1	29.3
Social Security wealth	29.8	32.5
Total	100.0	100.0
Fourth income quintile		
Net worth minus defined contribution wealth	47.6	38.6
Pension wealth*	25.6	32.4
Social Security wealth	26.8	29.0
Total	100.0	100.0
Fifth income quintile		
Net worth minus defined contribution wealth	75.7	70.6
Pension wealth*	15.0	20.5
Social Security wealth	9.3	8.9
Total	100.0	100.0
All households, aged 47–64		
Net worth minus defined contribution wealth	62.6	58.3
Pension wealth*	18.4	22.9
Social Security wealth	19.0	18.8
Total	100.0	100.0

NOTE: Augmented wealth* includes employer contributions to defined contribution pension plans. Households are classified into age groups by the age of the head of household. Income quintiles are based on income for age group 47–64 only and are calculated separately for each year. Key: Augmented wealth = nonpension wealth + retirement wealth*. Augmented wealth* = nonpension wealth + retirement wealth*. Totals may not sum to 100.0 due to rounding.
SOURCE: Author's computations from the 1989 and 2007 SCF.

tant among upper-income households, and pension wealth relatively more important among middle-income households.

Except for the bottom income quintile, pension wealth's importance as a share of total retirement resources rose over time. For example, the third income quintile's share of AW* grew from 24 percent in 1989 to 29 percent in 2007. With the exception of the bottom and top quintiles, the importance of SSW also increased. Again, for the middle income quintile, the share of SSW in AW* advanced from 27 to 29 percent over this period. Correspondingly, except for the bottom quintile, the share of nonpension wealth in AW* declined over these years (from 46 to 38 percent for the middle quintile, for example). Thus, there was generally a shift in retirement resources away from standard wealth holdings to pension and SSW.

We next look at mean retirement wealth by wealth and income class to determine whether gains in retirement resources have been greater at the bottom or top. Not surprisingly, there is a big spread of retirement wealth levels by wealth class—by a factor of five or so between the highest and lowest (see Table 6.4). A U-shaped profile is in evidence for gains in retirement wealth over the 1989–2007 period. This is true for all three age groups. The largest gains by far were made by the top wealth group. The retirement wealth of the wealth class with assets of $1,000,000 and above grew by 117 percent over the period among age group 56–64 and by 48 percent among elderly households. The smallest gains were made by the middle wealth class, those who have $100,000–$249,999. The mean retirement wealth of the bottom wealth class, in contrast, showed strong gains over the period (a 93 percent increase among age group 56–64). Thus, while retirement wealth among the lowest wealth group was catching up to the middle, the retirement wealth of the highest wealth groups was also moving further ahead of the middle. These changes reflected large gains in SSW at the lower end of the wealth distribution and very big increases in DC pension wealth at the top (see Figure 4.1a, for example).

The pattern is similar by income class (Table 6.5). Once again, gains in mean retirement wealth over the 1989–2007 period were strong among the top two or three income classes. There were also sizable gains for the bottom income class (except among the elderly). The three middle income classes ($25,000–$75,000) all experienced actual declines in their mean retirement wealth (with one exception).

**Table 6.4 Mean Retirement Wealth by Wealth Class, 1989 and 2007
(in thousands, 2007$)**

	1989	2007	% change, 1989–2007
Aged 47–55			
Under 50,000	115.8	166.1	43.4
50,000–99,999	196.3	234.1	19.3
100,000–249,999	239.0	273.9	14.6
250,000–499,999	329.6	362.3	9.9
500,000–999,999	355.0	470.7	32.6
1,000,000 or over	484.0	805.8	66.5
Aged 56–64			
Under 50,000	104.2	200.6	92.5
50,000–99,999	260.3	223.8	−14.0
100,000–249,999	290.1	301.9	4.0
250,000–499,999	396.0	400.4	1.1
500,000–999,999	517.5	581.4	12.4
1,000,000 or over	509.7	1,106.3	117.0
Aged 65+			
Under 50,000	105.6	159.8	51.4
50,000–99,999	183.0	176.8	−3.4
100,000–249,999	197.0	220.9	12.1
250,000–499,999	256.5	253.8	−1.1
500,000–999,999	422.4	378.3	−10.4
1,000,000 or over	518.6	769.1	48.3

NOTE: Households are classified by net worth in 2001 dollars. Key: Retirement wealth
= pension wealth + Social Security wealth.
SOURCE: Author's computations from the 1989 and 2007 SCF.

Given all other data trends discussed so far, especially the sharp
increases in SSW, it seems reasonable to assume that the changes in
retirement wealth among households nearing retirement were driven by
two separate forces. Increases were due to gains in SSW as a result of a
strong labor market, at least through 2001, and strong returns in 401(k)
and other DC plans, also mainly up through 2001, which in turn were
due to a strong financial market performance. Given the distribution of
financial wealth, it is very likely that the latter was more of a factor for
higher-income households.

**Table 6.5 Mean Retirement Wealth by Income Class, 1989 and 2007
(in thousands, 2007$)**

	1989	2007	% change, 1989–2007
Aged 47–55			
Under 25,000	73.9	91.8	24.3
25,000–34,999	140.0	138.9	−0.8
35,000–49,999	206.0	166.4	−19.2
50,000–74,999	247.9	234.2	−5.5
75,000–99,999	311.9	327.0	4.8
100,000–249,999	421.8	504.3	19.6
250,000 or over	796.2	900.6	13.1
Aged 56–64			
Under 25,000	102.1	130.4	27.7
25,000–34,999	226.6	234.9	3.7
35,000–49,999	325.8	211.2	−35.2
50,000–74,999	414.0	373.9	−9.7
75,000–99,999	448.0	475.1	6.1
100,000–249,999	519.3	681.6	31.3
250,000 or over	802.1	1,536.4	91.5
Aged 65+			
Under 25,000	120.2	90.1	−25.0
25,000–34,999	279.6	180.9	−35.3
35,000–49,999	285.3	263.9	−7.5
50,000–74,999	414.2	339.2	−18.1
75,000–99,999	365.5	462.1	26.4
100,000–249,999	642.4	696.1	8.4
250,000 or over	1,109.5	1,392.5	25.5

NOTE: Households are classified by income in 2001 dollars. Key: Retirement wealth = pension wealth + Social Security wealth.
SOURCE: Author's computations from the 1989 and 2007 SCF.

Disparate gains in wealth tend to reduce the overall effect of wealth gains on retirement income adequacy, especially if households that are likely to be already well prepared for retirement see the largest gains. If wealth gains are concentrated among households that already have a large amount of wealth or income, average retirement wealth increases have less of an effect on retirement income adequacy compared to a situation where wealth increases are less concentrated. The results so far show that percentage gains in retirement wealth have been generally greater at the upper ends of the wealth and income distributions as well as the very bottom, but small in the middle. As a result, the gains in retirement income adequacy from 1989 to 2007 were likely less than they could have been if the gains had been more equally distributed across wealth and income classes.

Importantly, this result holds only for retirement wealth outside of SSW. Improvements in SSW to be appear fairly equally distributed. Thus, it is fair to conclude that Social Security improvements had a more broad-based effect on retirement income adequacy than improvements in private pension wealth or other private savings, regardless of whether the changes on average were smaller or larger. In Chapter 7, we shall analyze these factors more fully.

DISPARITIES IN RETIREMENT WEALTH BY DEMOGRAPHIC GROUP

I next consider how different demographic groups have fared with regard to retirement and augmented wealth. I look at three divisions of the population: 1) race/ethnicity, 2) marital status, and 3) educational attainment.

Race/Ethnicity

The population is divided here into two groups: 1) non-Hispanic white households ("whites," for short) and 2) African American and Hispanic households ("minorities," for short).[4] In 2007 over three-quarters of white households in age groups 47–55 and 56–64 held some form of pension wealth (see Table 6.6). Over 70 percent of white elderly households and 60 percent of white younger households (age 46 and under) likewise owned pension wealth. In contrast, 57 percent of minority households in age group 47–55 and 59 percent in age group 56–64 held pension wealth, as did 38 percent of younger minority households and a half of minority elderly ones.

**Table 6.6 Percentage of Households with Pension Wealth by Race/
Ethnicity and Age Class, 1989 and 2007**

	Non-Hispanic white		African American or Hispanic	
	1989	2007	1989	2007
Aged 46 and under				
Defined contribution accounts	35.9	55.8	17.8	33.8
Defined benefit plans	42.0	25.7	26.3	15.2
Pension wealth	58.5	60.5	34.3	38.2
Share of defined contribution owners who receive employer contributions	77.1	64.8	81.5	75.8
Aged 47–55				
Defined contribution accounts	35.5	70.1	21.2	47.5
Defined benefit plans	60.3	36.3	40.4	32.5
Pension wealth	74.1	77.7	46.6	56.8
Share of defined contribution owners who receive employer contributions	58.1	61.8	36.2	72.4
Aged 56–64				
Defined contribution accounts	23.7	64.6	12.0	43.8
Defined benefit plans	65.1	46.3	39.3	33.1
Pension wealth	71.0	78.2	46.0	59.3
Share of defined contribution owners who receive employer contributions	0.0	43.6	0.0	62.0
Aged 65+				
Defined contribution accounts	1.6	45.3	0.0	9.3
Defined benefit plans	56.1	51.0	30.1	46.2
Pension wealth	56.8	71.1	30.1	49.9

NOTE: Households are classified by the age of the head of household. Asians and other
races are excluded from the table because of small sample sizes. Key: Pension wealth
= defined contribution + defined benefit wealth.
SOURCE: Author's computations from the 1989 and 2007 SCF.

It is at once evident that in 2007 whites were much more likely to have a pension plan than minorities. Among age group 56–64, the difference in pension wealth ownership rates was 19 percentage points. Differences were even higher for the other age groups—22 percentage points among age group 46 and under, 21 percentage points among age group 47–55, and 21 percentage points among the elderly. The main disparity was in ownership of DC accounts.[5] The gap in the ownership of DC plans was over 20 percentage points among the three youngest age groups and 36 percentage points among the elderly. The racial gap in entitlements to DB plans was much smaller, 4 percentage points among age group 47–55, 13 percentage points among age group 56–64, and 11 percentage points among younger households. Among the elderly, 46 percent of minority and 51 percent of white households held DB pension wealth, with a gap of only 5 percentage points.[6]

The disparity in DC pension ownership widened considerably between the two groups, as the take-up rate for DC plans grew much faster among white workers. Among younger households, DC ownership among whites expanded from 36 percent in 1989 to 56 percent in 2007, while among minorities it grew from 18 to 34 percent; among age group 47–55, it increased from 36 to 70 percent among the former and from 21 to 48 percent among the latter; among age group 56–64, it rose from 24 to 65 percent and from 12 to 44 percent, respectively; and among the elderly, from 2 to 45 percent and from 0 to only 9 percent, respectively. The gap in participation in DC plans between whites and minorities thus rose among all age groups, though particularly among the elderly (by 34 percentage points).

In contrast, the racial gap in participation in DB plans fell quite substantially between 1989 and 2007, as participation in these plans plummeted among both whites and minorities. As a result, the racial gap in the share of households with pension wealth (either DC or DB) narrowed somewhat over these years.

Despite improvements, minority households still had a lot less wealth accumulated than nonminority households as they approached retirement in 2007. For households between the ages of 47 and 55, the average retirement wealth of non-Hispanic whites was about twice as large as for minorities (Table 6.7). For households aged 56–64, the ratio of average retirement wealth was 2.3, for households 65 and older it was 1.4, and for households aged 46 and under it was 2.0. Similar

186

Table 6.7 Retirement Wealth by Race/Ethnicity and Age Class, 1989 and 2007 (in thousands, 2007$)

	Non-Hispanic white			African American or Hispanic		
	1989	2007	% change, 1989–2007	1989	2007	% change, 1989–2007
Aged 46 and under						
Mean pension wealth	41.4	67.5	63.1	14.5	27.3	88.6
Mean Social Security wealth	106.2	144.5	36.1	50.9	79.7	56.5
Mean retirement wealth	147.6	212.1	43.7	65.4	107.0	63.6
Median retirement wealth	124.3	155.6	25.1	48.0	79.2	65.0
Aged 47–55						
Mean pension wealth	114.8	204.5	78.1	70.2	93.6	33.4
Mean Social Security wealth	145.9	213.3	46.2	73.9	138.8	87.8
Mean retirement wealth	260.7	417.8	60.3	144.1	232.4	61.3
Median retirement wealth	193.6	304.4	57.2	95.7	166.3	73.8
Aged 56–64						
Mean pension wealth	166.2	329.1	98.0	56.6	111.0	96.0
Mean Social Security wealth	167.9	261.1	55.5	71.2	147.6	107.3
Mean retirement wealth	334.1	590.3	76.6	127.8	258.6	102.3
Median retirement wealth	269.6	417.1	54.7	68.1	183.9	169.8
Aged 65+						
Mean pension wealth	88.5	185.8	110.0	33.6	104.2	209.7
Mean Social Security wealth	141.5	171.4	21.1	56.7	149.3	163.3
Mean retirement wealth	230.0	357.2	55.3	90.4	253.5	180.5
Median retirement wealth	184.8	219.0	18.5	44.3	158.9	258.8

NOTE: Households are classified by the age of the head of household. Asians and other races are excluded from the table because of small sample sizes. Key: Pension wealth = defined contribution + defined benefit wealth. Retirement wealth = pension wealth + Social Security wealth.

SOURCE: Author's computations from the 1989 and 2007 SCF.

disparities existed for median retirement wealth. Discrepancies were much larger for pension wealth than SSW. In 2007, the ratio of average pension wealth was 2.5 for the youngest age group, 2.2 for age group 47–55, 3.0 for age group 56–64, and 1.8 among elderly households. These differences reflect to a large extent disparities in pension ownership. In contrast, the ratio of average SSW was 1.8 for the youngest age group, 1.5 for age group 47–55, 1.8 for age group 56–64, and only 1.2 among elderly households.

Over time, the racial gap in retirement wealth generally narrowed. Among younger households, pension wealth and SSW both increased faster among minorities than among whites, and the ratio of mean retirement wealth increased from 44 percent in 1989 to 51 percent in 2007 and the ratio of median retirement wealth from 39 to 51 percent. Among age group 47–55, the story was somewhat different. In this case, mean SSW grew faster for minorities but mean pension wealth grew slower. On net, the ratio of mean retirement wealth stayed at around 55 percent from 1989 to 2007, while that of median retirement wealth advanced from 49 to 55 percent. In contrast, among age group 56–64, mean pension wealth gained about the same for both groups from 1989 to 2007, while percentage gains in SSW were greater for minorities. As a result, the ratio of both mean and median retirement wealth between minorities and whites showed a sizable rise, particularly the ratio of medians. Elderly minority households also fared well in relative terms. Both mean pension wealth and mean SSW grew much faster for minorities in this age group than among whites, and the ratio of mean retirement wealth climbed from 39 percent in 1989 to 71 percent in 2007 and that of median retirement wealth from 24 to 73 percent.

Even larger differences exist for total wealth. The ratio of average total (augmented) wealth of whites to the average augmented wealth of minorities was 2.7 for households aged 46 and under in 2007, 2.7 for households aged 47–55, 2.9 for households aged 56–64, and 2.5 for households 65 and older (see Table 6.8).[7] Ratios of median augmented wealth were a bit lower (except for the youngest age group): 2.7 for ages 46 and under, 2.1 for ages 47–55 and ages 56–64, and 2.0 for elderly households. The gap in augmented wealth was uniformly smaller than the gap in net worth, where the ratios ran from 3.5 for the youngest age group to 4.2 for the oldest, but larger than the gap in income, where the ratios ranged from 1.8 for the youngest to 2.6 for the oldest. The smaller

188

Table 6.8 Income and Wealth by Race/Ethnicity and Age Class, 1989 and 2007 (in thousands, 2007$)

	Non-Hispanic white			African American or Hispanic		
	1989	2007	% change, 1989–2007	1989	2007	% change, 1989–2007
Aged 46 and under						
Mean income	70.9	76.4	7.7	34.2	42.3	23.8
Mean net worth	202.8	265.0	30.7	38.6	76.8	98.7
Mean augmented wealth	338.6	439.1	29.7	101.6	170.1	67.4
Median augmented wealth	195.8	215.0	9.8	48.5	80.3	65.7
Mean augmented wealth*	374.2	483.4	29.2	112.1	189.3	68.9
Mean net augmented wealth*	347.3	443.0	27.6	104.6	174.7	66.9
Aged 47–55						
Mean income	102.8	124.1	20.7	41.2	62.1	50.8
Mean net worth	543.7	822.2	51.2	106.8	222.3	108.2
Mean augmented wealth	778.9	1,112.0	42.8	244.0	415.3	70.2
Median augmented wealth	402.8	484.4	20.3	125.4	226.3	80.4
Mean augmented wealth*	812.3	1,163.9	43.3	247.9	435.5	75.7
Mean net augmented wealth*	761.5	1,071.8	40.7	228.5	399.7	74.9
Aged 56–64						
Mean income	79.5	125.5	58.0	29.9	52.7	76.1
Mean net worth	595.3	1,087.8	82.7	129.7	305.1	135.3
Mean augmented wealth	905.9	1,481.5	63.5	252.8	516.0	104.1
Median augmented wealth	503.7	676.8	34.4	104.7	323.4	209.0
Mean augmented wealth*	905.9	1,513.8	67.1	252.8	528.2	108.9
Mean net augmented wealth*	860.3	1,396.6	62.3	241.6	493.7	104.4

Aged 65+

Mean income	49.3	72.1	46.4	17.9	27.8	55.2
Mean net worth	539.0	877.2	62.7	58.9	207.2	252.1
Mean augmented wealth	766.3	1,139.5	48.7	149.2	448.5	200.6
Median augmented wealth	375.4	457.1	21.8	83.2	228.2	174.1

Households are classified by the age of the head of household. Asians and other races are excluded from the table because of small sample sizes. Key: Augmented wealth = nonpension wealth + retirement wealth. Augmented wealth* includes employer contributions to defined contribution pension plans.

SOURCE: Author's computations from the 1989 and 2007 SCF.

gap in augmented wealth than in net worth is attributable mainly to the equalizing effect of Social Security. The racial gap in augmented wealth thus narrowed over the years. The ratio of mean augmented wealth between minorities and whites rose from 0.30 in 1989 to 0.39 in 2007 among the 46-and-under age group, from 0.31 to 0.37 among the 47–55 age group, from 0.28 to 0.35 among the 56–64 age group, and from 0.20 to 0.39 among elderly households.[8] Relative gains made by minorities were even more pronounced for median augmented wealth. The closure of the augmented wealth racial gap was due to the sizable relative gains made by minorities in net worth, which occurred for all age groups, and to relative gains in retirement wealth, which occurred for all age groups except for ages 56–64.[9] The racial income gap also narrowed among all age groups.[10]

Family Status

I next analyze levels and trends of retirement wealth and total wealth for married couples, single females, and single males. I begin, as before, by looking at trends in pension ownership.[11] As shown in Table 6.9, wide gaps in holdings of pension plans are evident between married couples and both single men and single women, particularly with regard to DC plans.

In 2007, the gap in holdings of DC pension wealth between married couples and single men was 14 percentage points for the youngest age group, 20–22 percentage points among the middle-aged (47–64), and 26 percentage points among the elderly. Married couples were also more apt to have matching contributions to their DC plans from their employers. Among the three nonelderly age groups, the gap in DC pension coverage generally remained unchanged or widened slightly. However, among the elderly, the gap mushroomed from 2 percentage points in 1989 to 26 percentage points in 2007. In contrast, the gap in DB plan entitlement generally narrowed over the period from 1989 to 2007 as DB plans atrophied. All told, the gap in pension wealth holdings narrowed among nonelderly households over the 1989–2007 period, mainly because of the sharp contraction in DB plans, but widened among elderly households.

Results are similar when single females are compared with married couples. In 2007, the gap in ownership rates of DC plans between

Table 6.9 Percentage of Households with Pension Wealth by Family Status and Age Class, 1983–2007

	Married couples		Single males		Single females	
	1989	2007	1989	2007	1989	2007
Aged 46 and under						
Defined contribution accounts	37.8	57.4	21.0	43.4	21.5	33.9
Defined benefit plans	45.6	25.9	29.0	19.7	24.4	15.8
Pension wealth	62.4	61.7	41.7	49.0	33.6	39.5
Share of defined contribution owners who receive employer contributions	80.6	70.5	77.2	58.9	65.8	61.1
Aged 47–55						
Defined contribution accounts	41.5	74.3	19.4	52.6	17.3	51.9
Defined benefit plans	59.9	39.3	50.7	29.5	43.7	28.6
Pension wealth	75.6	80.6	57.4	61.9	54.3	62.7
Share of defined contribution owners who receive employer contributions	48.2	65.3	43.7	58.6	82.5	59.6
Aged 56–64						
Defined contribution accounts	26.7	69.7	10.5	49.6	20.2	46.1
Defined benefit plans	70.2	46.3	45.8	43.4	39.2	37.5
Pension wealth	77.8	79.5	45.8	68.0	51.5	66.9
Share of defined contribution owners who receive employer contributions	0.0	51.4	0.0	23.5	0.0	38.0
Aged 65+						
Defined contribution accounts	1.9	53.4	0.0	27.3	1.0	29.3
Defined benefit plans	65.3	57.2	66.1	57.3	33.4	40.7
Pension wealth	65.8	78.9	66.1	70.4	34.1	55.4

NOTE: Households are classified by the age of the head of household. Key: Pension wealth = defined contribution + defined benefit wealth.
SOURCE: Author's computations from the 1989 and 2007 SCF.

married couples and single women varied between 22 and 24 percentage points across age groups. Married couples were again more apt to have matching contributions to their DC plan from their employer than single females. Here, too, the gap in the share of DC plan holders generally widened over the years from 1989 to 2007 (except for age group 47–55). The gap in DB plan entitlement was about 10 percentage points among the three nonelderly age groups in 2007 and 17 percentage points for the oldest. These gaps in DB coverage narrowed over the years 1989 to 2007 among all age groups as DB plans were eliminated. As a consequence, the gap in pension wealth holdings between married couples and single females fell by 7 percentage points among young households from 1989 to 2007, by 3 percentage points among age group 47–55, by 14 percentage points among age group 56–64, and by 8 percentage points among the elderly.

The results from Tables 6.10 and 6.11 show that married couples had substantially more retirement wealth and total (augmented) wealth than single male–headed households, and they in turn had more retirement and augmented wealth than single female–headed households in 2007. However, the figures also show that single men and single women generally did catch up somewhat to married couples from 1989 to 2007.

The ratio of pension wealth, SSW, and both mean and median retirement wealth between single men and married couples improved between 1989 and 2007. This was true across all age groups. However, even in 2007, the mean pension wealth, SSW, and retirement wealth of single men averaged about half that of married couples, and median retirement wealth averaged about 40 percent that of married couples. This discrepancy is, of course, partly explainable by the fact that married couples have two adults in the household, and even if they did not have two earners, SSW at least is higher for a single earner in a married couple than a for single man living alone.[12]

In contrast, in 2007, the mean pension wealth, SSW, and retirement wealth, as well as the median retirement wealth, of single women averaged about 33–40 percent that of married couples. From 1989 to 2007, the relative position of single women aged 47 and under and aged 65 and older improved across the board with respect to married couples. Among age group 47–55, there was a mild deterioration in the relative position of single females, while among age group 56–64 the mean retirement wealth of single females declined relative to married

Table 6.10 Retirement Wealth by Family Status and Age Class, 1989 and 2007 (in thousands, 2007$)

	Married couples			Single males			Single females		
	1989	2007	% change, 1989–2007	1989	2007	% change, 1989–2007	1989	2007	% change, 1989–2007
Aged 46 and under									
Mean pension wealth	45.7	70.1	53.3	23.8	43.0	80.5	12.5	23.7	89.4
Mean Social Security wealth	122.1	160.8	31.7	47.4	69.8	47.2	49.2	69.4	41.0
Mean retirement wealth	167.8	230.9	37.5	71.2	112.8	58.3	61.7	93.1	50.8
Median retirement wealth	140.3	175.2	24.9	51.8	72.2	39.3	50.3	70.8	40.6
Aged 47–55									
Mean pension wealth	131.0	229.3	75.1	56.5	125.3	121.8	44.9	78.7	75.4
Mean Social Security wealth	161.5	251.9	56.0	65.9	111.9	69.7	71.4	108.0	51.3
Mean retirement wealth	292.5	481.3	64.5	122.4	237.2	93.7	116.3	186.8	60.6
Median retirement wealth	214.5	365.8	70.6	77.7	144.9	86.5	89.1	130.6	46.6
Aged 56–64									
Mean pension wealth	186.3	385.9	107.2	71.5	198.8	178.0	69.5	114.9	65.2
Mean Social Security wealth	195.8	311.3	59.0	75.3	134.0	78.0	72.5	128.7	77.6
Mean retirement wealth	382.1	697.2	82.5	146.8	332.8	126.7	142.0	243.6	71.5
Median retirement wealth	310.1	493.1	59.0	107.5	208.6	94.0	82.0	174.7	113.0
Aged 65+									
Mean pension wealth	138.2	265.4	92.0	59.8	124.3	107.7	34.8	81.9	135.3
Mean Social Security wealth	206.5	248.4	20.3	87.3	110.1	26.2	55.0	91.3	66.0
Mean retirement wealth	344.7	513.8	49.0	147.1	234.5	59.4	89.8	173.2	92.9
Median retirement wealth	282.3	352.1	24.7	125.8	157.4	25.1	56.7	102.7	81.1

NOTE: Households are classified by the age of the head of household. Key: Pension wealth = defined contribution + defined benefit wealth. Retirement wealth = pension wealth + Social Security wealth.

SOURCE: Author's computations from the 1989 and 2007 SCF.

Table 6.11 Income and Wealth by Family Status and Age Class, 1989 and 2007 (in thousands, 2007$)

	Married couples			Single males			Single females		
	1989	2007	% change, 1989–2007	1989	2007	% change, 1989–2007	1989	2007	% change, 1989–2007
Aged 46 and under									
Mean income	77.9	85.3	9.5	46.7	44.4	−5.1	30.4	33.5	10.1
Mean net worth	217.2	272.2	25.3	177.4	123.9	−30.1	50.3	100.2	99.0
Mean augmented wealth	372.4	464.3	24.7	243.9	210.4	−13.8	108.6	181.6	67.1
Median augmented wealth	222.8	241.2	8.3	73.1	83.2	13.8	56.3	68.3	21.2
Mean augmented wealth*	412.5	511.4	24.0	255.9	238.2	−6.9	121.1	199.1	64.4
Mean net augmented wealth*	381.9	468.4	22.7	244.4	214.7	−12.2	114.1	185.6	62.7
Aged 47–55									
Mean income	114.9	143.6	25.0	74.4	74.1	−0.4	31.7	42.8	35.1
Mean net worth	617.5	929.1	50.5	303.0	453.8	49.8	120.5	226.9	88.3
Mean augmented wealth	880.5	1,268.6	44.1	411.4	611.9	48.7	233.6	375.2	60.6
Median augmented wealth	449.7	592.7	31.8	135.0	282.4	109.1	141.4	192.7	36.3
Mean augmented wealth*	911.7	1,324.2	45.2	421.5	646.2	53.3	251.1	396.2	57.8
Mean net augmented wealth*	853.3	1,219.6	42.9	400.7	593.2	48.0	238.2	367.3	54.2
Aged 56–64									
Mean income	90.1	155.7	72.8	42.5	58.5	37.6	30.9	38.3	24.0
Mean net worth	665.1	1,335.0	100.7	242.8	541.2	122.9	215.2	281.1	30.6
Mean augmented wealth	1,022.6	1,797.7	75.8	382.5	773.1	102.1	343.5	471.3	37.2
Median augmented wealth	552.3	833.6	50.9	228.8	392.6	71.6	154.2	301.6	95.6
Mean augmented wealth*	1,022.6	1,839.1	79.8	382.5	785.1	105.3	343.5	478.4	39.2
Mean net augmented wealth*	972.7	1,695.8	74.3	364.2	723.4	98.6	324.8	449.6	38.4

Aged 65+

Mean income	66.8	102.5	53.3	27.4	46.3	69.1	23.7	29.6	25.1
Mean net worth	751.0	1,249.2	66.3	207.8	592.0	184.9	202.2	338.2	67.2
Mean augmented wealth	1,091.3	1,627.0	49.1	354.9	769.2	116.7	291.4	481.4	65.2
Median augmented wealth	510.2	674.4	32.2	179.2	386.9	115.9	167.1	299.5	79.2

NOTE: Households are classified by the age of the head of household. Key: Augmented wealth = nonpension wealth + retirement wealth. Augmented wealth* includes employer contributions to defined contribution pension plans.

SOURCE: Author's computations from the 1989 and 2007 SCF.

couples while median retirement wealth improved substantially. In the case of the latter group, the widening in the mean retirement wealth gap between single women and married couples was attributable to a relative decline in private pension wealth since their relative SSW had improved.

Augmented wealth also differed widely by marital status in 2007 (see Table 6.11). Single women typically had less than single men, who had less than married couples. Single men had only about half the level of augmented wealth (both mean and median) as married couples in 2007, while single women had about a third. Typically, single men or women should have about half of what married couples have in retirement wealth to achieve a similar level of retirement income adequacy, all else being equal. My figures show that, after controlling for family size in this simplistic manner, single men had approximately the same level of wealth per person as married couples. However, single women had approximately two-thirds of what their married or male counterparts had in terms of wealth.

However, single women generally showed an improvement relative to married couples with regard to augmented wealth over the period 1989–2007. Among younger households (under age 47), the ratio of mean augmented wealth advanced from 0.29 to 0.39 and that of median augmented wealth from 0.25 to 0.28. This improvement was attributable to relative gains in both net worth and retirement wealth. Among age group 47–55, the ratio of mean augmented wealth increased moderately from 27 to 30 percent, and that of median augmented wealth from 31 to 33 percent. These relative gains reflected relative improvements in mean net worth.

Among age group 56–64, the ratio of mean augmented wealth actually fell from 34 to 26 percent (the only case of a decline), but that of median augmented wealth rose from 28 to 36 percent. These changes were attributable to a sharp drop in relative mean net worth and strong relative gains in median retirement wealth. Among the elderly, the ratio of mean augmented wealth showed a modest improvement, from 27 to 30 percent, but that of median augmented wealth climbed from 33 to 44 percent. These trends were attributable to strong relative gains in mean and median retirement wealth.

The story for single men is even stronger. Their position relative to married couples in terms of retirement wealth, net worth, and augmented wealth improved across almost all age groups (except young households) over the years 1989–2007. However, single men saw their income relative to married couples generally decline over the period 1989–2007 (for single women the trends were mixed).

Educational Attainment

Trends based on distinctions by educational attainment are very different from those based on race and ethnicity and also those between married couples and single women. Households with less educational attainment had substantially less retirement wealth and total wealth in 2007 than their counterparts. In addition, they generally fell further behind college graduates over the years 1989–2007. Indeed, retirement wealth and total wealth splayed out over time, as college graduates pulled ahead of other educational groups.

As shown in Table 6.12, the gap in pension ownership rates widened over time between college graduates and the less educated. Holdings of DC plans increased among all educational levels and age groups from 1989 to 2007. Despite this, the gap in holdings of DC plans among young households (age 46 and under) between households with less than 12 years of schooling and households headed by a college graduate widened greatly, from 23 percentage points in 1983 to 57 percentage points in 2007. Most of the widening took place during the 1990s, as the take-up rate for DC plans was much higher for college graduates. Similar trends are evident for other age groups (among the elderly, the gap widened from 3 percentage points in 1989 to 50 percentage points in 2007!).

Trends differed somewhat for high school graduates. The gap in DC pension coverage between high school and college graduates was already generally quite large in 1989 but declined over the ensuing years among young households and those aged 47–55. However, the gap in DC plans between high school and college graduates rose from 12 to 30 percentage points among age group 56–64, and from 4 to 29 percentage points among elderly households. The gap in DC plan holdings between those with 13–15 years of schooling and college graduates rose by between 8 and 35 percentage points over the 1989–2007 period.[13]

The percentage of households with entitlements to DB plans plummeted among all educational levels and age groups from 1989 to 2007.

Table 6.12 Percentage of Households with Pension Wealth by Years of Schooling and Age Class, 1983–2007

	Less than 12 years		12 years		13–15 years		16 years or more	
	1989	2007	1989	2007	1989	2007	1989	2007
Aged 46 and under								
Defined contribution accounts	21.1	17.5	0.0	37.8	33.0	47.7	44.4	74.4
Defined benefit plans	26.1	5.2	78.0	50.6	44.1	21.5	45.7	34.1
Pension wealth	35.5	19.3	78.0	67.1	57.7	54.1	67.3	79.2
Share of defined contribution owners who receive employer contributions	70.1	85.6	0.0	10.9	83.1	69.5	80.6	65.3
Aged 47–55								
Defined contribution accounts	20.2	36.6	32.1	57.1	43.3	70.0	59.9	80.6
Defined benefit plans	48.2	14.9	52.4	31.2	71.8	33.7	64.1	46.3
Pension wealth	60.2	43.5	65.0	65.3	80.1	75.9	85.9	89.3
Share of defined contribution owners who receive employer contributions	57.7	65.4	53.2	63.5	53.1	58.2	47.3	65.8
Aged 56–64								
Defined contribution accounts	15.4	26.7	20.8	48.2	46.2	64.5	32.7	78.4
Defined benefit plans	47.7	12.8	61.4	40.1	73.9	50.5	81.9	51.1
Pension wealth	55.1	37.4	66.4	68.8	91.1	80.6	86.7	86.7
Share of defined contribution owners who receive employer contributions	0.0	51.4	0.0	46.2	0.0	53.9	0.0	41.1

Aged 65+

Defined contribution accounts	1.0	16.4	0.0	37.8	4.3	50.2	3.7	66.3
Defined benefit plans	43.9	36.5	78.0	50.6	58.4	52.3	65.9	65.4
Pension wealth	44.4	46.7	78.0	67.1	59.7	75.2	67.4	90.4

NOTE: Households are classified by the age and education of the head of household. Key: Pension wealth = defined contribution + defined benefit wealth.

SOURCE: Author's computations from the 1989 and 2007 SCF.

As a result, the gap in DB plan entitlements between college graduates and less-educated households generally fell over time. The gap in the share of households owning one or the other form of pension between less-educated households and college graduates rose over time. Between those with less than 12 years of schooling and college graduates, the gap widened by 28 percentage points from 1989 to 2007 among young households, by about 20 percentage points among middle-aged households, and by 21 percentage points among the elderly. Between high school graduates and college graduates, the gap widened by 23 percentage points among young households and by 34 percentage points among elderly ones, but it remained relatively unchanged among middle-aged households.[14] Between those with 13–15 years of schooling and college graduates, the gap increased by between 4 and 17 percentage points.

Not surprisingly, households with less education had accumulated much less pension wealth than those headed by a college graduate, and the gap widened between 1989 and 2007 (see Table 6.13). In 2007, the mean pension wealth of households with less than 12 years of schooling averaged less than 10 percent that of college graduates, the mean pension wealth of high school graduates about a quarter that of college graduates, and the mean pension wealth of those with 13–15 years of schooling only about a third of college graduates. The mean pension wealth among households headed by someone with less than 12 years of schooling declined among all age groups from 1989 to 2007 (about 55 percent for age groups 46 and under, 47–55, and 56–64 and by 4 percent for those aged 65 and over), and the ratio of mean pension wealth between this educational group and college graduates fell by between 7 and 17 percentage points.

For high school graduates, mean pension wealth remained more or less unchanged among the youngest age group and those aged 47–55, but declined by 12 percent among those aged 56–64 and by 27 percent among those aged 65 and over. Moreover, the ratio of mean pension wealth between high school and college graduates fell by 15–24 percentage points from 1989 to 2007. Despite the fact that the mean pension wealth of households with 13–15 years of schooling generally increased from 1989 to 2007, the ratio of mean pension wealth between this educational group and college graduates also declined across all age groups, from 9 to 29 percentage points.

Less-educated households did relatively better in terms of SSW than in terms of pension wealth. In 2007, the ratio of mean SSW among households with less than 12 years of schooling was about half that of college graduate households; the ratio between high school and college graduates varied between three-fifths and two-thirds; and the ratio between those with 13–15 years of schooling and college graduates ranged from about three-fifths to four-fifths. Mean SSW grew among all educational and age groups in 1989–2007 except among the elderly, where it stayed unchanged or declined. The ratio of mean SSW between those with less than a high school degree and college graduates actually increased moderately between 1989 and 2007. However, the ratio in mean SSW between high school and college graduates fell among all age groups, as it did between those with 13–15 years of schooling and college graduates.

Households with less than 12 years of schooling still had the least amount of retirement wealth in 2007, compared to households with more education. For instance, the typical household between the ages of 56 and 64 with less than 12 years of schooling had $164,000 in retirement wealth, compared to $271,500 for households with 12 years of schooling, $359,700 for households with 13–15 years of schooling, and $565,100 for households with 16 and more years of schooling. These differences held by and large, regardless of the age group or whether median or mean retirement wealth is used.

The ratio of mean and median retirement wealth ranged from 23 to 33 percent in 2007 between the least educated group and college graduates, from 33 to 48 percent between high school and college graduates, and from 49 to 64 percent between those with some college and college graduates. Due mainly to the increasing spread in pension wealth between college graduates and the less educated, the ratio of both mean and median retirement wealth between the least educated group and college graduates fell for every age group between 1989 and 2007 (with the single exception of median retirement wealth for age group 56–64). A similar pattern holds for the ratio between high school and college graduates. In the case of elderly households, the ratio in mean retirement wealth plummeted by 32 percentage points and that in median retirement wealth by 49 percentage points. A similar story ensues between those with some college and college graduates.

202

Table 6.13 Retirement Wealth by Years of Schooling and Age Class, 1989 and 2007 (in thousands, 2007$)

Category	Less than 12 years of schooling			12 years of schooling		
	1989	2007	% change 1989–2007	1989	2007	% change 1989–2007
Aged 46 and under						
Mean pension wealth	12.8	5.5	−57.5	31.0	31.9	3.0
Mean Social Security wealth	56.3	81.7	45.2	102.4	107.3	4.7
Mean retirement wealth	69.1	87.1	26.1	133.4	139.2	4.3
Median retirement wealth	61.8	78.9	27.7	111.2	115.7	4.0
Aged 47–55						
Mean pension wealth	54.5	24.2	−55.7	94.7	92.4	−2.3
Mean Social Security wealth	83.9	128.6	53.3	160.9	166.1	3.3
Mean retirement wealth	138.4	152.8	10.4	255.6	258.6	1.2
Median retirement wealth	106.2	116.1	9.3	203.5	219.5	7.9
Aged 56–64						
Mean pension wealth	73.3	33.3	−54.5	150.5	133.2	−11.5
Mean Social Security wealth	105.9	162.9	53.8	190.7	203.5	6.7
Mean retirement wealth	179.2	196.2	9.5	341.2	336.7	−1.3
Median retirement wealth	126.9	164.0	29.2	275.2	271.5	−1.3
Aged 65+						
Mean pension wealth	43.7	42.2	−3.5	111.8	81.9	−26.8
Mean Social Security wealth	94.0	123.7	31.6	210.1	153.6	−26.9
Mean retirement wealth	137.7	166.0	20.5	321.9	235.5	−26.8
Median retirement wealth	94.6	106.8	12.8	309.5	195.0	−37.0

	13–15 years of schooling			16 or more years of schooling		
Aged 46 and under						
Mean pension wealth	41.6	41.7	0.3	63.6	113.5	78.6
Mean Social Security wealth	96.7	111.5	15.3	134.4	177.1	31.8
Mean retirement wealth	138.3	153.2	10.8	197.9	290.6	46.8
Median retirement wealth	124.5	118.0	–5.2	169.1	239.1	41.4
Aged 47–55						
Mean pension wealth	111.5	137.5	23.3	220.8	328.1	48.5
Mean Social Security wealth	150.3	168.3	12.0	185.0	264.8	43.2
Mean retirement wealth	261.8	305.8	16.8	405.8	592.9	46.1
Median retirement wealth	250.1	241.2	–3.6	315.5	480.5	52.3
Aged 56–64						
Mean pension wealth	167.6	214.0	27.7	329.8	532.1	61.3
Mean Social Security wealth	173.0	211.3	22.1	221.8	309.3	39.4
Mean retirement wealth	340.6	425.2	24.8	551.7	841.4	52.5
Median retirement wealth	297.2	359.7	21.0	513.6	565.1	10.0
Aged 65+						
Mean pension wealth	188.3	172.8	–8.2	276.7	487.5	76.2
Mean Social Security wealth	195.1	189.8	–2.7	224.1	232.8	3.8
Mean retirement wealth	383.4	362.6	–5.4	500.8	720.2	43.8
Median retirement wealth	320.9	280.7	–12.5	335.4	452.8	35.0

NOTE: Households are classified by the age and education of the head of household. Key: Pension wealth = defined contribution + defined benefit wealth. Retirement wealth = pension wealth + Social Security wealth.
SOURCE: Author's computations from the 1989 and 2007 SCF.

Table 6.14 Income and Wealth by Years of Schooling and Age Class, 1989 and 2007 (in thousands, 2007$)

	Less than 12 years of schooling			12 years of schooling		
	1989	2007	% change, 1989–2007	1989	2007	% change, 1989–2007
Aged 46 and under						
Mean income	33.6	29.5	−12.2	55.6	51.1	−8.0
Mean net worth	57.6	40.8	−29.2	87.7	117.5	34.0
Mean augmented wealth	123.5	124.9	1.1	213.1	241.1	13.1
Median augmented wealth	68.7	83.2	21.1	150.0	128.0	−14.6
Mean augmented wealth*	135.4	129.7	−4.2	236.0	255.6	8.3
Mean net augmented wealth*	128.5	125.7	−2.2	219.7	239.5	9.0
Aged 47–55						
Mean income	41.0	38.8	−5.5	70.4	65.1	−7.5
Mean net worth	143.4	100.4	−30.0	397.1	266.9	−32.8
Mean augmented wealth	278.4	242.1	−13.0	638.1	478.2	−25.1
Median augmented wealth	177.0	170.8	−3.5	389.8	332.0	−14.8
Mean augmented wealth*	291.0	248.3	−14.7	646.7	497.9	−23.0
Mean net augmented wealth*	277.3	238.8	−13.9	614.1	461.2	−24.9
Aged 56–64						
Mean income	36.5	30.8	−15.8	64.5	56.9	−11.7
Mean net worth	198.9	123.1	−38.1	438.4	374.0	−14.7
Mean augmented wealth	369.5	298.0	−19.3	767.4	646.7	−15.7
Median augmented wealth	241.0	224.2	−7.0	532.7	424.6	−20.3
Mean augmented wealth*	369.5	300.7	−18.6	767.4	653.3	−14.9
Mean net augmented wealth*	355.5	291.6	−18.0	740.1	619.5	−16.3

205

	13–15 years of schooling			16+ years of schooling		
Aged 65+						
Mean income	25.3	25.8	2.0	43.5	36.9	−15.1
Mean net worth	200.8	241.7	20.4	505.9	375.7	−25.7
Mean augmented wealth	338.0	393.3	16.4	827.7	586.2	−29.2
Median augmented wealth	229.3	247.0	7.7	530.8	387.8	−26.9
Aged 46 and under						
Mean income	65.7	56.5	−14.0	105.9	109.8	3.7
Mean net worth	172.7	125.6	−27.3	422.3	454.5	7.6
Mean augmented wealth	301.9	258.9	−14.2	600.9	677.1	12.7
Median augmented wealth	184.9	136.9	−26.0	329.9	346.9	5.2
Mean augmented wealth*	330.8	287.6	−13.1	662.0	759.7	14.8
Mean net augmented wealth*	309.2	264.0	−14.6	611.6	687.4	12.4
Aged 47–55						
Mean income	92.3	73.0	−20.9	232.0	193.3	−16.7
Mean net worth	466.1	437.4	−6.1	1,306.7	1,411.8	8.0
Mean augmented wealth	706.9	657.0	−7.0	1,639.3	1,798.3	9.7
Median augmented wealth	522.5	340.5	−34.8	875.1	857.1	−2.1
Mean augmented wealth*	745.2	684.0	−8.2	1,712.0	1,886.7	10.2
Mean net augmented wealth*	694.6	632.2	−9.0	1,587.6	1,731.6	9.1

(continued)

Table 6.14 (continued)

	13–15 years of schooling			16+ years of schooling		
	1989	2007	% change, 1989–2007	1989	2007	% change, 1989–2007
Aged 56–64						
Mean income	85.2	79.8	−6.3	163.5	198.3	21.3
Mean net worth	504.0	488.0	−3.2	1,482.3	1,931.5	30.3
Mean augmented wealth	827.1	816.0	−1.3	1,971.6	2,434.8	23.5
Median augmented wealth	557.8	566.4	1.6	890.9	1,103.7	23.9
Mean augmented wealth*	827.1	832.2	0.6	1,971.6	2,495.3	26.6
Mean net augmented wealth*	776.3	771.6	−0.6	1,856.9	2,287.3	23.2
Aged 65+						
Mean income	81.9	60.3	−26.4	149.3	169.0	13.2
Mean net worth	1,360.8	666.4	−51.0	1,648.4	2,295.4	39.3
Mean augmented wealth	1,734.4	956.7	−44.8	2,136.6	2,741.8	28.3
Median augmented wealth	676.6	580.7	−14.2	971.0	1,149.3	18.4

NOTE: Households are classified by the age and education of the head of household. Key: Augmented wealth = nonpension wealth + retirement wealth. Augmented wealth* includes employer contributions to defined contribution pension plans.
SOURCE: Author's computations from the 1989 and 2007 SCF.

Likewise, similar disparities exist in net worth and augmented wealth between the less educated and college graduates (see Table 6.14). In 2007, the ratio of net worth between the least educated group and college graduates ranged from 6 to 11 percent; that between high school and college graduates from 19 to 26 percent; and that between some college and college graduates from 25 to 31 percent. Mean net worth generally declined among the less-educated groups and increased among college graduates from 1989 to 2007, so that the ratio of mean net worth between the three less-educated groups and college graduates generally fell between 1989 and 2007.

Ratios of both mean and median augmented wealth between the less educated and college graduates are generally higher than the corresponding net worth ratios. The ratio of mean and median augmented wealth between the least educated and college graduates ranged from 12 to 24 percent in 2007; that between high school and college graduates from 21 to 39 percent; and that between those with some college and college graduates from 33 to 51 percent. Here, too, because of a relative decline in both retirement wealth and net worth between the less educated and college graduates, the former groups fell further behind the latter in terms of both mean and median augmented wealth from 1989 to 2007. This occurred for all educational groups and age groups, with only two exceptions (median augmented wealth among the least educated aged 46 and under, and mean augmented wealth for high school graduates aged 46 and under). The mean income of the less-educated groups also declined relative to college graduates between 1989 and 2007. This was true for all age groups (again with two exceptions).

SUMMARY AND CONCLUDING REMARKS

The chapter began with a review of time series trends in retirement wealth and augmented wealth and comparisons of the portfolio composition of augmented wealth by age class and income quintile. It is clear that SSW was more important for younger households than older ones. It is also particularly important among the lowest income quintile, accounting for almost half or more of augmented wealth in some years. In contrast, pension wealth was a major component of augmented wealth for the third and fourth income quintiles. For the top income quintile, nonpension net worth was by far the leading component, accounting for about 70–75 percent of augmented wealth.

When dividing households by net worth class, a U-shaped pattern emerged between wealth class and the growth in retirement wealth from 1989 to 2007. Gains were by far the strongest at the top but also relatively strong at the bottom. They were weakest in the middle (in many cases negative). Dividing households by income class, I also find that advances in retirement wealth were strongest at the top. Advances were once again weakest in the middle and, in most cases, negative.

Dividing households by race and ethnicity, I find large gaps in pension ownership, pension wealth, retirement wealth, and augmented wealth between minorities and (non-Hispanic) whites. However, there is strong evidence of relative gains made by minorities on whites in terms of SSW, retirement wealth, net worth, and augmented wealth from 1989 to 2007. Relative gains in net worth appear to be due to a large expansion of the home ownership rate among minorities during the 2000s (see Chapter 2). Though a full analysis is beyond the scope of the present volume, it is likely that the relative gains in SSW among minorities are due to three factors: 1) some convergence in labor earnings between minorities and whites, particularly during the 1990s; 2) more continuous work histories for minority workers over time; and 3) a reduction in the life expectancy gap between minorities and whites.

There was also a substantial gap in retirement wealth and augmented wealth between single females and married couples. Similar to the experience of minorities, single females progressed relative to married couples between 1989 and 2007 along almost every dimension. A similar pattern holds for single men. Their position relative to married couples improved along almost every dimension as well.

Trends based on educational attainment are very different from those by race and ethnicity and by family status. Households with less educational attainment had substantially less retirement wealth and augmented wealth in 2007 than their counterparts. In addition, they generally fell further behind college graduates between 1989 and 2007 in terms of pension wealth, retirement wealth, net worth, and augmented wealth. Indeed, retirement wealth and augmented wealth splayed out over time, as college graduates pulled ahead of the other educational groups. Much of this change reflects the rising returns to education that have occurred since 1980 or so (see Goldin and Katz [2008], for example). This pattern also shows up in relative household incomes by schooling level, which shows increasing dispersion between 1989 and 2007.

With regard to pension wealth, the decline in DB plans was particularly detrimental to the less educated, since DB had been a bulwark of retirement security among the less-educated, blue-collar workers up to the 1980s. We also saw a similar pattern for current workers classified by years of schooling (see Table 4.2).

Notes

1. Although they are quite distinct financial instruments, we combine DC and DB plans under private pensions, as both are employer-sponsored savings initiatives with the explicit purpose of saving for retirement.
2. As was discussed in Chapters 4 and 5, most of the gains in both pension wealth and SSW occurred in the 1990s, with only modest advances from 2001 to 2007.
3. In general, incomes are skewed toward high-income earners in the SCF compared to the CPS because of oversampling of the rich and the fact that income values are not top-coded. Thus, average income levels (and inequality) in the SCF are higher than the corresponding figures in the CPS.
4. I combine these two minority groups because of the small sample of each. Also, Asians and other races are excluded from the table because of their small sample size. The race/ethnicity of the household is based on that recorded by the reference person in the household.
5. Interestingly, of those with DC accounts, minority households were much more likely to receive employer contributions (DCEMP).
6. Similar results are evident for (current) workers classified by race and ethnicity. (see Table 4.2).
7. Ratios of mean AW* and mean net AW* are almost identical.
8. Trends in mean AW* and mean net AW* are once again almost identical.
9. The racial net worth ratio by age group in 2007 was 0.29 for the youngest age group, 0.27 for age group 47–55, 0.28 for age group 56–64, and 0.24 for the elderly. These ratios compare to an overall net worth ratio of 0.19 in 2007 between African Americans and whites and of 0.26 between Hispanics and (non-Hispanic) whites (see Chapter 2). The apparent inconsistency is accounted for by the fact that there was a much higher share of minority households (notably Hispanics) in the low-wealth youngest age group (59.8 versus 40.1 percent), and correspondingly lower percentages in the high-wealth middle-aged group 47–64 (30.0 versus 35.2 percent) and the elderly group (11.2 versus 24.7 percent).
10. Minorities made considerable advances during the 1990s (the 1989–2001 period) as well as during the 2000s (2001 to 2007). During the 1990s, growth was strong

across the board for both whites and minorities but stronger among minority households. As a result, the gap in pension wealth, SSW, mean and median retirement wealth, income, and mean and median augmented wealth generally narrowed, particularly among the elderly. During the 2000s, the racial gap further narrowed. This was true almost across the board in terms of pension wealth, SSW, mean and median retirement wealth, income, and mean and median augmented wealth. Among households in age group 46 and under and age group 47–55, this closure was due to actual declines in pension wealth and SSW among white households in contrast to positive growth among minority households. For the older age groups, both whites and minorities generally saw positive growth, but it was higher among minorities than among whites.

11. As indicated, households are divided into three types: 1) married couples, including cohabiting adults; 2) male householders without a spouse (or a cohabiting adult) present; and 3) female householders without a spouse (or a cohabiting adult) present.

12. The reason, as discussed in Chapter 4, is that Social Security benefits for a single earner qualifying for benefits in a married couple are increased by 50 percent relative to benefits for a single earner living alone.

13. Similar trends are reported in Table 4.2 for this gap as measured by the educational level of (current) workers.

14. As was true among current workers, in 1989 high school graduates had a higher rate of pension ownership than college graduates because of a higher share of households with DB entitlements.

7
Retirement Prospects

Retirement income security occupies the public debate on a regular basis. It refers to the ability of households to provide an adequate stream of income during the period of their retirement from the labor force. There has been, for example, periodic discussion about the possibility for Social Security privatization. What is largely absent from the discussion, though, is a broader perspective that puts Social Security benefits in the frame of retirement income security. Social Security's value and thus the options to reform it can only be fully understood when it is put in the larger context of all retirement savings. This requires an understanding of the retirement savings that households have accumulated, how this has changed over time, and what role Social Security has played in these changes.

The first question is whether workers have saved enough for retirement. My results indicate that the retirement system in the United States outside of Social Security is a system with many holes, despite large tax incentives from the federal government for workers to save for retirement. Nearly one-fifth of households nearing retirement—i.e., households between the ages of 56 and 64—had no retirement savings other than Social Security. In contrast, almost all households can expect to receive some benefits from Social Security.

Even among the households that have private pensions, savings are very unevenly distributed. Indeed, one of the most dramatic transformations over the last three decades has been the replacement of traditional DB pension plans with DC plans such as 401(k)s. This changeover has actually been detrimental to a large share of the working population.

Minorities, single women, and workers with a high school education or less have substantially less retirement wealth than their counterparts. Much of this inequality results from an uneven distribution of retirement savings outside of Social Security. In fact, as is shown in Chapter 5, expected Social Security benefits are an equalizing force: when Social Security wealth is included, total retirement benefits are more equally distributed than without. Moreover, the typical household in 2007 could expect more retirement income from Social Security than from its private DC plan retirement savings. In addition, private pensions fell behind other private savings in the spectrum of retirement preparedness.

How have retirement savings changed over time? Retirement savings improved from 1989 to 2007, despite the fact that large trouble spots remain. The share of households that could expect to have retirement incomes that were less than the poverty line declined. Also, the share of households that could hope to replace at least three-quarters of their projected income at age 64 with benefits from their savings in retirement rose from 1989 to 2007. Moreover, minorities and the bottom quintile in terms of income saw larger improvements in retirement preparedness than their counterparts, although they generally remained less well prepared in 2007 than these other groups.

Social Security played an important role in the relative improvements of these two groups. Gains in Social Security benefits were more pronounced than improvements in private retirement savings among the groups that saw disproportionately larger gains—that is, relative improvements—in their retirement income adequacy. Social Security was at the heart of improving retirement income security for those who typically have less retirement wealth than their counterparts. In some cases, improvements in SSW even helped to offset declines in private pension wealth.

My empirical analysis involves three steps. The first is a calculation of how much wealth—in its various manifestations, including marketable wealth, pension wealth, and SSW—households held in 2007, and how that amount changed compared to 1983, 1989, and 2001. These computations of the components of augmented wealth are made in Chapters 4, 5, and 6. The second step is a calculation of the stream of retirement income that today's older workers can expect from their accumulated wealth at the time of their retirement. For this purpose, I convert the stock of wealth into an annuity flow on the basis of the historical rate of return on household assets and on the basis of life expectancy by age, race, and gender.

The third step is a comparison of the expected income stream generated from different wealth holdings to two standards of adequate retirement income: the poverty level income and the ratio of final income replaced by retirement income. These measures allow us to assess whether households have saved enough for retirement and how this has changed over time. The last two topics are the focus of the present chapter, as well as an analysis of changes in retirement income security for households with different demographic characteristics, as defined by age, gender, race or ethnicity, education, and marital status.

This chapter begins with a discussion of the methods used to measure retirement income adequacy. It then provides details on expected retirement income over the period 1989–2007 by demographic and household characteristic. I then make projections of the expected poverty rate at retirement by demographic and household characteristic. The last two sections present estimates of expected income replacement rates at retirement and offer a summary of results.

MEASURING RETIREMENT INCOME ADEQUACY

I now turn to a consideration of how well families are prepared for retirement. I first discuss the method for projecting future retirement income. I then show results on three dimensions of retirement income adequacy: 1) projected retirement income, 2) projected poverty status during retirement, and 3) the projected income replacement rate at retirement.

Retirement Income Projections

Retirement income is based on four components: 1) standard nonpension wealth holdings, 2) DC pension holdings, 3) DB pension entitlements, and 4) Social Security.[1] Current holdings of nonpension wealth are first divided into two parts: equity in owner-occupied housing and nonhome wealth. There is some disagreement in the literature about whether home equity should be considered part of the resource base for retirement income. On the one hand, home equity provides consumption services directly to the household and, as a result, does not augment other sources of income that can be used for nonhome consumption. On the other hand, home equity can be used to finance current consumption through new mortgages, home equity loans, and even reverse mortgages. In this regard, home equity can also add to the resource base for nonhome consumption. Because both views are legitimate, I will compute projected retirement income both including and excluding home equity and, as an intermediate position, including half the value of home equity.

I then convert nonhome, nonpension wealth and owner-occupied housing into an annuity equivalent (ANN) based on the formula

$$(7.1) \quad ANN_i = r_i \times \text{Asset } i \, / \, [1 - (1 + r_i)^{-\max(LERH, LERW)}] \, ,$$

where r_i is the rate of return on Asset i, *LERH* is the life expectancy of the husband at year of retirement, and *LERW* is the life expectancy of the wife at year of retirement. As discussed in Appendix D, each spouse records his or her expected date (or age) of retirement in the Survey of Consumer Finances (SCF). An annuity is calculated for each asset (and debt) based on the historical rate of return on that asset. The asset classes used for the calculation, as well as the corresponding estimated historical rate of return, are listed in Appendix Table D.1.

The rationale for converting household wealth into an annuity to gauge retirement adequacy is that the annuity value indicates the sustainable level of withdrawals from each asset that will last the (estimated) remainder of the person's life (or, in the case, of a couple, the life of the longest-living spouse) and that will totally exhaust the asset value at time of death.[2] In a sense, this is the wealth equivalent to the concept of permanent income. The rates of return include both capital gains and asset income like dividends and interest, so that the annuity value replaces any projected property income. Though a family need not actually withdraw the annuity value of its wealth each year, the annuity value does indicate the level of *potential* consumption that can be maintained over time from the family's wealth holdings. I treat the second component of augmented wealth, DC pension holdings, in exactly the same way, and convert it into an annuity.

The third component, DB plan benefits, is the sum of DB pension plan benefits currently received by the husband and wife and pension benefits expected in the future by the husband and wife. The former consists of pension benefits received by current retirees as well as benefits currently collected from past jobs by those currently working. Up to six pensions from past jobs and six benefits from current job benefits can be recorded in the SCF (see Chapter 4 and Appendix B for more details). The latter consists of future expected DB pension benefits as indicated by the respondent.

The fourth component, Social Security benefits, is the sum of Social Security benefits currently being received plus future expected Social Security benefits. The latter is based on a computation of the Primary Insurance Amount, which, in turn, is based on estimated work history for both husband and wife (see Chapter 4 and Appendix B for more details).

I then add to current nonpension wealth holdings and DC plan holdings the estimated amount of additional wealth accumulations up to the time of retirement. And, I estimate the future accumulations of each asset in nonpension wealth up to time of retirement. This is based on the historical real rate of return of each asset type (see Appendix Table D.1).[3] I also estimate the future gains on current holdings of DC pension wealth. Moreover, in the case of DC accounts, I add on DCEMP (future projected employer contributions to the worker's DC plan), as well as a new component which I call DCEMPW).[4] This is the present discounted value of future employee contributions into his or her DC plan. This is based on data provided in the SCF, which indicates what fraction of an employee's salary is currently contributed into the employee's DC account. It is assumed that the worker continues to work for the same employer until retirement and that his or her contribution rate remains unchanged over time.[5] I then define total DC wealth, DCTOT, as the sum of DC, DCEMP, and DCEMPW.

It should be noted that I do not try to estimate future savings rates or wealth transfers received from gifts or inheritances. Indeed, it should be stressed that I am not attempting to fully model the savings behavior of households nearing retirement, as one can do in a microsimulation model. As a result, my estimates of retirement income (and replacement rates) should be viewed as lower bounds. However, they are useful for comparing retirement preparedness of an age group at *different points in time*, such as 1989, 2001, and 2007, to determine whether there is improvement or deterioration.[6]

Retirement Adequacy

Retirement adequacy is measured in three different ways: 1) the annual projected retirement income, 2) the percentage of households whose projected retirement income is greater than the poverty threshold, and 3) the income replacement rate, which is based on projected retirement income at time of retirement and projected income up to the year of retirement (typically age 64).[7] For the latter, I use a 1.70 percent annual growth rate of real income, an estimate based on the growth of real income for age group 47–64 over the period 1989–2007.[8] It should be noted that this is a stringent measure of the replacement rate compared to most of the literature on the subject since it compares (projected) retirement income against (projected) preretirement income at the eve of retirement (see Chapter 3 for a review of the pertinent literature).[9] Other studies have used a measure akin to average income over the lifetime (or over the 10–20 years preceding retirement) or a measure of permanent income as the basis of comparison. However, I think a comparison of expected retirement income to projected income received in the year just before retirement is a more meaningful comparison than of expected retirement income to some measure of permanent income, because it is the drop in income just after retirement that most affects family well-being.

EXPECTED RETIREMENT INCOME

Table 7.1 presents a summary of results on future expected mean retirement income both overall and by selected demographic groups. The mean retirement income for all households in age group 47–64 is projected to be $111,300 in 2007. This compares to the actual mean income of this group in 2007 of $110,800. There is little difference in projected retirement income for age groups 47–55 and 56–64. However, there is a big difference between minorities and whites, with the latter projected to have 2.3 times the income of the former at retirement. (This compares to a ratio of 2.9 in augmented wealth between the two groups in 2007.)

There are also wide gaps by family type. The projected mean retirement income of married couples is $147,500, 1.9 times that of single males and 3.5 times that of single females. Wide variation is also seen by educational attainment. The projected mean retirement income of college graduates in 2007 is $206,000, 2.7 times that of those with some

Table 7.1 Expected Mean Retirement Income Based on Wealth and Expected Pension and Social Security Benefits (in thousands, 2007$)

	1989	2001	2007	Percentage change		
				1989–2001	2001–2007	1989–2007
Aged 47–64	73.2	102.8	111.3	40.4	8.2	52.0
Aged 47–55	83.9	104.8	112.6	24.9	7.4	34.2
Aged 56–64	61.1	99.9	109.6	63.6	9.7	79.4
Aged 47–64						
Non-Hispanic white[a]	83.5	117.8	125.5	41.0	6.5	50.2
African American or Hispanic[a]	31.2	41.6	53.8	33.3	29.5	72.6
Married couples	94.1	136.7	147.5	45.3	7.9	56.8
Single males	57.4	74.3	77.5	29.4	4.3	35.0
Single females	32.8	40.4	41.5	23.2	2.9	26.8
Less than 12 years of schooling[b]	36.2	31.3	26.3	-13.5	-16.0	-27.3
12 years of schooling[b]	76.5	53.7	56.0	-29.9	4.3	-26.9
13–15 years of schooling[b]	86.5	70.2	76.3	-18.8	8.7	-11.8
16 or more years of schooling[b]	173.9	202.6	206.0	16.5	1.7	18.4
Income quintile, aged 47–64						
Income quintile 1	12.3	22.7	24.2	84.5	6.6	96.7
Income quintile 2	33.7	37.9	39.8	12.3	5.0	18.0
Income quintile 3	52.5	60.5	66.8	15.2	10.4	27.2
Income quintile 4	71.0	93.8	99.1	32.2	5.6	39.6
Income quintile 5	200.7	310.3	335.8	54.6	8.2	67.3

NOTE: Total retirement income includes expected future gains on all components of net worth. Households are classified by the age of the head of household.

[a] Asian and other races are excluded from the table because of small sample sizes.

[b] Households are classified by the schooling level of the head of household.

SOURCE: Author's computations from the 1989, 2001, and 2007 SCF.

college, 3.7 times that of high school graduates, and 7.8 times that of those with the least schooling. There is also great variation by income quintile. The projected mean retirement income of the top quintile in 2007 is (a huge) $335,800, 3.4 times that of the fourth quintile, 5.0 times that of the middle quintile, 8.4 times that of the second quintile, and 13.9 that of the bottom quintile.

Projected retirement income advanced very strongly between 1989 and 2001. Among all households in age group 47–64, expected mean retirement income increased by 40 percent. However, changes in retirement income were generally much lower from 2001 to 2007. For age group 47–64 as a whole, mean retirement grew by only 8 percent. Relatively low growth is found for almost every group except minorities. For households with less than 12 years of schooling, a large 16 percent drop is projected for their mean retirement income.

Some gaps in retirement income between groups widened over time whereas others narrowed. Retirement income for households nearer retirement (aged 56–64) grew faster, 79 percent between 1989 and 2007, than households in age group 47–55, only 34 percent. Minorities saw greater gains in retirement income than whites, 73 percent versus 50 percent. While mean retirement income of whites grew somewhat faster than that of minorities over the 1990s, the reverse was true for the 2000s. Indeed, minorities were the only group with sizable gains (30 percent) in retirement income over the period 2001–2007. As a result, the ratio of retirement income between minorities and whites, after falling from 0.37 in 1989 to 0.35 in 2001, advanced to 0.43 in 2007. (This compares to an actual income ratio among 47-to-64-year-olds between the two groups of 47 percent in 2007.)

Married couples experienced greater gains in retirement income over the 1989–2007 period (57 percent) than single males (35 percent) and, especially, single females (27 percent), and the retirement income gaps widened among these groups. This result is consistent with the fact that the retirement wealth and augmented wealth of middle-aged single females declined relative to married couples between 1989 and 2007. In 2007, the mean expected retirement income of single females was only 28 percent that of married couples, down from 35 percent in 1989.

The only educational group with positive growth in retirement income from 1989 to 2007 was college graduates, which saw a modest 18 percent gain. The other groups experienced negative growth, ranging from −27 percent for the least educated group and for high school graduates to −12 percent for those with some college.[10] As a result, the gap in retirement income between college graduates and the other groups widened over these years. In contrast, the bottom income quintile recorded the fastest growth in retirement income at 97 percent, with the top income quintile second at 67 percent, whereas the middle three quintiles had the lowest gains over the period.

Further details are provided in the next two tables. The first of these, Table 7.2, shows the percentage composition of expected retirement income in 2007 (also see Appendix Table D.2 for details on 1989 and 1998). In 2007, 37 percent of total retirement income of all households in age group 47–64 is projected to come from this group's nonhome, nonpension wealth, including expected gains, and another 14 percent from home equity, also including expected capital gains, for a total of 52 percent from total nonpension wealth.[11] In addition, 18 percent is expected from the total value of DC plans, likewise including expected capital gains, and 17 percent from expected Social Security benefits, while 13 percent will come from DB pension benefits.[12]

There is a big variation in the composition of expected retirement income among different demographic groups. These tend to mirror the composition of augmented wealth. Expected Social Security benefits make up 27 percent of the expected retirement income of minorities in 2007, compared to 16 percent for whites, whereas the expected annuity from nonhome, nonpension wealth constitutes 21 percent, compared to 39 percent for whites. Likewise, expected Social Security benefits comprise 23 percent of the expected retirement income of single females, compared to 17 percent for married couples, whereas income from nonhome, nonpension wealth makes up 23 percent, compared to 39 percent for married couples. The share of expected Social Security benefits in expected retirement income falls from 49 percent for the least-educated group to 12 percent for college graduates, while the share from nonhome, nonpension wealth rises from 14 to 44 percent. The share from Social Security falls from 42 to 9 percent across the five income quintiles, while the share from nonhome, nonpension wealth rises from 24 to 52 percent.

Over time, DC plans are projected to become an increasingly important source of retirement income, since they have risen from 8 percent of projected retirement income in 1989 to 18 percent in 2007.

220

Table 7.2 **Composition of Expected Mean Retirement Income Based on Wealth Holdings and Expected Pension and Social Security Benefits, 2007 (%)**

	Nonhome, nonpension wealth	Home equity	Defined contribution plans	Defined benefit pensions	Social Security	Total
Aged 47–64	37.4	14.4	18.3	12.7	17.2	100.0
Aged 47–55	35.9	15.0	19.3	12.5	17.3	100.0
Aged 56–64	39.5	13.6	16.8	13.0	17.0	100.0
Aged 47–64						
Non-Hispanic white[a]	39.1	13.9	18.6	12.3	16.1	100.0
African American or Hispanic[a]	21.0	19.2	15.1	17.8	26.9	100.0
Married couples	39.0	13.9	18.3	12.1	16.7	100.0
Single males	38.3	13.9	19.8	12.8	15.1	100.0
Single females	22.9	19.9	17.1	17.4	22.7	100.0
Less than 12 years of schooling[b]	14.3	20.4	9.2	7.0	49.1	100.0
12 years of schooling[b]	22.5	19.3	15.2	14.2	28.7	100.0
13–15 years of schooling[b]	28.4	16.0	18.2	15.9	21.5	100.0
16 or more years of schooling[b]	43.8	12.7	19.4	11.8	12.2	100.0
Income quintile, aged 47–64						
Income quintile 1	24.4	19.9	4.4	9.0	42.3	100.0
Income quintile 2	17.7	19.5	11.5	15.3	36.0	100.0
Income quintile 3	15.4	17.3	19.7	19.4	28.2	100.0
Income quintile 4	15.4	17.0	23.8	19.5	24.3	100.0
Income quintile 5	52.0	12.0	18.2	9.3	8.5	100.0

221

Aged 47–64

1989	41.6	13.9	8.1	19.0	17.5	100.0
2001	39.2	11.7	17.0	13.8	18.4	100.0

NOTE: Households are classified by the age of the head of household. Each column equals the expected annuity (or annual benefit) from the current holdings of the indicated asset plus any future expected gains on the asset. Totals may not sum to 100.0 due to rounding. Key: Home equity: net equity in owner-occupied housing. Nonhome, nonpension wealth = net worth − defined contribution − home equity. Defined contribution plans: Total defined contribution wealth = defined contribution wealth + employer contributions to defined contribution pension plans + present discounted value of future employee contributions into employee's defined contribution plan.

[a] Asians and other races are excluded from the table because of small sample sizes.

[b] Households are classified by the schooling level of the head of household.

SOURCE: Author's computations from the 1989, 2001, and 2007 SCF.

This change reflects the sharp rise in the share of DC pension wealth in the overall household portfolio and the offsetting decline in the share of liquid assets in total household assets (see Chapter 2). Correspondingly, DB plans will become less important, having declined from 19 percent of projected retirement income in 1989 to 13 percent in 2007. Together, the contribution of total pension wealth to projected retirement income will rise from 27 percent in 1989 to 31 percent in 2007. Correspondingly, the proportion of projected retirement income from nonpension wealth will decline over time, from 55 percent in 1989 to 52 percent in 2007, while that from Social Security will remain almost unchanged at 17 percent.

Table 7.3 shows levels of retirement income by component in 2007 (See Appendix Table D.3 for results for 1989 and 1998 and Appendix Table D.4 for a similar set of results using a more detailed breakdown of the sources of retirement income). In 2007, the ratio of mean expected retirement income between minorities and whites was 43 percent. The ratio of the expected annuity from nonhome, nonpension wealth was much lower, at 23 percent, as was the ratio of the expected annuity from DC plans DCTOT, at 35 percent. However, the ratio of expected Social Security benefits was much higher, 71 percent, as was the ratio of expected DB plan benefits, 62 percent, and the expected annuity from home equity, 59 percent. This pattern mimics racial differences in pension wealth, Social Security wealth, and net worth (see Tables 6.7 and 6.8).

Similar patterns exist for other groupings. The ratio of mean expected retirement income between single females and married couples was 0.28 in 2007. However, the ratio of the expected annuity from nonhome, nonpension wealth was only 0.17 and that from DC plans DCTOT was 0.26, while the ratio of expected Social Security benefits was higher, at 0.38. The expected annuity from nonhome, nonpension wealth relative to college graduates was a mere 0.04 for the lowest education group, 0.14 for high school graduates, and 0.24 for those with some college, and the corresponding ratios of the expected annuity from DC plans DCTOT were 0.06, 0.21, and 0.35, respectively. In contrast, the expected Social Security benefits relative to college graduates were 0.51, 0.64, and 0.65, respectively.

The ratio of the expected annuity from nonhome, nonpension wealth of income quintiles 1 to 4 relative to the top income quintile ranged from 0.03 to 0.09 and that from DC plans DCTOT from 0.02 to 0.38. On the other hand, expected Social Security benefits relative to the top income quintile were much higher, ranging from 0.36 to 0.84, and expected DB plan benefits relative to the top quintile were also higher, ranging from 0.07 to 0.62.[13]

Overall, the expected retirement income of age group 47–64 climbed by 40 percent between 1989 and 2001 but advanced by only 8 percent from 2001 to 2007, for an overall gain of 52 percent (see Table 7.4). The expected annuity from nonhome, nonpension wealth grew strongly during the 1990s, by 33 percent, but by only 3 percent from 2001 to 2007, for an overall increase of 37 percent. The expected annuity from DC plans showed a huge gain in the first period, almost tripling in value, and a much smaller increase in the second period, 17 percent, for an overall advance of 244 percent. Expected DB pension benefits remained largely unchanged in both the earlier and later periods. Expected Social Security benefits rose sharply in the first period, by 48 percent, and then remained largely unchanged in the second period. As a result, the share of nonhome, nonpension wealth in total retirement income fell from 41 percent in 1989 to 37 percent in 2007, while the share of Social Security benefits stayed fairly constant. However, the share of DC pension wealth climbed 10 percentage points, from 8 to 18 percent, while that of DB pension benefits fell 6 percentage points, from 19 to 13 percent. Of the $38,000 increase in expected retirement income between 1989 and 2007, the increase in nonpension wealth (including home equity) made the largest contribution, 45 percent, followed by the growth of DC pension wealth, 38 percent (see Table 7.5).[14] The growth in Social Security wealth accounted for the other 17 percent.

The ratio of expected retirement income between minorities and whites jumped from 0.37 in 1989 to 0.43 in 2007. The convergence was due largely to the growth in expected Social Security benefits among minorities, which outstripped that among whites. From 1989 to 2007, expected Social Security benefits rose by 73 percent among minorities and 50 percent among whites. The share of expected Social Security benefits in expected retirement income also rose among minorities, from 24 percent in 1989 to 27 percent in 2007, whereas it was virtually unchanged among whites at about 17 percent. As a result, the ratio of expected Social Security benefits between the two groups climbed from 0.54 in 1989 to 0.71 in 2007. Minorities will obtain a much higher share

Table 7.3 Expected Mean Retirement Income Based on Wealth Holdings and Expected Pension and Social Security Benefits, 2007 (in thousands, 2007$)

	Nonhome, nonpension wealth	Home equity	Defined contribution plans	Defined benefit pensions	Social Security	Total
Aged 47–64	41.6	16.1	20.3	14.2	19.1	111.3
Aged 47–55	40.4	16.9	21.7	14.1	19.5	112.6
Aged 56–64	43.2	14.9	18.4	14.3	18.7	109.6
Aged 47–64						
Non-Hispanic white[a]	49.0	17.5	23.3	15.4	20.3	125.5
African American or Hispanic[a]	11.3	10.3	8.1	9.6	14.5	53.8
Married couples	57.5	20.4	26.9	17.9	24.7	147.5
Single males	29.7	10.8	15.4	10.0	11.7	77.5
Single females	9.5	8.3	7.1	7.2	9.4	41.5
Less than 12 years of schooling[b]	3.8	5.4	2.4	1.8	12.9	26.3
12 years of schooling[b]	12.6	10.8	8.5	8.0	16.1	56.0
13–15 years of schooling[b]	21.7	12.2	13.9	12.1	16.4	76.3
16 or more years of schooling[b]	90.3	26.2	39.9	24.4	25.2	206.0
Income quintile, aged 47–64						
Income quintile 1	5.9	4.8	1.1	2.2	10.2	24.2
Income quintile 2	7.1	7.8	4.6	6.1	14.3	39.8
Income quintile 3	10.3	11.5	13.1	13.0	18.9	66.8
Income quintile 4	15.3	16.8	23.5	19.3	24.1	99.1
Income quintile 5	174.6	40.4	61.2	31.1	28.6	335.8

225

Aged 47–64

1989	30.4	10.2	5.9	13.9	12.8	73.2
2001	40.3	12.0	17.4	14.2	18.9	102.8

SOURCE: Author's computations from the 1989, 2001, and 2007 SCF.

NOTE: Households are classified by the age of the head of household. Each column equals the expected annuity (or annual benefit) from the current holdings of the indicated asset plus any future expected gains on the asset. Key: Home equity = net equity in owner-occupied housing. Nonhome, nonpension wealth = net worth − defined contribution − home equity. Defined contribution plans: Total defined contribution wealth = defined contribution wealth + employer contributions to defined contribution pension plans + present discounted value of future employee contributions into employee's defined contribution plan.

[a] Asian and other races are excluded from the table because of small sample sizes.

[b] Households are classified by the schooling level of the head of household.

Table 7.4 Percentage Change in Expected Mean Retirement Income Based on Wealth Holdings and Expected Pension and Social Security Benefits, 1989–2007

	Nonhome, nonpension wealth	Home equity	Defined contribution plans	Defined benefit pensions	Social Security	Total
Aged 47–64	36.7	58.2	243.5	1.6	49.6	52.0
Aged 47–55	14.7	47.4	133.1	−0.7	42.1	34.2
Aged 56–64	73.0	72.4	801.8	4.5	59.3	79.4
Aged 47–64						
Non-Hispanic white[a]	36.5	54.4	225.4	2.0	44.2	50.2
African American or Hispanic[a]	47.1	93.9	1,017.1	−2.4	89.9	72.6
Married couples	44.2	65.3	258.4	0.1	50.2	56.8
Single males	2.8	16.5	412.1	16.1	52.4	35.0
Single females	−6.6	47.8	102.4	2.9	46.3	26.8
Less than 12 years of schooling[b]	−61.2	−12.1	−4.9	−80.0	49.4	−27.3
12 years of schooling[b]	−61.1	−4.2	141.3	−35.5	−5.6	−26.9
13–15 years of schooling[b]	−30.0	−10.7	57.0	−28.8	2.5	−11.8
16 or more years of schooling[b]	−1.9	41.6	131.7	−14.0	41.3	18.4
Income quintile, ages 47–64						
Income quintile 1	155.4	77.9	41,473.1	64.2	71.9	96.7
Income quintile 2	−15.7	30.3	317.9	−12.9	26.6	18.0
Income quintile 3	−22.8	24.7	373.5	−6.2	41.7	27.2
Income quintile 4	−16.1	70.1	222.6	−4.3	56.6	39.6
Income quintile 5	54.0	73.1	220.4	13.8	62.7	67.3

Aged 47–64

1989–2001	32.5	18.2	194.6	1.6	47.8	40.4
2001–2007	3.1	33.8	16.6	0.0	1.2	8.2

NOTE: Households are classified by the age of the head of household. Each column equals the expected annuity (or annual benefit) from the current holdings of the indicated asset plus any future expected gains on the asset. Key: Home equity = net equity in owner-occupied housing. Nonhome, nonpension wealth = net worth − defined contribution − home equity. Defined contribution plans: Total defined contribution wealth = defined contribution wealth + employer contributions to defined contribution pension plans + present discounted value of future employee contributions into employee's defined contribution plan.

[a] Asian and other races are excluded from the table because of small sample sizes.

[b] Households are classified by the schooling level of the head of household.

SOURCE: Author's computations from the 1989, 2001, and 2007 SCF.

228

Table 7.5 Contribution to the Change in Expected Mean Retirement Income Made by Component, 1989–2007 (%)

	Nonhome, nonpension wealth	Home equity	Defined contribution plans	Defined benefit pensions	Social Security	Total
Aged 47–64	29.3	15.5	37.9	0.6	16.7	100.0
Aged 47–55	18.0	18.9	43.3	-0.3	20.1	100.0
Aged 56–64	37.7	12.9	33.8	1.3	14.3	100.0
Aged 47–64						
Non-Hispanic white[a]	31.3	14.7	38.5	0.7	14.8	100.0
African American or Hispanic[a]	16.0	22.1	32.7	-1.0	30.2	100.0
Married couples	33.0	15.1	36.4	0.0	15.5	100.0
Single males	4.0	7.6	61.5	6.9	20.0	100.0
Single females	-7.6	30.5	40.9	2.3	34.0	100.1
Less than 12 years of schooling[b]	60.1	7.5	1.3	74.3	-43.1	100.0
12 years of schooling[b]	96.0	2.3	-24.3	21.3	4.7	100.0
13–15 years of schooling[b]	91.2	14.3	-49.4	47.9	-4.0	100.0
16 or more years of schooling[b]	-5.6	24.1	70.9	-12.4	23.0	100.0
Income quintile, aged 47–64						
Income quintile 1	30.2	17.7	8.9	7.2	36.0	100.0
Income quintile 2	-21.7	29.8	57.2	-15.0	49.7	100.0
Income quintile 3	-21.3	16.0	72.4	-6.0	38.8	100.0
Income quintile 4	-10.4	24.7	57.8	-3.1	31.0	100.0
Income quintile 5	45.3	12.6	31.1	2.8	8.1	100.0

NOTE: Households are classified by the age of the head of household. Each column equals the expected annuity (or annual benefit) from the current holdings of the indicated asset plus any future expected gains on the asset. Totals may not sum to 100.0 due to rounding. The contribution made by a component such as pension wealth to the overall change in expected retirement income is defined as the change in the mean value of the component divided by the change in the mean value of expected retirement income. Key: Home equity = net equity in owner-occupied housing.Nonhome, nonpension wealth = net worth − defined contribution − home equity. Defined contribution plans: Total defined contribution wealth = defined contribution + employer contributions to defined contribution pension plans + present discounted value of future employee contributions into employee's defined contribution plan.

[a] Asian and other races are excluded from the table because of small sample sizes.
[b] Households are classified by the schooling level of the head of household.
SOURCE: Author's computations from the 1989 and 2007 SCF.

of their retirement income from Social Security than whites—27 versus 16 percent in 2007—and also a somewhat higher proportion from pensions (DC plus DB)—33 versus 31 percent—and a correspondingly much smaller share from nonpension wealth holdings—40 versus 53 percent.

Nonhome, nonpension wealth grew much faster among whites from 1989 to 2001 but much faster among minorities from 2001 to 2007. On net the ratio of the expected annuity from nonhome, nonpension wealth between minorities and whites grew slightly, from 0.21 in 1989 to 0.23 in 2007. The ratio of the expected annuity from home equity also increased over these years, as did the ratio in the expected annuity from total DC pension wealth.

Of the overall increase in expected retirement income from 1989 to 2007, gains in Social Security accounted for 30 percent among minorities in comparison to 15 percent among whites. In contrast, the growth of nonhome, nonpension wealth contributed 31 percent of the overall advance in expected retirement income for whites but only 16 percent for minorities. Increases in DC pension wealth made a larger contribution for whites than minorities (39 versus 33 percent), while increases in home equity were more important for minorities than whites (22 versus 15 percent).

In contrast, the expected retirement income of single females grew much more slowly than that of married couples from 1989 to 2007, 18 versus 55 percent. As a result, the ratio in expected retirement income between the two groups fell from 0.35 in 1989 to 0.28 in 2007. The relative decline was due mainly to a steep drop in the expected annuity from nonhome, nonpension wealth, from a ratio of 0.26 in 1989 to 0.17 in 2007, and in the expected annuity from DC pension wealth from 0.47 to 0.26.

All told, the share of nonhome, nonpension wealth in expected retirement income as well as the share of expected Social Security benefits remained about the same among married couples from 1989 to 2007, but the former fell from 31 to 23 percent among single females, whereas the latter increased from 20 to 23 percent. Single females in 2007 will obtain a higher share of their retirement income from Social Security than will married couples (23 versus 17 percent), a higher fraction from (DC plus DB) pensions (35 versus 30 percent), but a much lower share from nonpension wealth (43 versus 53 percent).

Advances in Social Security benefits made a much larger contribution to gains in expected retirement income for single females, 34 percent, than for married couples, 16 percent, or single males, 20 percent. In contrast, DC plan accumulations were the largest source of growth in expected retirement income for single males, 62 percent, compared to 41 percent for single women and 36 percent for married couples. Increases in nonhome, nonpension wealth accounted for one-third of the growth in expected retirement income among married couples but made virtually no contribution to retirement income growth among single men or single women.

Absolute declines in expected retirement income were recorded for each of the three lowest educational groups between 1989 and 2007, whereas college graduates are expected to see an 18 percent increase. Here, too, there were steep declines in the expected annuity from nonhome, nonpension wealth relative to college graduates from 1989 to 2007 (the ratio between high school and college graduates plummeted from 0.35 to 0.14!), and that from total DC wealth relative to college graduates. Less-educated households became more dependent on Social Security, whose share in total expected retirement income more than doubled from 24 percent in 1989 to 49 percent in 2007 among the least educated, increased from 22 to 29 percent among high school graduates, and from 19 to 22 percent among those with some college (it also showed a modest rise among college graduates from 10 to 12 percent).

Correspondingly, the share of expected annuities from nonhome, nonpension wealth declined sharply among the three less-educated groups (it also fell among college graduates). However, overall the less-educated groups were much more dependent on Social Security in 2007 than were college graduates (29 percent for high school graduates versus 12 percent for college graduates) but the reverse was true for nonpension wealth holdings—42 percent for high school graduates versus 57 percent for college graduates.

The bottom income quintile showed a slight increase in expected retirement income relative to the top income quintile between 1989 and 2007 (from a ratio of 0.06 to 0.07), but the middle three income quintiles each lost ground (the relative expected retirement income of the third income quintile fell from 26 percent in 1989 to 20 percent in 2007). The expected annuity from nonhome, nonpension wealth of each of the four bottom quintiles was very low relative to the top quintile, ranging from a ratio of 0.03 to 0.09 in 2007. Except for the bottom quintile, these ratios all fell between 1989 and 2007. The expected annuity from DC plan wealth of each of the four bottom quintiles was also low relative to that of the top quintile, ranging from a ratio of 0.02 to 0.38 in 2007, but in this case there was little change between 1989 and 2007.

Middle-income households saw an increase in their dependence on Social Security as a source of retirement income. The share of total expected retirement income in the form of Social Security benefits rose from 34 percent in 1989 to 36 percent for the second quintile, from 25 to 28 percent for the middle quintile, and from 22 percent to 24 percent for the fourth quintile. Correspondingly, the importance of nonhome, nonpension wealth in future retirement income declined for each of the three middle quintiles. Interestingly, the share of Social Security in expected retirement income fell for the bottom quintile, from 48 to 42 percent, and the share from nonhome, nonpension wealth rose from 19 to 24 percent.

Nonetheless, the lower-income groups were all much more dependent on Social Security than the top quintile. The share of Social Security in expected retirement income descended with income quintile, from 42 percent for the bottom to 9 percent for the top quintile in 2007. In contrast, the share of expected annuity income from nonhome, nonpension wealth in expected retirement income ran in the range of 15 to 24 percent for the bottom four income quintiles in 2007, in contrast to 52 percent for the top quintile. Indeed, the gain in total expected retirement income of the bottom quintile relative to the top quintile (from a ratio of 0.06 to 0.07) can be traced largely to the faster growth of expected Social Security benefits in the bottom quintile relative to the top (a gain of 72 percent from 1989 to 2007 compared to 63 percent). In contrast, expected Social Security benefits grew slower for each of the middle quintiles than for the top or bottom.

Social Security was also much more important as a contributor to the growth in expected retirement income for the bottom four income quintiles (a range of 31 to 50 percent) than the top income quintile (only 8 percent). Gains in total DC pension wealth accounted for more than half the growth in expected retirement income among the middle three income quintiles, compared to 9 percent for the bottom and 31 percent for the top. Changes in nonhome, nonpension wealth made negative contributions to advances in expected retirement income among the middle three income quintiles but accounted for 45 percent of the gain for the top income quintile.

In summary, Social Security was more important as a source of expected retirement income among the lower-income groups—minorities, single females, the less educated, and the lower income quintiles—than among higher-income groups—whites, married couples, college graduates, and the top income quintile. It has thus served as an important equalizing factor in retirement adequacy. Moreover, the importance of Social Security benefits in expected retirement income grew over time between 1989 and 2007 for the low-income groups indicated above. The faster growth of expected Social Security benefits among minorities largely explains the decline in the gap in expected retirement income between them and whites from 1989 to 2007. Likewise, the faster growth of Social Security benefits for the bottom income quintile is the principal factor explaining the faster growth in their expected retirement income relative to that of the top quintile.

THE EXPECTED POVERTY RATE AT RETIREMENT

As discussed earlier, another important concern is the percentage of households that might be expected to fall below the poverty line after retirement. This is an important issue in social policy since such families will be at particular risk in that they are unlikely to be able to rely on the labor market in order to exit from poverty.

Trends in projected poverty rates at retirement tend to follow trends in mean retirement income (see Table 7.6). In 2007, 10.2 percent of households in age group 47–64 were projected to have retirement income of less than the poverty line for their family size. The percentage was smaller for age group 56–64 (8.2 percent) than for age group 47–55 (11.6 percent). Only 4.8 percent of white households are projected to fall below the poverty standard, compared to 13.9 percent of minorities (a 9.1 percentage point difference). Differences are also marked by marital status, with only 5.7 percent of married couples compared to 12.8 percent of single males and 19.7 percent of single females

Table 7.6 Percentage of Households with Expected Retirement Income Less Than the Poverty Line, Based on Wealth Holdings and Expected Pension and Social Security Benefits, 1989–2007

	1989	2001	2007	Change		
				1989–2001	2001–2007	1989–2007
Aged 47–64	14.8	10.2	10.2	−4.6	−0.0	−4.6
Aged 47–55	13.2	10.7	11.6	−2.5	0.8	−1.6
Aged 56–64	16.7	9.4	8.2	−7.3	−1.2	−8.5
Aged 47–64						
Non-Hispanic white[a]	3.2	4.0	4.8	0.8	0.8	1.6
African American or Hispanic[a]	48.1	21.6	13.9	−26.5	−7.6	−34.1
Married couples	7.3	3.9	5.7	−3.4	1.8	−1.6
Single males	11.4	11.9	12.8	0.4	1.0	1.4
Single females	33.2	24.4	19.7	−8.8	−4.7	−13.4
Less than 12 years of schooling[b]	26.7	23.8	28.1	−2.8	4.3	1.4
12 years of schooling[b]	1.6	10.6	9.0	9.1	−1.7	7.4
13–15 years of schooling[b]	0.4	6.8	9.0	6.4	2.1	8.5
16 or more years of schooling[b]	5.4	5.7	6.4	0.3	0.7	1.0

NOTE: Total retirement income includes expected future gains on all components of net worth. Households are classified by the age of the head of household. Percentage changes between years may reflect rounding.

[a] Asian and other races are excluded from the table because of small sample sizes.

[b] Households are classified by the schooling level of the head of household.

SOURCE: Author's computations from the 1989, 2001, and 2007 SCF.

falling below the poverty line. Poverty rates are smaller for the better educated, varying between 28.1 percent for the least educated and 6.4 percent for college graduates.

Most of the poverty reduction appears to have taken place between 1989 and 2001. The projected poverty rate at retirement for the whole age group 47–64 fell by 4.6 percentage points over these years. From 2001 to 2007 the projected poverty rate showed no change.

By and large, groups with the highest projected poverty rate in 1989 experienced the largest reduction in their projected poverty rate at retirement. Percentage point declines were much greater for age group 56–64, which had a higher poverty rate in 1989, than age group 47–55. In fact, the projected poverty rate was 3.5 percentage points greater for the older age group in 1989 and 3.4 percentage points lower in 2007. Minority households experienced a precipitous decline in their projected poverty rate, 34.1 percentage points, while white households experienced a slight increase of 1.6 percentage points. The gap between the two groups fell sharply, from 44.9 percentage points in 1989 to only 9.1 percentage points in 2007. Single females also saw a large decline—13.4 percentage points—especially compared to married couples (a 1.6 percentage point decline) and single males (a 1.4 percentage point increase).[15]

Table 7.7 shows the expected poverty rate at retirement on the basis of current and projected net worth, total DC wealth, expected DB pension benefits, and expected Social Security benefits for 2007 (see Appendix Table D.5 for details on 1989 and 2001). I have added in these components sequentially. Of course, the results depend on the order in which the components are included, so that these results give particular influence to Social Security, the last component.

On the basis of current and future gains on nonhome, nonpension wealth alone, I project a huge poverty rate at retirement of 75 percent for households in age group 47 to 64 in 2007.[16] In other words, standard nonpension financial wealth accumulation is quite insufficient to lift the vast majority of families out of poverty. Next, since the treatment of housing equity, owner-occupied housing, can be ambiguous (as discussed above), I first include only half the expected annuity on owner-occupied housing. This lowers the expected poverty rate by more than 15 percentage points, to 60 percent. Adding in the other half from home equity owner-occupied housing lowers it another 15 percentage points,

Table 7.7 Percentage of Households with Expected Retirement Income Less Than the Poverty Line, Based on Wealth Holdings and Expected Pension and Social Security Benefits, 2007

	Nonhome, nonpension wealth	Nonhome, nonpension wealth plus half of home equity	Nonpension wealth	Nonpension wealth plus defined contribution plans	Nonpension wealth plus all pensions	Total expected retirement income: nonpension wealth + pension wealth + Social Security
Aged 47–64	75.1	59.8	45.2	33.2	27.9	10.2
Aged 47–55	76.6	59.3	45.5	31.7	28.6	11.6
Aged 56–64	72.9	60.4	44.9	35.3	27.0	8.2
Aged 47–64						
Non-Hispanic white[a]	70.6	54.0	38.9	25.9	20.5	4.8
African American or Hispanic[a]	88.4	75.1	60.2	49.7	43.9	13.9
Married couples	70.9	54.0	37.1	24.9	20.6	5.7
Single males	72.1	57.8	50.3	44.0	36.8	12.8
Single females	86.9	74.9	62.4	48.0	41.0	19.7
Less than 12 years of schooling[b]	94.2	92.0	80.1	74.6	68.7	28.1
12 years of schooling[b]	86.3	72.6	54.3	39.9	32.8	9.0
13–15 years of schooling[b]	80.7	62.8	50.4	32.5	27.4	9.0
16 or more years of schooling[b]	56.4	37.5	23.9	15.5	11.7	6.4
Aged 47–64						
1989	67.5	57.0	45.1	40.7	27.5	14.8
2001	71.7	62.3	50.2	38.9	30.2	10.2

237

NOTE: Households are classified by the age of the head of household. Key: Home equity: net equity in owner-occupied housing. Non-home, nonpension wealth = net worth − defined contribution − home equity. Nonpension wealth plus defined contribution plans: Total defined contribution wealth = defined contribution wealth + employer contributions to defined contribution pension plans + present discounted value of future employee contributions into employee's defined contribution plan.

[a] Asians and other races are excluded from the table because of small sample sizes.

[b] Households are classified by the schooling level of the head of household.

SOURCE: Author's computations from the 1989, 2001, and 2007 SCF.

to 45 percent. Thus, standard nonpension financial wealth accumulation plus investing in a home still leaves the expected poverty rate at a very high level.

Another 12 percentage point decline comes from adding in the expected annuity from both the current value and the expected future gains on total DC pension wealth, bringing the expected poverty rate down to about one-third, and adding in DB pension benefits brings the poverty rate down a bit more, to 28 percent. Finally, adding in the expected Social Security benefit lowers the expected poverty rate by 18 percentage points, to 10 percent.

There is considerable disparity across groups in the importance of these various components to reducing expected poverty. In 2007, non-whites aged 47–64 were projected to have a poverty rate of 14 percent, compared to 5 percent for whites. The poverty rate on the basis of standard nonpension wealth (including home equity) is much lower for whites, 39 percent, than for nonwhites, 60 percent. Adding in the expected annuity from all expected pension benefits lowers the rate for whites by 18 percentage points to 21 percent, and that for blacks by 16 percentage points to 44 percent. Adding in Social Security causes a huge reduction in the expected poverty rate for nonwhites, by 30 percentage points, to 14 percent, compared to a 16 percentage point drop for whites, to 5 percent.

A similar pattern holds for the comparison between married couples and single females. The expected poverty rate for the former is 37 percent on the basis of nonpension wealth alone. Adding in private retirement wealth reduces it by 17 percentage points to 21 percent, and including Social Security further reduces it by 15 percentage points to 6 percent. For single females, the predicted poverty rate is 62 percent on the basis of nonpension wealth alone. It falls to 41 percent, a 21 percentage point reduction, when private pensions are included, and then to 20 percent when Social Security is included, another 21 percentage point reduction.

The expected poverty rate for college graduates on the basis of nonpension wealth NWX is quite low, 24 percent. Adding private pensions lowers it by 12 percentage points to 12 percent, and then including Social Security lowers it by 5 percentage points to 6 percent. In contrast, the poverty rate on the basis of nonpension wealth alone varies from a high of 80 percent for the least educated households to 50 percent for those with some college. Adding in private pensions reduces the expected poverty rate by 11 to 23 percentage points, and then including Social Security lowers it by another 18 to 41 (for the least-educated group) percentage points. Indeed, for the least educated group, Social Security reduces the projected poverty rate from 69 to 27 percent.

Over time, the importance of Social Security grows as a weapon to reduce poverty among the low-income elderly. Among all households aged 47–64, on the basis of nonhome, nonpension wealth alone, the expected poverty rate actually increases by 8 percentage points, from 68 percent in 1989 to 75 percent in 2007. With the addition of home equity owner-occupied housing, the expected poverty rate remains at 45 percent in 1989 and in 2007. Next, with the inclusion of private pensions, the expected poverty rate is slightly higher in 2007, at 28 percent, than in 1989, at 27 percent. The main effect comes from Social Security. When this is included, the expected poverty rate declines from 15 percent in 1989 to 10 percent in 2007.

The effects of Social Security are even more significant for minorities. Their expected poverty rate on the basis of private accumulations alone (nonhome, nonpension wealth plus private pensions) is 63 percent in 1989. Adding in Social Security reduces it by 15 percentage points to just a little less than half, 48 percent. In 2007, their expected poverty rate from private accumulations is 44 percent, 19 percentage points lower than in 1989, but adding in Social Security results in a 30 percentage point drop, to 14 percent.

Similar results hold for single females. On the basis of private accumulations, their expected poverty rate in 1989 is 48 percent; adding in Social Security lowers it by 15 percentage points, to 33 percent. In 2007, the expected poverty rate from private accumulations alone is lower, at 41 percent, but including Social Security results in a 21 percentage point fall, to 20 percent.

The results by educational group highlight the importance of DB pensions for less-educated workers in the 1980s. In 1989, the predicted poverty rate from total net worth for the least educated workers is 57 percent. Adding expected DB pensions lowers it by 15 percentage points, to 42 percent. In 2007, the drop in the expected poverty rate from including DB pensions is only 6 percentage points. Among high school graduates, the addition of DB pensions to net worth lowers the expected poverty rate by 13 percentage points in 1989 but only 7 percentage pints in 2007. Even among those with some college, including DB pensions reduces the expected poverty rate by 13 percentage points in 1989 but by only 5 percentage points in 2007. In fact, in 1989, the expected poverty rate is actually lower among high school graduates (1.6 percent) and those with some college (0.4 percent) than among college graduates (5.4 percent), because of the greater importance of DB pensions for these two groups than for college graduates.

The same pattern also holds with regard to the importance of Social Security for the less-educated households. The predicted poverty rate among the least educated workers in 1989 is 42 percent from private accumulations alone but 27 percent when Social Security is included, a 16 percentage point reduction. In 2007, it was higher, 69 percent from private accumulations, and also higher when Social Security is added, 28 percent, but the effect of adding Social Security is greater for 2007, a 41 percentage point reduction. For high school graduates, the expected poverty rate from private accumulations alone is also higher in 2007 than in 1989, 27 percent versus 17 percent, but the reduction from adding Social Security is also greater, 24 versus 15 percentage points. A similar result holds for households with some college.

REPLACEMENT RATES

The third dimension of retirement income security is the so-called replacement rate. This concept measures expected retirement income as a fraction of the income the household receives just on the eve of retirement. As such, it reflects the degree to which income during retirement replaces prior income and is thus of major concern to the individual household.

There was relatively little change over time in the share of households with expected retirement income greater than or equal to three-quarters of projected income at retirement (the "three-quarters replacement rate"), particularly in comparison to changes in projected poverty rates (see Table 7.8).[17] The reason is that a replacement rate is a relative standard, whereas the poverty rate is based on an absolute standard. Changes in the replacement rate reflect changes in both expected retirement income, which is projected to grow on average by 2.32 percent

241

Table 7.8 Percentage of Households with Expected Retirement Income Greater Than or Equal to 75 Percent of Projected Income at Age 64, Based on Wealth Holdings and Expected Pension and Social Security Benefits, 1989, 2001, and 2007

	1989	2001	2007	Change		
				1989–2001	2001–2007	1989–2007
Aged 47–64	45.4	46.5	49.3	1.2	2.8	3.9
Aged 47–55	38.8	40.7	43.7	1.9	2.9	4.9
Aged 56–64	53.0	55.3	57.1	2.3	1.8	4.0
Aged 47–64						
Non-Hispanic white[a]	49.7	50.5	53.6	0.8	3.1	3.9
African American or Hispanic[a]	35.2	37.4	41.5	2.3	4.1	6.4
Married couples	47.3	49.7	49.7	2.4	-0.0	2.4
Single males	54.0	47.1	57.2	-6.9	10.1	3.2
Single females	37.6	38.2	44.0	0.5	5.9	6.4
Less than 12 years of schooling[b]	42.1	44.3	34.6	2.2	-9.7	-7.5
12 years of schooling[b]	47.8	44.8	42.6	-3.0	-2.2	-5.2
13–15 years of schooling[b]	44.8	43.1	45.9	-1.7	2.8	1.2
16 or more years of schooling[b]	52.7	51.5	61.4	-1.2	9.9	8.7
Income quintile, ages 47–64						
Income quintile 1	51.8	62.2	57.3	10.4	-5.0	5.4
Income quintile 2	45.8	45.1	47.0	-0.7	1.9	1.1
Income quintile 3	56.4	38.4	47.8	-18.0	9.4	-8.7
Income quintile 4	33.6	41.3	47.1	7.7	5.8	13.5
Income quintile 5	39.2	45.1	47.3	5.9	2.2	8.1

NOTE: Total retirement income includes expected future gains on all components of net worth. Households are classified by the age of the head of household. Percentage changes between years may reflect rounding.
[a] Asian and other races are excluded from the table because of small sample sizes.
[b] Households are classified by the schooling level of the head of household.
SOURCE: Author's computations from the 1989, 2001, and 2007 SCF.

per year from 1989 to 2007, and preretirement income itself, which is projected to grow at 1.70 percent per year.

In 2007, only 49 percent of all households in age group 47–64 are expected to meet the three-quarters replacement rate. The share meeting this standard increased slightly from 1989 to 2001 (by 1.2 percentage points) and then showed a moderate gain from 2001 to 2007 (2.8 percentage points). This time trend differs from that found for projected average retirement income, which shows a much greater increase from 1989 to 2001 than from 2001 to 2007.

Surprisingly, the percentage of households meeting this replacement rate standard is generally greater for the higher-income groups, despite their higher preretirement income. The share projected to meet the three-quarters replacement rate in 2007 is greater for the higher-income older age group 56–64, 57 percent, than the lower-income younger age group, 44 percent. However, the younger age group experienced a somewhat greater increase in the share of households meeting this replacement standard from 1989 to 2007. Despite the higher preretirement income of white households, the share meeting the three-quarters replacement rate is 54 percent in 2007, compared to 42 percent for minorities. However, the share of minority households meeting this standard rose more than that of white households, 6.4 versus 3.9 percentage points between 1989 and 2007.

In similar fashion, despite the lower preretirement income of single females, the share of this group meeting the 75 percent replacement rate was lower in 2007, at 44 percent, than that for married couples, 50 percent, or single men, 57 percent. However, as with minorities, single women saw the greatest improvement in retirement income adequacy, at least if a 75 percent replacement standard is used, from 1989 to 2007, while both married couples and single men experienced smaller gains (6.4 percentage points versus 2.4 and 3.2 percentage points, respectively).

The share of households meeting the three-quarters replacement rate standard was much higher among college graduates in 2007 (61 percent) than among the other educational groups (35 to 44 percent), despite their much higher level of preretirement income. Moreover, the share meeting the replacement rate standard climbed much more for college graduates than for the other educational groups (indeed, changes were negative for the two lowest educated groups), reflecting the greater gains in expected retirement income among college graduates than among the other groups (which were all negative).

The percentage of households able to meet the 75 percent replacement rate benchmark was much higher among the bottom income quintile (57 percent) than among the other income quintiles (about 47 percent for the top four quintiles). The bottom quintile also saw an improvement in the share able to meet the replacement rate standard from 1989 to 2007 (5.4 percentage points), as did the fourth quintile (13.5 percentage points) and the top quintile (8.1 percentage points), whereas the second quintile showed no change and the share of the middle quintile meeting the standard fell by 8.7 percentage points.

As noted above, in 2007, the percentage of all households in age group 47–64 with a 75 percent replacement rate was projected to be 49 percent. However, the percentage of households in this age group projected to meet this replacement rate standard is only 6 percent on the basis of nonhome, nonpension wealth alone (see Table 7.9 and Appendix Table D.6 for details for 1989 and 2001). The share rises somewhat to 10 percent when the annuity from home equity is also included and then to 17 percent when total DC pension wealth is also included. The addition of DB pension wealth raises this fraction rather sizably to 29 percent. The addition of Social Security makes an even bigger difference, raising the share to 49 percent.

As noted above, the share of households in age group 47–64 meeting the 75 percent replacement standard rose from 45 to 49 percent between 1989 and 2007. Defined contributions pensions made a larger marginal contribution in the later year, increasing the replacement rate by 6.8 percentage points compared to 2.2 percentage points in 1989, whereas DB pensions made a correspondingly smaller marginal contribution, 11.7 percentage points in 2007 compared to 14.8 percentage points in 1989. The marginal contribution of Social Security increased between the two years as well—17.6 in 1989 versus 20.8 percentage points in 2007.

There is a sizable gap in the share of households meeting the replacement rate standard between whites and minorities, 14.5 percentage points in 1989 and 12.1 percentage points in 2007. Most of the gap comes from differences in the accumulation of standard nonpension wealth, and a smaller contribution emanates from the larger total DC wealth accumulations of whites. In 2007, the difference in expected

Table 7.9 Share of Households with Expected Replacement Income Greater Than or Equal to Three Quarters of Projected Income at Age 64, Based on Wealth Holdings and Expected Pension and Social Security Benefits, 2007 (%)

	Nonhome, nonpension wealth	Nonhome, nonpension wealth plus half of home equity	Nonpension wealth	Nonpension wealth plus defined contribution plans	Nonpension wealth plus all pensions	Total expected retirement income: nonpension wealth + pension wealth + Social Security
Aged 47–64	5.5	7.3	10.0	16.8	28.5	49.3
Aged 47–55	4.4	6.1	8.1	14.7	26.1	43.7
Aged 56–64	6.9	8.9	12.5	19.6	31.8	57.1
Aged 47–64						
Non-Hispanic white[a]	6.1	8.2	11.0	18.9	31.2	53.6
African American or Hispanic[a]	3.9	5.0	7.8	11.4	23.2	41.5
Married couples	5.1	6.6	8.7	16.5	28.4	49.7
Single males	9.9	11.2	14.9	20.8	35.8	57.2
Single females	4.1	6.9	10.5	15.4	25.1	44.0
Less than 12 years of schooling[b]	2.2	2.5	3.1	4.4	7.5	34.6
12 years of schooling[b]	3.2	4.6	7.6	11.7	19.9	42.6
13–15 years of schooling[b]	6.1	8.3	10.2	15.2	27.5	45.9
16 or more years of schooling[b]	8.1	10.3	13.9	25.7	42.7	61.4
Income quintile, ages 47–64						
Income quintile 1	6.7	10.4	16.8	19.4	25.6	57.3
Income quintile 2	4.8	6.5	9.3	14.8	25.1	47.0
Income quintile 3	4.0	5.7	7.6	16.0	29.2	47.8
Income quintile 4	2.1	2.8	3.2	12.4	29.2	47.1
Income quintile 5	10.1	11.2	12.9	21.5	33.8	47.3

245

Aged 47–64						
1989	6.8	8.0	10.8	13.0	27.8	45.4
2001	6.3	8.0	10.5	16.1	26.8	46.5

SOURCE: Author's computations from the 1989, 2001, and 2007 SCF. Households are classified by the age of the head of household.
Key: Home equity = net equity in owner-occupied housing. Nonhome, nonpension wealth = net worth − defined contribution − home equity. Nonpension wealth plus defined contribution plans: Total defined contribution wealth = defined contribution wealth + employer contributions to defined contribution pension plans + present discounted value of future employee contributions into employee's defined contribution plan.

[a] Asian and other races are excluded from the table because of small sample sizes.
[b] Households are classified by the schooling level of the head of household.

Social Security benefits between whites and minorities also contributes to the gap. The gap between married couples and single females is large in 1989, 9.7 percentage points. This is mainly due to the higher expected Social Security benefits of the former, which increase the percentage of households meeting the replacement standard by 21.3 percentage points, compared to a 12.0 percentage point increase for single females. However, by 2007 the gap in the share meeting the replacement rate standard between these two groups narrows to 5.7 percentage points.

Differences in the share of households meeting the replacement rate standard are 5–10 percentage points higher for college graduates than for the other education groups in 1989. By 2007, the differences expand to a range of 17–27 percentage points. In 1989, the differences are due almost entirely to the higher expected Social Security benefits of college graduates. However, by 2007, the differences are ascribable almost exclusively to the much higher value of DC pension wealth among college graduates.

In contrast, the share meeting the replacement standard is highest for the lowest income quintile, at 57 percent in 2007. It is almost constant among the top four income quintiles, at 47 percent. In 2007, the gap between the bottom and top quintiles is quite large, 10.0 percentage points. Differences in the share of households meeting the replacement rate standard are much smaller on the basis of private accumulations (the sum of nonpension wealth and total DC pension wealth), with the top income quintile having the highest share meeting this standard. As a result, the *relatively* higher level of expected Social Security benefits for lower-income households explains almost all of these gaps.

Similar patterns exist when we look at different cut-off points for replacement rates (Table 7.10). The share of all households aged 47–64 meeting the indicated replacement rate standard remains virtually unchanged from 1989 to 2001 and then increases from 2001 to 2007 at the 50 and 75 percent replacement rate standards, though it is almost unchanged at the 25 and 100 percent replacement standards. The share meeting these standards are uniformly higher for age group 56–64 than for age group 47–55, for whites than for minorities, and for married couples than for single females. The percentage of households meeting the standards were also generally higher for college graduates than for the other educational groups (particularly for 2007), and generally higher for the bottom income quintile than for higher income quintiles.

Table 7.10 Percentage of Households in Age Group 47–64 Meeting Minimum Expected Replacement Rate Standards, Based on Expected Income at Retirement, 1989, 2001, and 2007

	1989				2001				2007			
	25	50	75	100	25	50	75	100	25	50	75	100
Aged 47–64	89.6	69.4	45.4	27.6	92.2	70.1	46.5	30.4	92.2	73.7	49.3	30.9
Aged 47–55	88.8	64.7	38.8	22.4	91.3	64.5	40.7	25.4	91.1	70.1	43.7	25.9
Aged 56–64	90.5	74.9	53.0	33.7	93.5	78.7	55.3	38.0	93.8	78.7	57.1	37.8
Non-Hispanic white[a]	96.2	76.6	49.7	30.4	96.9	75.4	50.5	33.6	96.4	78.2	53.6	34.2
African American or Hispanic[a]	77.7	51.7	35.2	20.9	86.9	59.3	37.4	22.2	93.4	70.1	41.5	23.7
Married couple	92.7	75.0	47.3	26.9	94.3	75.4	49.7	33.3	93.0	75.3	49.7	30.1
Single male	92.2	66.3	54.0	40.8	93.0	66.8	47.1	29.7	90.2	72.5	57.2	42.1
Single female	81.5	58.0	37.6	24.2	86.2	59.5	38.2	23.8	91.4	70.3	44.0	27.0
Less than 12 years of schooling[b]	85.1	62.6	42.1	24.5	90.4	64.6	44.3	29.4	90.2	61.4	34.6	21.2
12 years of schooling[b]	94.8	74.9	47.8	30.0	91.3	69.7	44.8	28.9	92.1	70.4	42.6	24.6
13–15 years of schooling[b]	97.0	82.5	44.8	25.5	92.7	67.6	43.1	26.1	93.4	72.5	45.9	28.7
16 or more years of schooling[b]	91.2	74.1	52.7	35.8	93.3	75.0	51.5	35.3	92.2	80.9	61.4	40.5
Income quintile 1	80.3	63.9	51.8	33.7	90.6	77.6	62.2	47.9	92.7	78.3	57.3	42.2
Income quintile 2	90.9	76.6	45.8	26.6	91.8	68.0	45.1	29.5	91.2	67.8	47.0	31.7
Income quintile 3	95.3	80.9	56.4	31.2	91.8	62.9	38.4	24.5	92.1	75.4	47.8	29.9
Income quintile 4	91.7	59.9	33.6	24.6	93.1	69.3	41.3	24.4	92.0	75.5	47.1	26.8
Income quintile 5	88.2	64.1	39.2	22.6	93.7	72.6	45.1	25.1	93.2	71.3	47.3	23.6

NOTE: Total retirement income includes expected future gains on all components of net worth. Households are classified by the age of the head of household.

[a] Asian and other races are excluded from the table because of small sample sizes.

[b] Households are classified by the schooling level of the head of household.

SOURCE: Author's computations from the 1989, 2001, and 2007 SCF.

SUMMARY OF RESULTS AND CONCLUDING COMMENTS

In line with the main themes of the book, a marked slowdown in the growth of mean expected retirement income was found for age group 47–64 in the 2000s compared to the 1990s, even before the financial meltdown of 2008–2009. Whereas mean expected retirement income gained 40 percent from 1989 to 2001, it advanced by only 8 percent from 2001 to 2007. This result is consistent with our findings of a pronounced decline in the rate of growth of augmented wealth between the 1990s and the 2000s (see Chapter 5). Households in this age group also saw a large reduction in their expected poverty rate at retirement, from 15 percent in 1989 to 10 percent in 2001. However, there was no further reduction in the expected poverty rate from 2001 to 2007. In contrast, the percentage of households meeting the 75 percent replacement standard rose more in the later period, from 45.4 to 46.5 percent from 1989 to 2001 and from 46.5 to 49.3 percent from 2001 to 2007.

With regard to intergroup differences, the ratio of expected retirement income between minorities and whites jumped from 0.37 in 1989 to 0.43 in 2007. The convergence was due largely to the growth in expected Social Security benefits among minorities, which outstripped that among whites. These results are consistent with my finding of a convergence in augmented wealth between the two groups over this time period (see Chapter 6).

Minorities also made dramatic inroads in reducing their projected poverty rate at retirement. This fell from 48 percent in 1989 to 14 percent in 2007, a 34 percentage point reduction. In contrast, white households saw their expected poverty rate rise by 1.6 percentage points. Still, whites had a much lower expected poverty rate in 2007 than minorities, 5 versus 14 percent. Moreover, minorities saw slightly greater increases in the share of households with a replacement rate of 75 percent or more from 1989 to 2007—6.4 versus 3.9 percentage points. However, minorities still had a lower proportion who met this replacement standard in 2007—42 versus 54 percent.

In contrast, the expected retirement income of single females grew much more slowly than that of married couples from 1989 to 2007, by 27 versus 57 percent. As a result, the ratio in expected retirement income between the two groups fell from 0.35 in 1989 to 0.28 in 2007.

The relative decline was due mainly to a steep drop in the relative holdings of nonhome, nonpension wealth and total DC wealth.

Less-educated households did not fare well at all. The three lowest groups all saw absolute declines in their expected retirement income from 1989 to 2007. For those with a high school degree or less, expected retirement income plummeted by 27 percent. Indeed, the only group showing positive gains was college graduates. The less-educated groups were much more dependent on Social Security in 2007 than college graduates (29 percent of expected retirement income for high school graduates versus 12 percent for college graduates), but the reverse was true for nonpension wealth holdings—42 percent for high school graduates versus 57 percent for college graduates.

The expected poverty rate at retirement was much higher for the least-educated group, 28 percent in 2007, compared to 6–9 percent for the more-educated ones. However, those with 12 years of schooling and those with some college saw the biggest increase in expected poverty, 7 and 9 percentage points, respectively. Indeed, households with a high school degree and those with some college had by far the lowest expected poverty rates in 1989, 1.6 and 0.4 percent, respectively. The 1989 figures reflected the large role played by DB pension wealth in their portfolios.

The share of households meeting a 75 percent replacement rate at retirement was much higher for college graduates in 2007, 61 percent, than for the other schooling groups, between 35 and 46 percent. The percentage meeting this standard increased for college graduates between 1989 and 2007 but declined for the least-educated group and high school graduates and essentially remained the same for those with some college.

Expected retirement income also varies directly with income quintile, and the gaps were quite large. The ratio of expected retirement income of the top to the bottom quintile was 13.9 in 2007. Advances in expected retirement income had a U-shaped pattern, with the strongest gains at the bottom quintile and the second strongest at the top quintile. The share of households with a 75 percent expected replacement rate is actually greatest for the bottom quintile in 2007, at 57 percent, compared to 47–48 percent for the other income quintiles.

Social Security was much more important as a source of expected retirement income among the lower-income groups—minorities, single females, the less educated, and the lower income quintiles—than among higher-income groups—whites, married couples, college graduates, and the top income quintile. It thus serves as an important equalizing factor in retirement adequacy. The share of Social Security in expected retirement income descended with income quintile, from 42 percent for the bottom to 9 percent for the top in 2007.

Moreover, the importance of Social Security benefits in expected retirement income grew between 1989 and 2007 for the low-income groups indicated above. The faster growth of expected Social Security benefits among minorities largely explains the decline in the gap in expected retirement income between them and whites from 1989 to 2007. Likewise, the faster growth of Social Security benefits for the bottom income quintile was the principal factor explaining the faster growth in that group's expected retirement income relative to that of the top quintile.

In 2007, Social Security caused a huge reduction in expected poverty rate for low-income groups—nonwhites (30 percentage points), single females (21 percentage points), less than 12 years of school (41 percentage points), and high school graduates (24 percentage points). Between 1989 and 2007, the drop in the expected poverty rate from adding in expected Social Security benefits increased from 15 to 30 percentage points for minorities; 15 to 21 percentage points for single females; 16 to 40 percentage points for the least educated; and from 15 to 24 percentage points for high school graduates.

The unraveling of the DB pension system was particularly hurtful to those with less than a high school degree, high school graduates, and those with 3–5 years of college or less in terms of expected poverty rates. In 1989, high school graduates and those with some college had the lowest expected poverty rates at retirement. The effect of adding expected DB pension benefits on the expected poverty rate fell from 15 to 6 percentage points for the least educated households from 1989 to 2007, 13 to 7 percentage points for high school graduates, and from 13 to 5 percentage points for those with some college.

Overall, the marginal effect of adding total pension wealth (DB plus DC pensions) to nonpension wealth on the expected poverty rate actually fell a bit from 1989 to 2007 (from a 17.6 to a 17.3 percentage point reduction) among all households in age range 47–64. Among most demographic groups, there was little change from 1989 to 2007 in the marginal impact of pension wealth on the expected poverty rate. However, the drop in the marginal impact was particularly severe among those with less than a high school education (from a 21 to an 11 percentage point reduction), though among single females the marginal impact rose between 1989 and 2007 (from a 15 to a 21 percentage point reduction in the expected poverty rate).

In conclusion, it has been found, first, that Social Security fulfills its expected role of a solid, broadly shared retirement benefit. Second, private savings, including home ownership, is the second most important retirement savings vehicle. Third, private pensions still leave large holes, even after growing sharply from 1989 to 2007.

Notes

1. I am ignoring miscellaneous sources of income such as government transfer payments other than Social Security, alimony payments, and the like. These components of household income are quite small and are hard to predict many years into the future.

2. In fact, in principle, the family could convert its net worth into an annuity plan from a life insurance company if the plan was actuarially fair and the life insurance company made no profits on the annuity.

3. The average real rate of return on gross assets for age group 47–64 on the basis of their actual portfolio composition was 1.97 percent in 1989, 1.76 percent in 2001, and 1.79 percent in 2007. The real rate of return on net worth was much higher because of the high debt levels of U.S households—7.33 percent in 1989, 5.32 percent in 2001, and 6.09 percent in 2007 (see Chapter 2 for a discussion of household debt).

4. This projection is based on the assumption that the worker continues to work for the same employer (the so-called on-going concern assumption). See Chapter 4 for more discussion.

5. DCEMPW is defined in exactly analogous fashion to DCEMP except that in Equation (4.10), the term EMPAMT is replaced by EMPLAMT, or the dollar amount of the *employee* contribution to the DC plan, which is assumed to remain fixed in real terms over time; and in Equation (4.11), the term EMPPER is replaced by EMPLPER, which is the employee contribution to the DC plan as a percent of earnings, which is assumed to be fixed over time. See Chapter 4 for more details.

6. I also use an alternative method to project future retirement income. This method, referred to as Method A, is a straightforward projection of net worth (NW, including DC, DCEMP, and DCEMPW) based on historical changes in the net worth of age group 47–64. Using data from the SCF for age group 47–64 over the period 1989–2007, I calculate an annual growth rate of 2.59 percent for real net worth.

7. I use the official U.S. poverty thresholds for this analysis and assume that the family's marital status remains unchanged over time, and that at time of retirement there are no children living with the parents.

8. Though it is possible to project wages and salaries at retirement on the basis of the estimated human capital earnings functions (see Appendix B in Chapter 4 for details), it is not easy to project other forms of income, such as property income, government transfer income other than Social Security benefits, and miscellaneous income. As a result, I use the historical growth in income as the basis for projecting household income at retirement.

9. Scholz and Seshadri (2009), for example, used two denominators for their replacement rate calculations: the average of lifetime income up to the time of retirement and income averaged over the top five earnings years. They computed a much lower average replacement rate on the basis of the latter standard: 0.57 versus 0.68. My standard is closer to income averaged over the top five earnings years than to average lifetime income.

10. These results might appear to be inconsistent with an overall gain of 39 percent in mean retirement income for the whole age group 47–64. However, the paradox is explained by the fact that the share of households with a college degree also climbed sharply over the period (from 17 to 37 percent).

11. The estimated share of total expected retirement income from net worth is higher than most other estimates because I include the expected annuitized value from net worth in my definition of retirement income rather than expected future property income. As a result, the shares of Social Security and DB pensions in expected retirement income are correspondingly lower than in most other estimates.

12. Further details are provided in Appendix Table D.4. Of the 51.8 percent share of nonpension wealth in total retirement income in 2007, 40.6 percent will come from the current value of nonpension wealth and 11.3 percent will come from future gains on nonpension wealth. Likewise, of the 18.3 percent share of DCTOT in total retirement income, a little under half of this, 8.7 percent, is projected to come from current holdings in DC plans; another 2.5 percentage points from DCEMP, or expected future contributions into the plans from the employer; 1.4 percentage points from DCEMPW, or expected future contributions into the plans by the employee; and finally, 5.7 percentage points from expected future capital gains on all three components.

13. It is also of interest to compare estimates of mean retirement income using the standard method discussed in the text with the alternative method (Method A) discussed in Note 6. The two estimates were almost identical for 1989 and very close in the other two years (a 4 percent difference in 2001 and 2007). These results suggest that households in this age group engaged in very little net savings (and received relatively little in the form of wealth transfers like inheritances) other than accumulations in DC plans and receiving returns on existing forms of wealth.

14. The contribution made by a component such as pension wealth to the overall change in expected retirement income is defined as the change in the mean value of the component divided by the change in the mean value of expected retirement income. This term shows what share of the gain in expected retirement income is attributable to increases in the value of that component.

15. There is no clear pattern by educational group.
16. It should be noted that the poverty rates reported in Table 7.7 are household poverty rates, not individual (head count) poverty rates.
17. A 75 percent replacement rate is the standard most often used in the relevant literature on the subject. See Chapter 3 for a discussion of this issue. Moreover, it should be noted that the replacement rate computed here is based on the ratio of expected retirement income and projected income during the year before retirement.

8

Conclusions and Policy Recommendations

SUMMARY OF PRINCIPAL FINDINGS

The 1980s and 1990s witnessed the unraveling of the traditional DB pension system in favor of DC pension coverage. The study in this book addresses three key questions. First, have U.S. households in general gained from this transformation? Second, if not, which groups gained and which groups lost out? Third, has the transformation of the pension system lowered or raised overall wealth inequality?

The main finding is that DC plans did very well during the 1980s and 1990s, when the stock market boomed, and that they more than fully compensated for the decline of DB pension plans. The overall value of pension wealth rose sharply over these two decades, and overall pension coverage increased, at least during the 1990s. However, between 2001 and 2007, when the stock market slackened, there was a marked slowdown in the growth of both DC and overall pension wealth, and overall pension coverage dipped slightly. Moreover, when the stock market tanked from 2007 to 2009, there was a sharp projected drop in DC pension wealth. Indeed, from 2001 to 2009, there was virtually no change in average DC pension wealth and in average overall pension wealth.

I begin the study using conventional net worth in order to provide a backdrop to the analysis of retirement wealth. Over the 2001–2007 period, median net worth grew by 19 percent, even faster than during the 1990s (and 1980s). Wealth inequality was also up very slightly from 2001 to 2007. The most notable finding for the 2001–2007 period was the sharply rising debt-to-income ratio, which reached its highest level in almost 25 years at 119 percent in 2007 for all households. The debt-equity ratio also climbed, from 14.3 percent in 2001 to 18.1 percent in 2007. Among the middle three wealth quintiles there was a huge increase in the debt-income ratio, from 100 to 157 percent from 2001 to 2007, and an almost doubling of the debt-equity ratio, from 32 to 61 percent.

I also updated the wealth figures to July 1, 2009, on the basis of changes in housing and stock prices. My projections indicate that while mean wealth (in 2007 dollars) declined by 17 percent from 2007 to 2009, median wealth plunged by 36 percent. The projections also suggest a steep rise in wealth inequality, with the Gini coefficient advancing from 0.834 to 0.865.

The racial disparity in wealth holdings was almost exactly the same in 2007 as in 1983, with a ratio of average net worth holdings of 0.19 and a ratio of median wealth of about 0.07 in both years. In contrast, Hispanic households made progress relative to white (non-Hispanic) households, with the ratio of average net worth holdings rising from 0.016 in 1983 to 0.026 in 2007 (there was little change in the ratio of median wealth). Young households (under the age of 45), after some relative gains from 1983 to 1989, saw their relative wealth position deteriorate over the years 1989 to 2007.

In 2007, 56 percent of male workers (currently employed) under the age of 65 had some type of DC account, 19 percent had some form of DB entitlement, and altogether, 62 percent had some form of pension coverage. Corresponding figures for female workers were only slightly lower than those for men. Pension coverage was lower for workers under age 47 than those aged 47–64: 53 versus 75 percent. Figures for female workers were very similar to those for men.

From 1989 to 2001, overall coverage rose moderately, by 3.2 percentage points for male workers and 3.9 percentage points for females. However, trends were very different for DC and DB coverage. Defined contribution coverage climbed by 13 percentage points for men and 10 percentage points for women, while DB coverage plummeted by 12 and 11 percentage points, respectively. However, from 2001 to 2007, male pension coverage fell by 6.4 percentage points, while female pension coverage increased by 1.7 percentage points. As a result, whereas in 1989 and 2001 there was about a 10 percentage point gap in pension coverage between male and female workers, by 2007 the gap was almost completely eliminated. The loss in pension coverage for men from 2001 to 2007 was almost all from the decline in DB coverage, which, in turn, was likely due to the continuing decline in manufacturing jobs. Gains in coverage for female workers, in contrast, were all in the form of expanded DC plan coverage, which likely reflected the continuing movement of women up the occupational ladder and from part-time to full-time work.

On the household level, there were spectacular gains in the proportion of households covered by DC plans from 1983 to 2001, but the coverage rate stabilized from 2001 to 2007. However, the DB coverage rate plummeted from 1989 to 2001, and though it remained steady from 2001 to 2007, the overall pension coverage rate slipped by 1.4 percentage points from 2001 to 2007, to 64 percent, after rising by 10 percentage points from 1989 to 2001. Due mainly to the stock market boom and rising DC coverage, average DC pension wealth increased spectacularly from 1989 to 2001 (by 80 percent). It continued to increase from 2001 to 2007 but at a much slower pace (only 14 percent). Projections to mid-2009 suggest that DC wealth was eviscerated by the stock market plunge of 2007–2009. The average value of DC plans tumbled by 17 percent from 2007 to the midpoint of 2009. Over the years from 2001 to 2009, mean pension wealth was virtually unchanged. In all, 2001–2009 was truly a "lost decade." The results also illuminate the fact that DC pension wealth does well only when the stock market performs spectacularly.

While there were marked improvements in both mean and median net worth from 1983 to 2007, mean private accumulations (the sum of net worth and DB pension wealth) grew slower than mean net worth, as did median private accumulations in comparison to median net worth. This pattern also held for middle-aged and elderly households.

Mean Social Security wealth grew by 46 percent from 1989 to 2001 among all households, but there was virtually no change from 2001 to 2007. As a result, mean and median retirement wealth surged from 1989 to 2001 (by 59 and 46 percent, respectively, for all households) but mean retirement wealth grew very slowly from 2001 to 2007 and median retirement wealth fell slightly in absolute terms. Both mean and median augmented wealth (the sum of net worth and retirement wealth, the most comprehensive measure of retirement resources) advanced strongly from 1989 to 2001 (39 and 23 percent gains, respectively). However, the growth in both mean and median augmented wealth dissipated from 2001 to 2007. Indeed, median augmented wealth advanced by only 2 percent among middle-aged households and the elderly.

Clearly, by the decade of the 2000s, the DC pension system was not providing the boost to household well-being that it had in the 1990s.

There was also a marked slowdown in the growth of mean expected retirement income for age group 47–64 in the years 2001–2007 in comparison to the period 1989–2001, even before the financial meltdown of 2007–2009. Whereas mean expected retirement income climbed 40 percent during the earlier period, it advanced by only 8 percent in the later one. This result is consistent with the finding of a pronounced decline in the growth of augmented wealth between the 1990s and the 2001–2007 period. These households also experienced a substantial reduction in their expected poverty rate at retirement, from 15 percent in 1989 to 10 percent in 2001, but there was no further decline in 2001–2007. The percentage of households with replacement rates of 75 or more percent of their projected income at age 64 rose somewhat more in the later period than the earlier one (because preretirement income slowed). Still, in 2007, less than half of households could meet this replacement rate criterion.

Because of the switchover from lower-inequality DB plans to higher-inequality DC plans, pension wealth inequality among pension holders rose from 1989 to 2007. The Gini coefficient was up by 0.020 points among all households, 0.018 points among young households, 0.039 points among middle-aged ones, and 0.036 among the elderly.

The addition of DB pension wealth to net worth to obtain private accumulations reduces measured wealth inequality. In 2007, the Gini coefficient for net worth among all households was 0.834 while that for PA was 0.805, for a 0.029 difference. This difference is due to the smaller level of inequality in DB pensions than in net worth. However, the inequality-reducing effect of DB pensions declined from 0.039 in 1989 to 0.029 in 2007. This change was largely due to the declining share of DB wealth in total private accumulations. This effect on inequality is most notable among middle-aged households, the group that was most subject to the transition of the pension system. The difference in the Gini coefficients of net worth and private accumulations dwindled from 0.073 in 1983 to 0.036 in 2007.

When we next include Social Security wealth in retirement wealth, we find that the addition of retirement wealth also lowers wealth inequality. Adding retirement wealth to net worth lowered the Gini coefficient for 2007 from 0.834 to 0.684. Most of the equalizing effect came from adding in Social Security wealth. However, the equalizing effect of retirement wealth, like that of DB pension wealth, also fell off from 1989 to 2007. The addition of retirement wealth to net worth reduced the overall Gini coefficient in 1989 by 0.169 but by only 0.150 in 2007. Among middle-aged households, the difference in the Gini coefficient between net worth and augmented wealth fell off from 0.187 in 1983 to 0.145 in 2007.

As might be expected, younger households suffered the most damage from the transition from the DB to the DC system in terms of pension wealth. Among households aged 46 and under, DC pension coverage dropped by 4 percentage points from 2001 to 2007 and overall pension coverage dipped by 6 percentage points. Average DC wealth declined by 7 percent from 2001 to 2007, and overall pension wealth was up by only 4 percent over this period, compared to a 56 percent rise in the 1990s. This marked slowdown in pension wealth growth bodes ill for the future retirement security of this generation.

Moreover, among young households, mean net worth and mean private accumulations grew very slowly from 2001 to 2007, and median net worth and median private accumulations actually declined in absolute terms during both the 1990s and the 2000s. Mean augmented wealth was largely unchanged over these years, and median augmented wealth fell by 6 percent.

Young households were particularly vulnerable to the stock market crisis in 2007–2009. From 2001 to 2009, their mean net worth plummeted by 21 percent, and their median net worth by (an incredible) 78 percent. Their pension wealth, retirement wealth, and augmented wealth were all down over these years. Starting in 2007, young households, who had already slipped in terms of net worth and augmented wealth during the early and mid-2000s before the financial meltdown, got hammered by the stock market crash of the late 2000s.

Middle-aged households also experienced deleterious effects from the transformation of the pension system, though many were still protected under the older DB system. After rising 34 percentage points from 1989 to 2001, DC coverage barely moved in the 2000s, and the overall pension coverage rate, after advancing by 8 percentage points in the 1990s, declined by 2 percentage points in the 2000s. Mean DC pension wealth, after exploding in the 1990s (by 76 percent), grew much more slowly in the 2000s (only 6 percent).

The elderly were by and large fully protected from the transition of the pension system. In particular, those with DB pensions were sheltered because of "grandfather" provisions and pension legacies. Their DC accumulations also experienced strong growth during the 1990s. As a result, their overall pension coverage rate advanced in both the 1990s and the 2000s. However, gains in mean pension wealth also slowed down from 79 percent in the 1990s to a still respectable 16 percent in the 2000s.

In 2007, there was a 12 percentage point gap in pension coverage between black and (non-Hispanic) white male workers and a huge 30 percentage point gap between Hispanic and (non-Hispanic) white male workers. Racial and ethnic differences in pension coverage were very similar for female workers as well. The racial and ethnic gap in pension coverage increased from 1989 to 2007. On the household level, there were also large gaps in pension coverage, pension wealth, retirement wealth, and augmented wealth between minorities and (non-Hispanic) whites in 2007. However, minorities made strong relative gains on whites in terms of Social Security wealth, retirement wealth, net worth, and augmented wealth from 1989 to 2007, particularly from 2001 to 2007. Among age group 47–55, the ratio of mean augmented wealth advanced by 10 percentage points from 2001 to 2007 and that of median augmented wealth by 16 percentage points.

The ratio of expected retirement income between minorities and whites also climbed, from 0.37 in 1989 to 0.43 in 2007. The convergence was due largely to the growth in expected Social Security benefits among minorities, which outstripped that among whites. It is likely that the relative gains in Social Security wealth among minorities are due to three factors: 1) some convergence in labor earnings between minorities and whites, particularly during the 1990s; 2) more continuous work histories for minority workers over time; and 3) a reduction in the life expectancy gap between minorities and whites.

Minorities also made dramatic inroads in reducing their expected poverty rate at retirement, from 48 percent in 1989 to 14 percent in 2007. Still, whites had a much lower expected poverty rate in 2007 than minorities, 5 versus 14 percent. Moreover, minorities saw slightly greater increases in the share of households with a replacement rate of 75 percent or more from 1989 to 2007. However, minorities still had a lower proportion who met this replacement standard in 2007—42 versus 54 percent.

There was also a substantial gap in retirement wealth and augmented wealth between single females and married couples in 2007. However, similar to the experience of minorities relative to whites, single females generally made modest gains on married couples between 1989 and 2007 in terms of pension, retirement, and augmented wealth. However, despite this, the ratio of expected retirement income between the two groups dropped from 0.35 in 1989 to 0.28 in 2007.

In 2007, only 22 percent of male workers without a high school degree had some form of pension coverage, compared to 51 percent of those with a high school degree, 62 percent of those with some college, and 79 percent of college graduates. The gap in pension coverage between college graduates and the other educational groups widened substantially from 1989 to 2007. The reason is not that pension coverage grew strongly among college graduates but rather that it dropped among the other educational groups. Here, too, results are similar for female workers.

Households with less educational attainment had substantially less retirement wealth and augmented wealth in 2007 than those with more education. Moreover, they generally fell further behind college graduates over the years from 1989 to 2007 in terms of pension wealth, retirement wealth, and augmented wealth. Indeed, retirement wealth and augmented wealth splayed out over time, as college graduates pulled ahead of the other educational groups. With regard to pension wealth, the decline in DB plans was particularly detrimental to the less educated, since DB coverage had been a bulwark of retirement security among blue-collar workers up through the 1980s.

Less-educated households did not fare well at all with regard to expected retirement income. The three lowest educational groups aged 47–64 all experienced absolute declines in this dimension from 1989 to 2007, and the only group showing positive gains was college graduates. Likewise, the share of households meeting a projected 75 percent or better income replacement rate at retirement was much higher for college graduates in 2007, 61 percent, than for the other schooling groups, between 35 and 46 percent. The expected poverty rate at retirement was likewise much higher for the least educated group, 28 percent in 2007, compared to the more educated ones. In contrast, households with a high school degree and those with some college had by far the lowest expected poverty rates in 1989, 1.6 and 0.4 percent, respectively, because of their high level of DB coverage.

Pension coverage was also much higher among the top earnings quintile than the bottom—94 versus 40 percent for male workers in 2007 and 86 versus 46 percent among female workers. However, among male employees in 1989, overall pension coverage rates were over 90 percent among the top four earnings quintiles. This was attributable to the concentration of DB plans in the middle of the earnings distribution. During the 1980s, the DB pension system shored up the middle class. However, with the decline of the DB system, a growing gap in pension coverage emerged between the top earnings quintile and the bottom three. Expected retirement income varied directly with (household) income quintile, and the gaps were quite large. The ratio of expected retirement income of the top to the bottom quintile was 14 in 2007. However, gains in expected retirement income had a U-shaped pattern, with the strongest gains at the bottom quintile and the second strongest at the top quintile.

Social Security was a much more important source of expected retirement income among the lower-income groups—minorities, single females, the less educated, and the lower income quintiles—than among higher-income groups – whites, married couples, college graduates, and the top income quintile. It thus serves as an important equalizing factor in retirement adequacy. The share of Social Security in expected retirement income was much higher for the lowest income quintile (42 percent) than the top quintile (8 percent). Moreover, in the lowest income quintile, Social Security wealth accounted for almost half or more of augmented wealth in some years.

Social Security benefits became more important as a source of expected retirement income for the low-income groups indicated above between 1989 and 2007. The faster growth of expected Social Security benefits among minorities largely explains the decline in the gap in expected retirement income between them and whites from 1989 to 2007. Likewise, the higher growth of Social Security benefits for the bottom income quintile was the principal factor accounting for relatively faster growth in their expected retirement income compared to that of the top quintile.

In 2007, Social Security benefits substantially lowered the expected poverty rate among these low-income groups—30 percentage points for nonwhites, 21 percentage points for single females, 41 percentage points for those with less than 12 years of school, and 24 percentage points for high school graduates. Between 1989 and 2007, the reduction in the expected poverty rate from adding in expected Social Security benefits to other sources of retirement income climbed from 15 to 30 percentage points for minorities; 15 to 21 percentage points for single females; 16 to 40 percentage points for the least educated; and from 15 to 24 percentage points for high school graduates.

The unraveling of the DB pension system was particularly hurtful to non–college graduates in terms of expected poverty rates. In 1989, high school graduates and those with some college had the lowest expected poverty rates at retirement. The effect of adding expected DB pension benefits to nonpension wealth on the expected poverty rate declined from 15 to 6 percentage points between 1989 and 2007 for the least educated households, from 13 to 7 percentage points for high school graduates, and from 13 to 5 percentage points for those with some college.

It is thus found that Social Security fulfills its expected role of a solid, broadly shared retirement benefit. In contrast, private pensions still leave large holes, even after showing strong improvements from 1989 to 2001. Indeed, in 2007, many households still had to rely on Social Security as the sole source of their retirement income. One-quarter of all households nearing retirement (aged 47–64) had no private pension plans in 2007. In fact, private pension wealth still remained below the level of other private savings for households nearing retirement. The impact of private pensions on retirement income adequacy is further reduced by the fact that private pension wealth remained very unevenly distributed. Whites, the more highly educated, married couples and single men, and college graduates had substantially larger pension wealth accumulations than their respective counterparts.

Most of the groups with less wealth narrowed the gap in retirement income adequacy somewhat from 1989 to 2007. Most of these gains were due to improvements in Social Security wealth and not private pension wealth. Social Security offers almost universal coverage. Also, Social Security's benefits depend solely on one's earnings record. Thus, as the labor market improved throughout the economic expansion of the 1990s, Social Security wealth also saw large gains (though there was some retrenchment during the 2000s). Moreover, these gains were more equally distributed than income gains or other wealth gains due to the fact that Social Security redistributes wealth to lower lifetime earners. In other words, as many new job opportunities opened up for low-wage workers in the late 1990s, Social Security wealth increased, though some of these gains were modestly reversed in the 2000s.

Still, the data include a sobering note with respect to retirement income adequacy. Assuming that a replacement ratio of 75 percent of preretirement income is a threshold for retirement income adequacy, less than half of all households in age range 47–64 in 2007, 42 percent of minority households, 44 percent of single women, and only 35 percent of the least educated households will likely meet this target.

Young households, in particular, appear to face a daunting future. The share of households under the age of 47 with a DC account already fell by 4 percentage points from 2001 to 2007, before the financial crisis hit, and the share with any pension wealth was down by 6 percentage points. Though mean pension wealth was up by 4 percent over these years, mean retirement wealth fell by 0.5 percent and median retirement wealth by 4 percent. Mean net worth and mean augmented wealth were both up slightly but median net worth tumbled by 10 percent and median augmented wealth dropped by 6 percent.

The "Great Recession" of 2007–2009 hit this group particularly hard, with mean net worth plummeting by 23 percent, mean augmented wealth by 13 percent, median net worth by another (incredible) 75 percent, and median augmented wealth by another 12 percent. By 2009 young households, according to my projections, had likely slipped way behind where they were in 2001. Though the fortunes of young households may be reversed to some degree when the stock market rebounds (as it basically has partially as of November 2010, when I am writing this chapter) and housing prices recover (which may take much longer), it may take a decade or more for this group to fully recover the 2001 levels of their pension wealth, net worth, and augmented wealth.

POLICY RECOMMENDATIONS

Against this backdrop, how do we think about the most effective policies to recommend? We have already seen that even in 2007, before the financial meltdown, replacement rates with respect to preretirement income just before retirement were low. Assuming that a replacement rate of 75 percent is a threshold for retirement income adequacy, slightly less than half of all households in age range 47–64, 42 percent of minority households, 44 percent of single women, and only 35 percent of the least educated households will likely meet this target.

Much work is still left to do for public policy. First and foremost, retirement income adequacy cannot depend solely on Social Security, despite the fact that it is an important source of retirement income and of gains in retirement wealth for vulnerable groups. In fact, in 2007 Social Security by itself accounted for only 17 percent of projected retirement income, on average, among age group 47–64. Nonpension wealth picked up another 52 percent on average, though, as we saw in Chapters 2 and 4, it is very unequally distributed.

Pension wealth accounted for the remaining 31 percent on average, though it also, as we saw in Chapter 4, is quite unequally distributed, as are its increases over time. In fact, in 2007, only 45 percent of households (and 70 percent of pension holders) in age range 47–64 had pension wealth worth $100,000 or more (including DB wealth). A $100,000 balance would generate only about $700 in retirement benefits *per year*. This high degree of inequality in pension wealth is to a large extent a consequence of the transformation of the private pension system from traditional DB plans to the newer DC plans such as 401(k)s. Thus, private pension coverage needs to be broadened, and future improvements in retirement income adequacy will likely depend on ensuring more widely held private pension wealth with higher account balances.

In 2007, as we saw in Chapter 4, only 74 percent of households in age group 47–64 had any pension coverage (including IRAs and Keogh plans). Moreover, of those with pension coverage, many, as I just indicated, had very small pension balances. In fact, the pension coverage rate had already slipped a bit between 2001 and 2007. It is quite likely that the downturn of 2007–2009 caused even further slippage in the pension coverage rate, particularly as financially distressed families cashed out their DC plans. As we saw in Chapter 5, it is also likely the downturn resulted in a large reduction in average pension balances.

As the country moves toward universal health coverage, the next logical step may be universal pension coverage. For current workers, I argue in favor of guaranteed employer pension coverage for all workers in the company. For nonworkers below the age of retirement, I advocate a mixture of Individual Retirement Accounts (IRAs) and Individual Development Accounts (IDAs) supported, and in some cases, subsidized by the federal government. For nonworkers under retirement age without any preexisting DB or DC pension account, one or the other retirement account should be mandated by law.

It is unlikely that the country will be able to return to the "golden age" of DB plans. Moreover, it is not clear that the DB system is all that desirable. There are many problems associated with the DB system, particularly for younger workers. First, DB systems have vesting requirements. As a result, workers who switch jobs frequently (particularly younger ones) often do not work long enough at a company to become vested. Second, correspondingly, DB pensions as they are set up now are not portable, so that those workers who switch jobs before vesting lose the benefits of the time worked at the company. Third, even among workers who become vested but leave a company early in their work careers, the accrued benefits from the DB system are often very small. Indeed, the DB system is designed to encourage long-term employment at a company. Fourth, DB plans are expensive and seem to work best for high-wage, high-productivity employees. As a result, requiring an employer to provide a DB plan may result in substantial dislocations of low-wage and low-skilled workers.

Fifth, DB systems have, historically at least, been subject to many funding problems. By the same token, their funding is often heavily dependent on movements in the stock market. With the collapse of the stock market in 2008 and 2009, many private pension funds and, particularly, state and local government pension funds, found themselves severely underfunded. Though benefits from private pensions are largely guaranteed (at least up to a cap) by the Pension Benefit Guaranty Corporation (PBGC), the PBGC itself is (as of March 2011) in financial trouble, with its reserves severely depleted.

Though it may be possible through legislation to shore up the DB system and to encourage employers to offer such plans (or, at least, to not discontinue existing plans) through a combination of tax incentives and tax credits, it seems to be the case that many of the same advantages of the DB system can be garnered by a DC system. Moreover, the DC system has the advantage of portability and can be extended to low-income workers without creating an employment disincentive for the company (at least to the same degree as a DB plan would).

With regard to the DC pension system, there appear to be four major goals in reforming and improving the present system. The first is to increase participation rates so that pension coverage is universal. The second is to increase the amount contributed into the system. The third is to increase the returns on retirement accounts. The fourth is to stabilize the returns on these accounts and reduce the risk associated with such accounts.

There have been many proposals to accomplish these four objectives. With regard to the first objective, one common proposal is to change the default option at work for enrollment in a retirement plan to "opt out" rather than to "opt in" to the retirement plan. Automatically enrolling employees in a retirement plan unless they opt out is a useful objective. However, one problem with this approach is that a lot of low-income workers simply cannot afford a 401(k) or even an IRA. The same is true for young workers. Changing the default option is therefore likely to have only a modest impact on the take-up rate of these retirement plans for these groups of workers.

Another proposal is that tax incentives need to be changed. Under existing law, high-income employees receive the largest tax subsidy, while low-income ones receive the lowest. As a result, replacing the current tax deduction for retirement plan contributions with a tax credit would still provide everyone with a tax incentive but would shift the benefit down the income ladder. This should presumably increase the savings of low-income workers and increase their take-up rate for an employer-provided retirement plan.

I would, in fact, make the amount of tax credit dependent on family income and would turn the tax credit into a refundable tax credit in the case of low-income families. This would mean that the government would subsidize low-income workers for part of the savings in a retirement account, much like the way an IDA works (see, for example, Sherraden 1991). Moreover, a special tax credit might be provided to young families as well in order to boost their take-up rate of retirement accounts.

Another recommendation is to push for comprehensive retirement coverage, an emphasis at least early on in the Obama administration. Less than half of employees have a retirement plan at work. The so-called universal IRA advanced by Barack Obama during the presidential campaign would help make a retirement account available to all workers (see Mandell et al. [2009] for a discussion of this proposal).

Personally, I would make an even stronger proposal: universal, guaranteed employer pension coverage (much like one would propose for health care). The first step is to make participation universal within a firm, so that all workers are covered. Second, it should *not* be necessary to require employee contributions in order to have funds provided (or matched) by the employer. Instead, employer contributions should be *mandatory*. A certain minimum contribution should be required from each employer (in much the same way as minimum standards should be drawn up for an employer-provided health policy). Employee contributions, in turn, should be *voluntary*. Third, the provisions should be universal within a firm. The plans should be the same for rank-and-file workers as for top management.

In addition, nonworkers under the age of retirement would be required to have an IRA unless they have a preexisting DB or DC plan from earlier employment. In the case of low-income and young households, the contribution to the IRA should be subsidized by the federal government in much the same way as an IDA. This subsidy would take the form of a refundable tax credit like the Earned Income Tax Credit. Low-income households would receive a tax credit (or actual payment from the government) as a percentage of their contribution to the IRA, where the credit would vary inversely to household income (starting as high as 100 percent for a household with no income). A minimum contribution would also be required—perhaps $1,000 per year in the initial year, indexed for inflation over time.

With regard to the second objective, increasing balances in retirement accounts, it is first of note that a 2009 *New York Times* editorial reports evidence from Fidelity Investments that from the first quarter of 2008 through the first quarter of 2009 more employees reduced their contributions to 401(k) plans than increased them. By the second quarter, employees were still contributing less of their pay than they did in

2008. Moreover, some employers cut their 401(k) matching contributions as well. Indeed, some recent reports indicate that many large companies were suspending their matches entirely for employee retirement accounts.[1]

With this in mind, I would propose that employers be required to contribute a minimum percentage to the retirement accounts of the workers in their employ. I favor a minimum of 3 percent of worker pay. Moreover, a minimum dollar amount should be stipulated by law, say, $1,000 in the initial year and indexed for inflation over time. This would help insure adequate accumulations in retirement accounts among low-wage workers. As noted above, a similar minimum pay-in should be required for nonworkers into their IRAs.

Another proposal is that preretirement payouts from retirement accounts should be discouraged (I would even say prohibited), except in cases of real hardship like disability. This proposal is important in light of the Great Recession of 2007–2009, during which many financially distressed families "cashed out" a large part or even all of their retirement accounts. One method of implementing this proposal would be to require that employees roll over a 401(k) or similar retirement account into a new account when they change jobs. I would also add that loans against retirement accounts like 401(k)s should be severely limited, since these also reduce the payout from these plans at the time of retirement.

The third and fourth objectives enumerated above are to increase the returns on retirement accounts and to reduce the risk associated with such accounts. These objectives are particularly germane in light of the 2007–2009 years, when DC plans were devastated by the stock market crash. In light of the recent financial crisis, should we think about limiting the stock market exposure of DC plans? Should we mandate a guaranteed rate of return on pension assets?

In order to avoid wide variations in payouts from retirement plans at the time of retirement, one possibility would be to develop a savings plan in which the federal government shared the risk. This could be implemented by providing a guarantee that returns would not fall below a certain level. A similar proposal has been advanced by Ghirladucci (2007, 2008), which she calls a Guaranteed Retirement Account. In her proposal, participation in the program is mandatory except for workers participating in an equivalent or better employer DB plan. Contributions are set equal to 5 percent of earnings, split equally by employer and employee. Participants are guaranteed a minimum 3 percent annual rate of return adjusted for inflation. The guarantee is provided by the federal government.[2]

I support such an approach only in part. I think that a fixed rate of return should be mandated (and guaranteed) for only a fixed amount (or percentage) of pension assets. To achieve this, one possibility is to offer federal bonds with fixed yields. Such bonds actually already exist as Treasury Inflation-Protected Securities, though the yields have historically been quite low. Another possibility is to have the federal government or company make up the difference between the actual yield on a retirement account like a 401(k) and some preset minimum. This plan, however, would require some further refinement. However, we should give individuals the freedom for speculation and risk-taking on the remaining part of their pension accounts if they so desire. This would allow individuals to invest part of their pension accounts in equities, for example, where, at least historically, rates of returns have been higher than on bonds and other financial securities.

Though this book is about the pension system and not Social Security, it might be helpful to say a few words about Social Security as well. I think that in general the current Social Security system should be left largely intact. For example, the periodic discussions over benefit cuts for middle-class families as part of Social Security privatization seem to be misplaced, since it would hurt middle-class families, for whom private pensions have not filled the supplemental income role that they were always intended to play. Indeed, this should give pause to those who want to carve up Social Security through privatization, since Social Security has proven to be superior to private retirement benefits in many ways. It is universal and it has risen faster than other forms of retirement savings for those households who need additional retirement benefits the most. It also has a pronounced equalizing effect on the distribution of (augmented) wealth. As a result, it would be most desirable to protect Social Security as much as possible and fill the holes in the retirement savings system outside of Social Security, so that a decent standard of living in retirement as a reward for a life of hard work becomes a reality for America's middle class and working poor.

Though no major overhaul of the Social Security system is needed, there may be small fixes required to keep the system fiscally in balance. I have three recommendations. First, as life expectancy rises, split the difference with regard to the normal retirement age. In particular, for each 12-month rise in life expectancy, raise the normal retirement age for that birth cohort by some fixed fraction (perhaps one-third).[3] A similar proposal is voiced by Turner (2009) in the case of DB pension plans. Second, gradually raise the earnings cap (without a corresponding increase in Social Security benefits at the top). Third, make the Social Security tax more progressive (currently it is a regressive tax).

Last, because large improvements in retirement income adequacy resulted primarily from more Social Security wealth as a result of a tight labor market in the late 1990s, and because these gains may have been largely dissipated by the Great Recession and the high unemployment rate of this period, public policy should also focus on increasing employment and lowering unemployment as a way not only to lift current living standards, but also the living standards of future retirees.

Notes

1. See, for example, Munnell and Quinby (2010), who report that in 2008 and 2009, over 200 employers suspended their 401(k) matches, affecting 5 percent of active 401(k) participants.
2. A critique of a guaranteed rate of return plan is provided in Munnell et al. (2009).
3. One proposal before Congress as of November 2010 is to gradually raise the age of full Social Security benefits from the current 67 to 69.

Appendix A
Sources and Methods Used for the
Survey of Consumer Finances Data

CHOICE OF WEIGHTS

In some years, the SCF supplied alternative sets of weights. For the 1983 SCF, I use the "Full Sample 1983 Composite Weights" because this set of weights provides the closest correspondence between the national balance sheet totals derived from the sample and those in the Federal Reserve Board Flow of Funds. For the same reason, results for the 1989 SCF are based on the average of SRC-Design-S1 series (X40131 in the database itself) and the SRC design-based weights (X40125). Results for the 2001 and 2007 SCF rely on the Designed-Base Weights (X42001)—partially design-based weights that are constructed on the basis of original selection probabilities and frame information and adjusted for nonresponse and that account for the systematic deviation from the CPS estimates of homeownership rates by racial and ethnic groups.

ALIGNMENT WITH THE FLOW OF FUNDS DATA

The Federal Reserve Board imputes information for missing items in the SCF. However, despite this procedure, there still remain discrepancies for several assets between the total balance sheet value computed from the survey sample and the Flow of Funds data. Because of this, the results presented in Table A.1 are based on my adjustments to the original asset and liability values in the surveys. This takes the form of the alignment of asset and liability totals from the survey data to the corresponding national balance sheet totals. In most cases, this entails a proportional adjustment of reported values of balance sheet items in the survey data (see Wolff [1987a, 1994, 1996, 1998] for details). The adjustment factors by asset type and year are as follows:

No adjustments were made to other asset and debt components, or to the 2001 or 2007 SCF.

It should be noted that the alignment has very little effect on the measurement of wealth inequality—both the Gini coefficient and the quantile shares.

Table A.1 Asset Adjustment Factors by Asset Type and Year

	1983 SCF	1989 SCF
Checking accounts	1.68	
Savings and time deposits	1.50	
All deposits		1.37
Financial securities	1.20	
Stocks and mutual funds	1.06	
Trusts		1.66
Stocks and bonds		
Nonmortgage debt	1.16	

NOTE: Blanks = not applicable.

However, it is important to make these adjustments when comparing changes in mean wealth, both overall and by asset type.

CHOICE OF PRICE INDEX

I use the standard price deflator, the CPI-U, which the BLS has been computing since 1947, to deflate wealth values. The CPI-U has been criticized for overstating the rate of inflation. As a result, the BLS also provides an alternative consumer price series called the CPI-U-RS (the RS stands for research series). The CPI-U-RS series makes quality adjustments for housing units and consumer durables such as automobiles and personal computers and employs a geometric mean formula to account for consumer substitution within CPI item categories. As a result, the CPI-U-RS deflator is not subject to the same criticisms as the CPI-U series. Indeed, the CPS data are now normally deflated to constant dollars by the U.S. Census Bureau using the CPI-U-RS price index.

While the CPI-U-RS deflator incorporates quality and other adjustments, the adjustments are made only from 1978 to the present. The CPI-U index is used for years prior to 1978. The CPI-U-RS shows a much slower rate of inflation after 1973 than the CPI-U: 288 versus 238 percent. If we use the CPI-U-RS deflator, then constant dollar median family income would show a 22 percent growth between 1973 and 2000, in comparison to the 6 percent growth rate on the basis of the CPI-U deflator.

While the use of the CPI-U-RS will show a higher growth in real incomes (and wealth) since 1978, it is not clear that the degree of bias in the CPI has risen in recent years. If similar adjustments were made on the pre-1978 price data, it is possible that the inflation rate over the 1947–1978 period would be adjusted downward by a similar amount as the post-1978 inflation rate. Since my aggregate time-series data on wealth began in 1922 and I have made calculations of household wealth trends on the basis of microdata beginning in 1962, I have elected to use the CPI-U series to convert nominal values to real dollars to be consistent with my earlier work on the subject, since the CPI-U series is the only consumer price series that runs from 1922 to the present (see, for example, Wolff [1987a, 1994, 2002a]).

Appendix B
Estimation of Pension and Social Security Wealth

I generally follow the methodology laid out in the 1983 SCF codebook. However, even though estimates of both pension and Social Security wealth are provided in the 1983 SCF, I reestimate the values of both to be consistent with later years. The computations of retirement wealth use the following steps:

DEFINED BENEFIT PENSION WEALTH

Defined benefit pension wealth consists of two main components.[1]

1) The present value of DB pensions from past jobs: The sum of the present value of past DB job pensions for head and spouse.

2) The present value of DB pensions from current jobs: The sum of the present value of current job nonthrift benefits for head and spouse. Expectations data are used for calculations.

The procedure is as follows. Pension coverage is first ascertained for current jobs. There are five possible categories:

1) covered and vested, anticipates benefits;

2) covered but not vested yet, anticipates benefits;

3) covered but not vested yet, does not anticipate benefits;

4) not covered but anticipates will be (the age when expected to be covered is ascertained); and

5) not covered, never will be.

For those who are covered by a pension plan or expect coverage, the person is asked how many distinct pension plans he or she is covered by. For each plan, the age at which the pension benefits are expected to be given is then asked.

The actual expected annual retirement benefit is then determined by the following steps. First, the age at which the respondent will be vested in each plan is determined. Second, the age at which the respondent could retire with full benefits is ascertained. Third, the respondent was asked the nature of the formula used to determine the retirement benefits. There are six possibilities:

1) retirement formula based on age,

2) retirement formula based on years of service,

3) retirement formula based on meeting both age and years of service criteria,

4) retirement formula based on the sum or age and years of service,

5) retirement formula based on meeting either age or years of service criteria, and

6) other combinations or formulas.

Fourth, the age at which the respondent could retire with some benefits was asked. The same six choices of the formula used were then given. Fifth, the age at which the respondent expected benefits to start was then asked.

Sixth, the expected retirement benefit was computed depending on the type of formula. This consists of three possibilities:

1) The annual pay in the final year of the job was computed. This variable, used in pension benefit calculations, is computed by projecting current pay to the year respondents say they will leave the job or retire. This projection is based on human capital earnings equations detailed below and a real discount rate of 2.0 percent. Wage growth is based on the historical change in the Bureau of Labor Statistics' mean hourly wages series for nonsupervisory workers for the period and of hours worked per week from 1979 to 2007.[2]

2) In some cases, the respondent reported expected retirement benefits. This variable is the expected dollar retirement benefits in the first year of eligibility as answered by the respondent. For some observations the dollar amount was reported directly, but for others it was computed by multiplying reported benefits as a percentage times the calculated projected final wage. The variable is given as an annual amount except when a lump sum is expected (in which case the lump sum amount is given).

3) In some cases, the respondent reported expected retirement benefits as a percentage of final pay. This variable is the expected retirement benefits in the first year of eligibility as answered by the respondent, expressed as a percentage of their projected wages in their final year of work. For some observations the percentage was reported directly, but for others it was computed by dividing the reported dollar benefit by the calculated projected final wage.

Seventh, on the basis of the responses above, the present value of pension benefits from each current and past plan applicable to both head and spouse was then computed. This variable is measured assuming an annual (or lump sum) pension benefit as given above, starting in the year of first benefits. Benefits for that and each succeeding year are adjusted for the probability of death and are discounted back to the survey year. For this, I have used mortality rates by age, gender, and race in the computation of the present value of both pensions and Social Security wealth.[3] These are capped at 109 years. Spousal survival benefits are assumed to be opted for 75 percent of the time and are randomly assigned when appropriate. Spousal survival benefits are also adjusted for death probabilities. Benefits are discounted at a real discount rate of 2 percent.

Eighth, pension wealth was also computed for those individuals currently receiving pension benefits from past jobs. This was based on the following responses: number of years receiving benefits, and amount of pension benefit pay received in the year preceding the survey year. For pensions already being received, the nominal value of the pension is assumed to be fixed, and is indexed to the year it started by the actual price changes observed, as measured by the CPI. The present value of pension benefits from each job is then measured, assuming an annual pension benefit from the survey year onward. Benefits for that and each succeeding year (adjusted for probability of survival) are discounted back to the survey year. As before, I have used mortality rates by age, gender, and race in the computation of the present value of both pensions and Social Security wealth. These are capped at 109 years. Spousal survival benefits are assumed to be opted for 75 percent of the time and are randomly assigned when appropriate. Spouse mortality tables are also used, and benefits are discounted at a real discount rate of 2 percent.

SOCIAL SECURITY WEALTH

The present value of Social Security benefits is defined as the sum of the present value of Social Security benefits for head and spouse. Social Security formulae and current receipts are used for calculations.

Among current Social Security benefit recipients, the steps are as follows. First, the respondent was asked which kind of Social Security benefit he or she received. (The possibilities are retirement, disability, both retirement and disability, and other.) Second, the respondent was asked the number of years he or she had received Social Security benefits. Third, both head and spouse were asked the amount received in the survey year.

Among future recipients, the steps are as follows. First, both head and spouse were asked to report the age at which they expected to receive Social Security benefits (zero if he or she does not expect benefits). Second, the number of years until the start of Social Security benefits was determined. Third, the respondent was asked the total number of years he or she had spent working on jobs covered by Social Security to the current date. If this was not answered, then an estimate of Social Security coverage was used, summing over current and three possible past jobs. Fourth, an estimate of future years on Social Security jobs was computed from retirement years indicated by head and spouse.

Fifth, data on the number of years on Social Security jobs, wage rates for each known job, estimates of retirement dates, and dates of starting benefits were used as inputs to Social Security formulae to compute benefits. Sixth, estimates of Social Security benefits were provided. A calculated value was based on current job wage. All persons were assumed to work continuously until their stated age of full-time retirement, and then part-time until their stated age of final retirement. All persons were assumed to retire no later than 72, or age plus one if currently over 72. Persons not currently working and over 50 were assumed not to work again. Wages were calculated by projecting current wages by the same method used to calculate final wages. This projection is based on human capital earnings equations detailed in the following section and a real discount rate of 2.0 percent. Wage growth is based on the historical change in the Bureau of Labor Statistics' mean hourly wage series for non-supervisory workers for the period and of hours worked per week from 1979 to 2007. Part-time years (if currently working full time) were assigned wages equal to one-half the projected full-time wages or the maximum amount for full benefit receipt allowed by Social Security, whichever was smaller.

Seventh, the Social Security AIME used as the basis for calculating the Social Security benefit base was computed. The variable is the average covered Social Security earnings per month (including zero) for all years from 1951 or age 22–60 (whichever is later). These are indexed by a Social Security wage index to the year the respondent is 60. Years after 60 can be substituted at nominal value. The five lowest years are dropped before an average AIME is computed. These procedures are mimicked using the SCF data on job earnings and future retirement plans to estimate an AIME value. Past and current job wages are projected back (and forward) to estimate earnings for each known year of work. As before, these projections are based on human capital earnings equations detailed below and a real discount rate of 2.0 percent. Wage changes are based on the historical change in the Bureau of Labor Statistics' mean hourly wages series for nonsupervisory workers for the period and of hours worked per week from 1979 to 2007. Other years of unknown jobs are filled in with terms from the closest known job to fill in the total number of Social Security covered years. Wages are then capped at the actual or projected Social Security maximum and minimum coverage amounts. The AIME was then computed using actual or projected Social Security wage indices. The variable is currently estimated for all persons projected to have future Social Security benefits.

Eighth, the Social Security Primary Insurance Amount (PIA) on an annual basis is the basis of the calculation of Social Security benefits. It is computed from the AIME. In 1982 the monthly PIA was computed as 90 percent of the first $254 of AIME plus 32 percent of the next $1,274 plus 15 percent of the amount above that. Calculations here take into account legislatively planned changes in this formula. The PIA is currently computed for all nonreceivers projected to have future Social Security benefits.

Ninth, the present value of Social Security benefits is then determined assuming an annual benefit as given by the PIA estimate and starting in the year of first benefits (or the survey year). Benefits for that and each succeeding year (adjusted for probability of receipt) are discounted back to the survey year. As before, I have used mortality rates by age, gender, and race in the computation of the present value of Social Security wealth; these are capped at 109 years. Benefits are discounted at a real discount rate of 2 percent.

Tenth, spousal benefits are also assumed at 50 percent of the primary benefit if a spouse is present. However, this variable will be zero if no spousal benefits are expected (such as when the individual's own benefits are larger than his or her spousal benefits). The age at which spousal benefits begin is estimated. Spouse mortality tables are also used for these calculations. The age at which widow's benefits first could be drawn is also estimated. It is an estimate of the age at which the individual could start to receive Social Security widow's benefits upon the death of the spouse. This variable will be zero if widow's benefits could never be drawn. An adjustment is also made if it appeared that the recipient's benefits had been reduced because of work. Benefits are discounted at a real discount rate of 2 percent.

HUMAN CAPITAL EARNINGS EQUATIONS

The regression equations used to compute future and past earnings are as follows:

Human capital earnings functions are estimated by gender, race, and schooling level. In particular, the sample is divided into 16 groups by the following characteristics: white and Asian versus African American and Hispanic; male and female; and less than 12 years of schooling, 12 years of schooling,

13–15 years of schooling, and 16 or more years. For each group, an earnings equation is estimated as follows:

$$\ln(E_i)=b_0+b_1 \ln(H_i)+b_2 X_i+b_3 X_i^2+b_4 SE_i+\Sigma_j b_j OCCUP_{ij}+b_{10} MAR_i+b_{11} AS_I+\varepsilon_i,$$

where ln is the natural logarithm; E_i is the current earnings of individual i; H_i is annual hours worked in the current year; X_i is years of experience at current age (estimated as age minus years of schooling minus 5); SE_i is a dummy variable indicating whether the person is self-employed or working for someone else; $OCCUP$ is a set of five dummy variables indicating occupation of employment: 1) professional and managerial; 2) technical, sales, or administrative support; 3) service; 4) craft; and 5) other blue-collar, with farming the omitted category; MAR is a dummy variable indicating whether the person is married or not married; AS is a dummy variable indicating whether the person is Asian (used only for regressions on the first racial category); and ε is a stochastic error term. Future earnings are projected on the basis of the regression coefficients.[4]

QUESTIONS ON WORK HISTORY

Following is a sample of questions on work history drawn from the 1989 SCF codebook that is used to calculate the earnings profile of both head and spouse and to calculate the AIME for each:

1) Including any periods of self-employment, the military, and your current job, since you were 18, how many years have you worked full-time for all or most of the year?

2) Not counting your current job, have you ever had a full-time job that lasted for three years or more?

3) I want to know about the longest such job you had. Did you work for someone else, were you self-employed, or what?

4) When did you start working at that job?

5) When did you stop working at that job?

6) Since you were 18, have there been years when you only worked part-time for all or most of the year?

7) About how many years in total did you work part time for all or most of the year?

8) Thinking now of the future, when do you expect to stop working full time?

9)   Do you expect to work part time after that?

10)   When do you expect to stop working altogether?

QUESTIONS ON DEFINED CONTRIBUTION PLANS

1)   Does your employer make contributions to this [DC] plan? Does the business make contributions to this plan?

2)   What percentage of pay or amount of money per month or year does your employer currently contribute?

Appendix Notes

1. A third though minor component is also provided: pensions from other nonspecified sources.
2. These figures are based on the Bureau of Labor Statistics (BLS) hourly wage series. The source is Table B-47 of the Economic Report, available at http://www .gpoaccess.gov/eop/tables09.html. The BLS wage figures are converted to constant dollars on the basis of the Consumer Price Index for All Urban Consumers (CPI-U). I use the BLS series rather than one of the alternatives to project future wages because it likely corresponds closest to changes in the Social Security wage base over time, due to the cap on Social Security earnings that enter the Social Security benefit formula.
3. The source is U.S. Census Bureau, *Statistical Abstract*, various years and table numbers. I use the mortality tables as of the survey year (or the one nearest to the survey year).
4. This implicitly assumes that deviations from the regression line in the current year are a result of a transitory component to current income only. This procedure follows the conventions of the 1983 SCF codebook.

Table B.1 Percentage of Workers with Pension Coverage by Race, Education, Age, and Gender, 1989, 2001, and 2007

	1989		2001		2007	
	Male	Female	Male	Female	Male	Female
By race[a]						
Aged 46 and under						
Non-Hispanic whites						
All DC accounts	45.3	40.9	60.2	48.4	53.1	52.0
All DB plans	35.4	23.7	18.1	15.1	14.0	12.8
DC and/or DB Plans	64.2	51.5	66.1	55.4	56.9	57.7
(Non-Hispanic) African Americans						
All DC accounts	37.8	33.3	50.8	45.3	47.1	37.9
All DB plans	33.0	37.2	17.2	15.1	15.3	8.6
DC and/or DB plans	56.6	53.6	61.2	53.6	50.7	42.7
Hispanics						
All DC accounts	15.2	13.6	28.4	26.2	29.2	28.6
All DB plans	22.6	23.5	11.7	12.1	6.9	9.1
DC and/or DB plans	34.0	33.2	32.7	34.4	32.1	34.1
Aged 47–64						
Non-Hispanic whites						
All DC accounts	66.4	56.6	69.1	65.2	71.9	67.9
All DB plans	45.1	38.8	40.1	27.2	29.6	22.8
DC and/or DB plans	82.8	71.8	81.4	75.3	79.4	75.3
(Non-Hispanic) African Americans						
All DC accounts	28.8	20.8	47.7	52.4	43.4	50.3
All DB plans	45.0	46.5	46.2	21.7	28.3	25.7
DC and/or DB plans	63.3	52.9	73.9	61.5	59.6	61.1
Hispanics						
All DC accounts	44.6	36.3	48.1	31.0	42.8	35.1
All DB plans	34.5	34.1	24.9	21.2	11.1	10.3
DC and/or DB plans	57.1	57.4	58.5	42.6	49.8	45.3
By educational attainment						
Aged 46 and under						
No high school diploma (or GED)						
All DC accounts	17.6	21.0	21.4	21.4	14.0	14.2
All DB plans	20.3	13.7	6.6	1.6	1.2	0.3
DC and/or DB plans	32.5	32.0	25.8	23.0	15.2	14.5

Table B.1 (continued)

	1989		2001		2007	
	Male	Female	Male	Female	Male	Female
By educational attainment *(cont.)*						
Aged 46 and under *(cont.)*						
High school diploma (or GED)						
All DC accounts	34.7	29.0	48.2	34.6	35.9	34.0
All DB plans	32.4	23.0	15.3	10.7	12.0	10.2
DC and/or DB plans	55.7	44.3	55.4	41.4	40.3	40.5
Some college						
All DC accounts	42.8	37.5	49.7	37.5	51.2	42.9
All DB plans	33.5	25.1	19.5	11.0	11.6	10.2
DC and/or DB plans	61.8	48.4	59.1	43.5	54.9	48.3
College degree						
All DC accounts	53.3	51.9	74.7	63.4	70.3	62.3
All DB plans	39.1	30.5	20.7	22.1	17.6	15.2
DC and/or DB plans	71.7	61.9	78.8	72.6	73.9	68.7
Aged 47–64						
No high school diploma (or GED)						
All DC accounts	41.6	26.6	33.3	18.8	33.9	35.0
All DB plans	38.2	31.3	37.9	14.1	7.9	7.0
DC and/or DB plans	68.3	50.7	60.0	33.0	40.1	39.2
High school diploma (or GED)						
All DC accounts	55.4	44.0	60.6	54.2	55.4	55.7
All DB plans	38.6	35.1	33.1	19.0	26.6	18.7
DC and/or DB plans	73.9	61.7	72.6	66.2	67.0	63.0
Some college						
All DC accounts	63.5	53.3	61.9	67.9	68.5	64.7
All DB plans	46.5	37.0	31.5	21.4	29.7	18.8
DC and/or DB plans	83.5	69.2	72.8	71.6	75.6	70.9
College degree						
All DC accounts	78.0	72.1	78.6	72.4	80.0	74.9
All DB plans	50.3	47.9	45.5	35.2	30.5	28.8
DC and/or DB plans	87.6	85.2	90.2	82.9	86.2	84.1

NOTE: The table includes only current workers aged 64 and under.
[a] Asians and other races are excluded from the table because of their small sample size.
SOURCE: Author's computations from the 1989, 2001, and 2007 SCF.

Table B.2   Percentage of Workers with Pension Coverage by Industry, Occupation, Employment Status, and Age, 1989, 2001, and 2007

	1989		2001		2007	
	Male	Female	Male	Female	Male	Female
By industry of employment[a]						
Aged 46 and under						
Goods-producing industries						
All DC accounts	40.2	37.5	52.0	53.1	38.1	51.9
All DB plans	28.6	25.4	17.4	11.2	7.8	7.0
DC and/or DB plans	55.1	53.3	58.9	56.0	41.2	53.8
Wholesale and retail trade						
All DC accounts	35.4	22.4	45.7	33.3	46.4	27.8
All DB plans	15.8	12.3	7.6	4.9	6.1	3.9
DC and/or DB plans	44.5	29.4	47.8	35.9	47.5	30.0
Nongovernmental services						
All DC accounts	43.9	40.3	62.5	46.2	56.7	50.9
All DB plans	39.9	25.7	17.1	16.0	11.1	11.4
DC and/or DB plans	65.6	52.4	67.7	54.9	59.8	56.7
Public administration						
All DC accounts	41.4	52.0	72.2	53.0	73.8	62.1
All DB plans	76.5	59.6	51.2	45.7	57.9	52.8
DC and/or DB plans	96.2	77.0	93.8	73.9	86.1	88.9
Aged 47–64						
Goods-producing industries						
All DC accounts	58.6	45.7	62.7	54.6	59.8	67.5
All DB plans	46.2	22.7	37.3	25.0	21.7	7.9
DC and/or DB plans	79.6	51.3	78.3	62.5	66.9	70.3
Wholesale and retail trade						
All DC accounts	51.6	45.3	62.5	53.7	66.3	63.9
All DB plans	14.5	21.7	28.6	13.7	15.9	12.1
DC and/or DB plans	60.9	60.2	74.0	59.1	69.4	67.0
Nongovernmental services						
All DC accounts	65.3	53.5	68.4	63.5	72.0	63.5
All DB plans	49.7	43.7	38.9	27.3	30.2	24.5
DC and/or DB plans	82.5	72.8	79.8	74.5	80.2	72.5
Public administration						
All DC accounts	80.7	34.8	82.0	66.4	70.5	73.2
All DB plans	64.3	67.6	74.6	36.5	55.1	57.4
DC and/or DB plans	96.9	70.1	100.0	78.4	89.8	88.7

Table B.2 (continued)

	1989		2001		2007	
	Male	Female	Male	Female	Male	Female
By occupation of employment						
Aged 46 and under						
Professional and managerial						
All DC accounts	56.7	51.7	70.0	56.6	67.7	57.4
All DB plans	40.6	33.9	18.5	21.3	13.7	15.0
DC and/or DB plans	75.0	64.8	74.4	66.6	70.1	63.8
Technical and clerical						
All DC accounts	42.5	37.0	58.7	44.7	53.4	47.4
All DB plans	23.6	23.6	14.4	11.7	11.0	8.4
DC and/or DB plans	55.3	49.4	62.7	50.5	56.0	52.1
Service workers						
All DC accounts	30.9	19.1	35.2	20.7	38.4	21.8
All DB plans	43.2	13.3	22.5	7.2	26.5	9.4
DC and/or DB plans	63.8	28.0	48.2	25.5	47.9	27.3
Craft, operative, and agricultural						
All DC accounts	30.5	24.9	46.3	42.2	35.7	31.5
All DB plans	31.2	24.7	16.4	8.4	8.7	9.8
DC and/or DB plans	50.0	41.0	53.6	46.9	38.8	38.2
Aged 47–64						
Professional and managerial						
All DC accounts	78.2	73.3	77.2	71.3	79.3	67.7
All DB plans	55.5	39.9	40.6	30.1	31.8	27.4
DC and/or DB plans	91.8	83.1	87.1	80.3	86.6	77.4
Technical and clerical						
All DC accounts	57.5	53.5	74.8	63.5	68.5	71.5
All DB plans	25.2	45.5	32.7	22.4	22.4	20.1
DC and/or DB plans	71.8	75.9	81.2	71.8	73.6	77.4
Service workers						
All DC accounts	27.9	19.9	53.3	39.6	56.2	35.8
All DB plans	48.4	34.0	54.8	20.1	43.4	15.7
DC and/or DB plans	61.2	44.8	76.1	52.7	73.3	42.9
Craft, operative, and agricultural						
All DC accounts	51.7	28.5	53.5	40.1	53.5	58.2
All DB plans	40.1	17.1	36.3	24.6	20.4	7.2
DC and/or DB plans	72.2	35.6	71.0	55.7	61.5	60.6

(continued)

Table B.2 (continued)

	1989		2001		2007	
	Male	Female	Male	Female	Male	Female
By work status[a]						
Aged 46 and under						
Part-time, full-year						
All DC accounts	17.4	24.1	27.5	31.4	37.0	32.7
All DB plans	24.3	8.8	7.5	8.3	2.7	4.1
DC and/or DB plans	35.2	29.8	31.8	35.5	37.0	35.6
Full-time, part-year						
All DC accounts	33.0	42.9	49.8	42.9	34.9	57.8
All DB plans	26.6	41.8	11.8	31.6	10.4	20.6
DC and/or DB plans	47.9	64.1	53.3	63.5	38.3	67.8
Part-time, part-year						
All DC accounts	18.7	35.8	19.8	34.5	30.9	33.0
All DB plans	15.3	10.1	1.2	8.7	17.7	9.5
DC and/or DB plans	27.1	42.8	20.1	38.7	40.3	38.1
Full-time, full-year						
All DC accounts	43.1	40.7	58.8	49.9	51.9	50.8
All DB plans	34.9	30.1	18.6	14.7	13.4	12.8
DC and/or DB plans	62.5	55.0	65.4	56.7	55.5	56.9
Self-employed workers						
All DC accounts	31.3	52.1	40.6	46.4	31.3	37.6
All DB plans	9.9	20.3	6.7	11.5	1.3	12.6
DC and/or DB plans	34.6	62.0	43.2	50.9	32.4	40.8
Aged 47–64						
Part-time, full-year						
All DC accounts	58.8	31.1	48.2	48.0	60.2	50.6
All DB plans	25.4	24.1	37.3	16.8	17.9	17.0
DC and/or DB plans	70.9	46.7	64.1	57.1	64.1	54.9
Full-time, part-year						
All DC accounts	70.5	54.2	66.7	64.4	55.8	58.6
All DB plans	37.1	72.1	42.5	48.5	30.0	32.3
DC and/or DB plans	81.8	91.0	83.4	87.3	66.8	73.6
Part-time, part-year						
All DC accounts	46.9	50.7	72.8	65.1	72.2	60.5
All DB plans	8.8	14.0	49.7	23.3	24.1	18.8
DC and/or DB plans	46.9	55.7	84.7	72.6	78.7	63.1

Table B.2 (continued)

	1989		2001		2007	
	Male	Female	Male	Female	Male	Female
By work status[a] *(cont.)*						
Aged 47–64 *(cont.)*						
Full-time, full-year						
All DC accounts	60.5	54.8	67.8	63.8	68.2	68.8
All DB plans	46.9	42.2	38.4	24.5	28.0	22.6
DC and/or DB plans	80.0	72.3	80.4	72.1	76.3	76.9
Self-employed workers						
All DC accounts	58.8	44.8	63.6	49.8	54.1	48.2
All DB plans	12.3	20.9	20.5	22.6	11.1	20.3
DC and/or DB plans	63.7	50.4	71.2	62.1	57.6	52.4

NOTE: The table includes only current workers aged 64 and under. Industries are grouped into four classifications: 1) agriculture, mining, and manufacturing; 2) wholesale and retail trade; 3) communications, information services, finance, insurance, real estate, repair services, transportation, utilities, professional services, and personal services; and 4) public administration.

[a] Part-time = less than 35 hours per week; part-year = less than 50 weeks per year. Self-employment may be part-time or full-time.

SOURCE: Author's computations from the 1989, 2001, and 2007 SCF.

Table B.3 Percentage of Workers with Pension Coverage by Age and Earnings Quintile, 1989, 2001, and 2007

	1989		2001		2007	
	Male	Female	Male	Female	Male	Female
Aged 46 and under						
Bottom earnings quintile						
All DC accounts	32.4	34.2	37.4	36.6	26.7	32.7
All DB plans	29.3	22.8	8.8	11.4	6.3	6.9
DC and/or DB plans	51.3	46.8	42.7	43.3	29.8	37.9
Second earnings quintile						
All DC accounts	75.3	71.7	67.9	67.4	58.6	61.4
All DB plans	47.5	64.6	22.3	23.1	15.6	20.4
DC and/or DB plans	92.8	87.0	76.0	76.3	64.0	71.5
Third earnings quintile						
All DC accounts	64.6	98.8	79.5	82.9	71.6	85.6
All DB plans	57.8	40.3	32.7	31.9	18.4	19.0
DC and/or DB plans	89.2	99.8	88.2	92.3	75.0	89.4
Fourth earnings quintile						
All DC accounts	89.8	100.0	88.1	95.7	85.0	81.4
All DB plans	28.0	11.8	24.3	8.8	27.1	27.2
DC and/or DB plans	89.8	100.0	89.2	95.7	88.0	83.6
Top earnings quintile						
All DC accounts	67.7	99.5	91.3	57.7	93.2	85.0
All DB plans	72.5	96.5	26.4	29.1	19.2	6.0
DC and/or DB plans	96.4	100.0	91.8	78.2	93.5	85.0
Aged 47–64						
Bottom earnings quintile						
All DC accounts	52.4	47.7	55.9	53.0	49.2	52.8
All DB plans	35.7	36.6	31.5	20.2	17.3	16.7
DC and/or DB plans	72.2	65.5	70.3	62.9	57.4	60.1
Second earnings quintile						
All DC accounts	73.9	84.9	68.1	78.6	68.2	76.5
All DB plans	63.3	69.6	41.5	36.3	32.6	31.2
DC and/or DB plans	92.4	96.4	80.7	89.9	78.6	88.0
Third earnings quintile						
All DC accounts	89.9	96.4	71.4	78.5	75.1	85.6
All DB plans	71.2	62.7	55.6	39.4	34.2	32.9
DC and/or DB plans	98.3	99.9	92.1	87.5	84.6	92.1

Table B.3 (continued)

	1989		2001		2007	
	Male	Female	Male	Female	Male	Female
Fourth earnings quintile						
All DC accounts	93.3	99.8	91.6	92.3	84.9	85.7
All DB plans	55.3	49.2	44.4	40.1	36.4	26.2
DC and/or DB plans	93.3	99.8	92.5	92.3	90.7	89.1
Top earnings quintile						
All DC accounts	91.4	100.0	91.2	95.6	96.0	85.4
All DB plans	52.7	0.0	31.5	48.4	25.1	15.2
DC and/or DB plans	99.9	100.0	94.9	100.0	96.5	85.4

NOTE: The table includes only current workers age 64 and under. Self-employed are excluded from this table. Earnings quintiles are based on the combined distribution of annual earnings for men and women.
SOURCE: Author's computations from the 1989, 2001, and 2007 SCF.

Appendix C
Augmented Wealth Including Employer Contributions to DC Plans and Net of Taxes

Table C.1 Augmented Wealth, Net of Federal Income Taxes on Receipt and Including Employer Contribution to DC Plans (DCEMP), 1983–2007 (in thousands, 2007$)

	1983	1989	2001	2007
All households				
Mean values including DCEMP				
Net pension wealth*	—	68.3	119.7	132.0
Net private accumulations*	—	367.4	502.1	591.5
Net retirement wealth*	—	171.0	262.0	276.8
Net augmented wealth*	—	470.0	644.4	736.3
Median values including DCEMP				
Pension wealth	—	10.6	34.2	33.7
Private accumulations	—	122.4	138.7	158.6
Retirement wealth	—	124.2	185.6	184.5
Augmented wealth	—	227.1	287.3	312.5
Aged 46 and under				
Mean values including DCEMP				
Net pension wealth*	—	49.7	78.2	74.3
Net private accumulations*	—	211.7	250.1	253.5
Net retirement wealth*	—	134.4	189.5	185.2
Net augmented wealth*	—	296.3	361.4	364.3
Median values including DCEMP				
Pension wealth	—	4.5	18.3	6.3
Private accumulations	—	60.1	62.4	54.3
Retirement wealth	—	100.8	141.5	131.0
Augmented wealth	—	148.5	178.5	167.6

(continued)

Table C.1 (continued)

	1983	1989	2001	2007
Aged 47–64				
Mean values including DCEMP				
Net pension wealth	75.2	106.6	188.2	204.0
Net private accumulations	503.1	563.2	775.6	873.4
Net retirement wealth	233.8	231.8	373.3	389.7
Net augmented wealth	661.6	688.4	960.7	1,059.1
Aged 47–64				
Median values including DCEMP				
Pension wealth	39.1	41.2	77.8	84.9
Private accumulations	202.6	212.1	253.2	287.3
Retirement wealth	196.1	176.2	275.6	279.2
Augmented wealth	359.6	364.0	448.1	471.2

NOTE: Augmented wealth includes employer contributions to defined contribution pension plans (DCEMP). Households are classified into age groups by the age of the head of household. Key: Private accumulations = nonpension wealth + pension wealth. Retirement wealth = PW + SSW. Augmented wealth = NWX + PW + SSW. — = data not available. Augmented wealth* includes employer contributions to defined contribution pension plans.
SOURCE: Author's computations from the 1983, 1989, 2001, and 2007 SCF.

Appendix D
Extended Results on
Retirement Adequacy

Table D.1 Average Annual Real Rates of Return Used in Annuity Calculations

Asset type	Period available	Period chosen	Nominal	Real
	Average rates of return (%)			
Owner-occupied housing[a]	1968–2007	1968–2007	5.96	1.39
Business and nonhome real estate[b]	1953–2007	1960–2007	6.96	2.63
Liquid assets[c]	1965–2007	1965–2007	5.48	0.88
Financial assets[d]	1955–2007	1960–2007	7.54	3.19
Defined contribution accounts[e]	1986–2007	1986–2007	6.72	3.58
Mortgage debt		1960–2007	0.00	−4.04
Nonmortgage debt		1960–2007	0.00	−4.04
Inflation rate (CPI-U average)[f]		1960–2007	4.21	
		1965–2007	4.55	
		1968–2007	4.58	
		1986–2007	3.03	

NOTE: Real Rate of Return = $(1 + \text{Nominal Rate}) / (1 + \Delta \text{CPI}) - 1$.

[a] Owner-occupied housing: U.S. Census Bureau (2009, Table 943). Updated with data from the National Association of Realtors, Washington, DC: Median Sales Price of Existing Single-Family Homes for Metropolitan Areas, at www. Realtor.org/research.

[b] Business and nonhome real estate: Holding gains (taken from the Flow of Funds table R.100) divided by equity in noncorporate business (taken from the Flow of Funds Table B.100).

[c] Liquid assets: The weighted average of the rates of return on checking deposits and cash, time and saving deposits, and life insurance reserves. The weights are the proportion of these assets in their combined total (calculated from the Flow of Funds Table B.100). The assumptions regarding the rates of return are zero for checking deposits, the rate of return on a one-month CD (taken from the table "H.15 Selected Interest Rates," published by the Federal Reserve and available at http://www .federalreserve.gov/releases/h15/data.htm) for time and saving deposits, and one plus the inflation rate for life insurance reserves.

[d] Financial assets: The weighted average of the rates of return on open market paper, Treasury securities, municipal securities, corporate and foreign bonds, corporate equities, and mutual fund shares. The weights are the proportion of these assets in total

Table D.1 (continued)

financial assets held by the household sector (calculated from the Flow of Funds Table B.100). The assumption regarding the rate of return on open market paper is that it equals the rate of return on one-month finance paper (taken from the Table H.15 "Selected Interest Rates," published by the Federal Reserve and available at http://www .federalreserve.gov/releases/h15/data.htm). The data for the rates of return on other assets are taken from the Economic Report of the President 2005, Table B.73. The assumptions regarding Treasury securities, municipal securities, corporate and foreign bonds, and corporate equities are, respectively, the average of Treasury security yields, high-grade municipal bond yields, the average of corporate bond yields, and annual percent change in the S&P 500 index. Mutual fund shares are assumed to earn a rate of return equal to the weighted average of the rates of return on open market paper, Treasury securities, municipal securities, corporate and foreign bonds, and corporate equities. The weights are the proportions of these assets in the total financial assets of mutual funds (calculated from the Flow of Funds Table L.123).

[e] Pension (defined contribution) accounts: Net acquisition of financial assets (taken from the Flow of Funds Table F.119c) divided by total financial assets of private defined-contribution plans (taken from the Flow of Funds table L.119c).

[f] Inflation rate: Calculated from the CPI-U, published by the Bureau of Labor Statistics.

SOURCE: Wolff, Zacharias, and Masterson (2009).

Table D.2 Composition of Expected Mean Retirement Income Based on Wealth Holdings and Expected Pension and Social Security Benefits, 1989, 2001, and 2007 (%)

	Nonhome, nonpension wealth	Home equity	Defined contribution plans	Defined benefit pensions	Social Security	Total
1989						
Aged 47–64	41.6	13.9	8.1	19.0	17.5	100.0
Aged 47–55	42.0	13.7	11.1	16.9	16.3	100.0
Aged 56–64	40.9	14.2	3.3	22.4	19.2	100.0
Aged 47–64						
Non-Hispanic white[a]	43.0	13.5	8.6	18.1	16.8	100.0
African American or Hispanic[a]	24.6	17.1	2.3	31.5	24.4	100.0
Married couples	42.4	13.1	8.0	19.0	17.5	100.0
Single males	50.4	16.1	5.2	14.9	13.4	100.0
Single females	31.1	17.1	10.7	21.5	19.7	100.0
Less than 12 years of schooling[b]	26.8	16.9	7.1	25.4	23.9	100.0
12 years of schooling[b]	42.3	14.8	4.6	16.1	22.2	100.0
13–15 years of schooling[b]	35.8	15.8	10.2	19.6	18.5	100.0
16 or more years of schooling[b]	52.9	10.6	9.9	16.3	10.2	100.0
Income quintile, aged 47–64						
Income quintile 1	18.8	22.0	0.0	10.8	48.4	100.0
Income quintile 2	24.8	17.7	3.2	20.8	33.5	100.0
Income quintile 3	25.4	17.6	5.3	26.3	25.4	100.0
Income quintile 4	25.7	14.0	10.3	28.4	21.7	100.0
Income quintile 5	56.5	11.6	9.5	13.6	8.7	100.0

(continued)

Table D.2 (continued)

2001					
Aged 47–64	39.2	11.7	17.0	13.8	18.4	100.0
Aged 47–55	36.6	11.8	18.6	14.7	18.3	100.0
Aged 56–64	43.4	11.4	14.4	12.4	18.5	100.0
Aged 47–64						
Non-Hispanic white[a]	40.9	11.6	17.2	13.0	17.4	100.0
African American or Hispanic[a]	20.6	12.9	14.6	21.8	30.0	100.0
Married couples	40.7	11.0	17.2	12.8	18.3	100.0
Single males	32.5	12.7	18.1	20.6	16.1	100.0
Single females	35.6	15.6	13.6	13.3	21.9	100.0
Less than 12 years of schooling[b]	17.2	15.7	9.2	16.8	41.1	100.0
12 years of schooling[b]	26.6	13.6	14.9	15.8	29.1	100.0
13–15 years of schooling[b]	31.3	14.5	15.6	15.2	23.4	100.0
16 or more years of schooling[b]	45.8	10.2	18.4	12.6	13.0	100.0
Income quintile, aged 47–64						
Income quintile 1	14.1	15.3	9.3	13.1	48.3	100.0
Income quintile 2	14.9	16.5	11.1	18.2	39.2	100.0
Income quintile 3	15.8	13.2	13.0	28.7	29.3	100.0
Income quintile 4	24.5	14.5	20.5	15.8	24.6	100.0
Income quintile 5	53.8	9.5	17.9	9.6	9.1	100.0
2007						
Aged 47–64	37.4	14.4	18.3	12.7	17.2	100.0
Aged 47–55	35.9	15.0	19.3	12.5	17.3	100.0

Aged 56–64	39.5	13.6	16.8	13.0	17.0	100.0

Aged 56–64	39.5	13.6	16.8	13.0	17.0	100.0
Aged 47–64						
Non-Hispanic white[a]	39.1	13.9	18.6	12.3	16.1	100.0
African American or Hispanic[a]	21.0	19.2	15.1	17.8	26.9	100.0
Married couples	39.0	13.9	18.3	12.1	16.7	100.0
Single males	38.3	13.9	19.8	12.8	15.1	100.0
Single females	22.9	19.9	17.1	17.4	22.7	100.0
Less than 12 years of schooling[b]	14.3	20.4	9.2	7.0	49.1	100.0
12 years of schooling[b]	22.5	19.3	15.2	14.2	28.7	100.0
13–15 years of schooling[b]	28.4	16.0	18.2	15.9	21.5	100.0
16 or more years of schooling[b]	43.8	12.7	19.4	11.8	12.2	100.0
Income quintile, aged 47–64						
Income quintile 1	24.4	19.9	4.4	9.0	42.3	100.0
Income quintile 2	17.7	19.5	11.5	15.3	36.0	100.0
Income quintile 3	15.4	17.3	19.7	19.4	28.2	100.0
Income quintile 4	15.4	17.0	23.8	19.5	24.3	100.0
Income quintile 5	52.0	12.0	18.2	9.3	8.5	100.0

NOTE: Households are classified by the age of the head of household. Each column equals the expected annuity (or annual benefit) from the current holdings of the indicated asset plus any future expected gains on the asset. Totals may not sum to 100.0 due to rounding.
Key: Home equity: net equity in owner-occupied housing. Nonhome, nonpension wealth = net worth − defined contribution − home equity. Defined contribution plans: Total defined contribution wealth = defined contribution wealth + employer contributions to defined contribution pension plans + present discounted value of future employee contributions into employee's defined contribution plan.
[a] Asian and other races are excluded from the table because of small sample sizes.
[b] Households are classified by the schooling level of the head of household.
SOURCE: Author's computations from the 1989, 2001, and 2007 SCF.

Table D.3 Expected Mean Retirement Income Based on Wealth Holdings and Expected Pension and Social Security Benefits, 1989, 2001, and 2007 (in thousands, 2007$)

	Nonhome, nonpension wealth	Home equity	Defined contribution plans	Defined benefit pensions	Social Security	Total	Total: Method A
1989							
Aged 47–64	30.4	10.2	5.9	13.9	12.8	73.2	73.1
Aged 47–55	35.2	11.5	9.3	14.2	13.7	83.9	80.6
Aged 56–64	25.0	8.7	2.0	13.7	11.7	61.1	64.4
Aged 47–64							
Non-Hispanic white[a]	35.9	11.3	7.2	15.1	14.0	83.5	81.4
African American or Hispanic[a]	7.7	5.3	0.7	9.8	7.6	31.2	34.4
Married couples	39.9	12.4	7.5	17.9	16.4	94.1	90.9
Single males	28.9	9.2	3.0	8.6	7.7	57.4	59.7
Single females	10.2	5.6	3.5	7.0	6.4	32.8	34.2
Less than 12 years of schooling[b]	9.7	6.1	2.6	9.2	8.6	36.2	37.0
12 years of schooling[b]	32.4	11.3	3.5	12.3	17.0	76.5	75.8
13–15 years of schooling[b]	31.0	13.7	8.9	17.0	16.0	86.5	81.4
16 or more years of schooling[b]	92.1	18.5	17.2	28.3	17.8	173.9	166.1
Income quintile, aged 47–64							
Income quintile 1	2.3	2.7	0.0	1.3	6.0	12.3	14.6
Income quintile 2	8.4	6.0	1.1	7.0	11.3	33.7	33.9
Income quintile 3	13.4	9.2	2.8	13.8	13.3	52.5	50.9
Income quintile 4	18.2	9.9	7.3	20.2	15.4	71.0	67.4
Income quintile 5	113.4	23.3	19.1	27.3	17.5	200.7	190.6

2001							
Aged 47–64	40.3	12.0	17.4	14.2	18.9	102.8	99.2
Aged 47–55	38.4	12.4	19.4	15.4	19.2	104.8	99.1
Aged 56–64	43.3	11.4	14.3	12.4	18.4	99.9	99.3
Aged 47–64							
Non-Hispanic white[a]	48.2	13.6	20.2	15.3	20.5	117.8	112.9
African American or Hispanic[a]	8.6	5.4	6.1	9.1	12.5	41.6	39.9
Married couples	55.7	15.1	23.5	17.4	25.0	136.7	130.7
Single males	24.1	9.5	13.4	15.3	12.0	74.3	70.4
Single females	14.4	6.3	5.5	5.4	8.9	40.4	40.5
Less than 12 years of schooling[b]	5.4	4.9	2.9	5.3	12.9	31.3	31.9
12 years of schooling[b]	14.3	7.3	8.0	8.5	15.6	53.7	52.1
13–15 years of schooling[b]	22.0	10.2	11.0	10.7	16.4	70.2	67.3
16 or more years of schooling[b]	92.7	20.7	37.2	25.6	26.3	202.6	191.4
Income quintile, aged 47–64							
Income quintile 1	3.2	3.5	2.1	3.0	11.0	22.7	23.2
Income quintile 2	5.7	6.2	4.2	6.9	14.9	37.9	36.9
Income quintile 3	9.6	8.0	7.9	17.4	17.7	60.5	57.9
Income quintile 4	23.0	13.6	19.3	14.8	23.1	93.8	88.0
Income quintile 5	166.9	29.6	55.6	29.8	28.3	310.3	293.0
2007							
Aged 47–64	41.6	16.1	20.3	14.2	19.1	111.3	106.9
Aged 47–55	40.4	16.9	21.7	14.1	19.5	112.6	106.5
Aged 56–64	43.2	14.9	18.4	14.3	18.7	109.6	107.4

(continued)

Table D.3 (continued)

	Nonhome, nonpension wealth	Home equity	Defined contribution plans	Defined benefit pensions	Social Security	Total	Total: Method A
Aged 47–64							
Non-Hispanic white[a]	49.0	17.5	23.3	15.4	20.3	125.5	119.9
African American or Hispanic[a]	11.3	10.3	8.1	9.6	14.5	53.8	52.5
Married couples	57.5	20.4	26.9	17.9	24.7	147.5	140.8
Single males	29.7	10.8	15.4	10.0	11.7	77.5	74.6
Single females	9.5	8.3	7.1	7.2	9.4	41.5	40.5
Less than 12 years of schooling[b]	3.8	5.4	2.4	1.8	12.9	26.3	27.0
12 years of schooling[b]	12.6	10.8	8.5	8.0	16.1	56.0	54.2
13–15 years of schooling[b]	21.7	12.2	13.9	12.1	16.4	76.3	73.3
16 or more years of schooling[b]	90.3	26.2	39.9	24.4	25.2	206.0	193.9
Income quintile, aged 47–64							
Income quintile 1	5.9	4.8	1.1	2.2	10.2	24.2	25.3
Income quintile 2	7.1	7.8	4.6	6.1	14.3	39.8	39.4
Income quintile 3	10.3	11.5	13.1	13.0	18.9	66.8	62.5
Income quintile 4	15.3	16.8	23.5	19.3	24.1	99.1	91.6
Income quintile 5	174.6	40.4	61.2	31.1	28.6	335.8	317.7

NOTE: Households are classified by the age of the head of household. Each column equals the expected annuity (or annual benefit) from the current holdings of the indicated asset plus any future expected gains on the asset. Key: Home equity = net equity in owner-occupied housing. Nonhome, nonpension wealth = net worth − home equity − defined contribution − defined contribution plans: Total defined contribution wealth = defined contribution wealth + employer contributions to defined contribution pension plans + present discounted value of future employee contributions into employee's defined contribution plan.

[a] Asian and other races are excluded from the table because of small sample sizes.

[b] Households are classified by the schooling level of the head of household.

SOURCE: Author's computations from the 1989, 2001, and 2007 SCF.

Table D.4 Expected Mean Retirement Income Based on Wealth Holdings, Expected Pension Benefits, and Expected Social Security Benefits, by Detailed Component, 1989, 2001, and 2007 (in thousands, 2007$)

	Expected annuity from nonhome, nonpension wealth	Expected annuity from home equity	Expected annuity from DC plans	Actual plus expected annual defined benefit	Actual plus expected annual Soc. Sec. benefit	Expected annuity from DCEMP	Expected annuity from DCEMPW	Expected annuity from future gains in NWX	Expected annuity from future gains in DCTOT	Total expected retirement income	Total expected retirement income: Method A
1989											
Aged 47–64	23.0	8.4	1.6	13.9	12.8	1.2	0.9	9.2	2.2	73.2	73.1
Aged 47–55	24.0	8.7	1.5	14.2	13.7	2.2	1.8	14.0	3.8	83.9	80.6
Aged 56–64	21.9	8.0	1.7	13.7	11.7	0.0	0.0	3.7	0.4	61.1	64.4
Aged 47–64											
Non-Hispanic white[a]	27.2	9.3	1.9	15.1	14.0	1.5	1.1	10.7	2.7	83.5	81.4
African American or Hispanic[a]	5.8	4.5	0.1	9.8	7.6	0.1	0.2	2.7	0.3	31.2	34.4
Married couples	30.0	10.1	2.0	17.9	16.4	1.4	1.3	12.2	2.9	94.1	90.9
Single males	22.3	7.7	1.1	8.6	7.7	0.6	0.2	8.1	1.0	57.4	59.7
Single females	8.0	4.8	0.8	7.0	6.4	1.0	0.5	3.0	1.2	32.8	34.2
Less than 12 years of schooling[b]	7.5	5.3	0.6	9.2	8.6	0.7	0.4	3.1	0.9	36.2	37.0
12 years of schooling[b]	23.9	9.1	1.0	12.3	17.0	0.3	0.9	10.6	1.3	76.5	75.8
13–15 years of schooling[b]	22.5	10.8	1.3	17.0	16.0	2.2	1.6	11.4	3.8	86.5	81.4
16 or more years of schooling[b]	70.8	15.2	5.6	28.3	17.8	3.2	2.1	24.6	6.3	173.9	166.1
Income quintile, aged 47–64											
Income quintile 1	1.8	2.4	0.0	1.3	6.0	0.0	0.0	0.9	0.0	12.3	14.6
Income quintile 2	6.4	5.1	0.2	7.0	11.3	0.2	0.3	2.9	0.4	33.7	33.9
Income quintile 3	10.4	7.6	0.3	13.8	13.3	0.6	0.7	4.6	1.2	52.5	50.9
Income quintile 4	14.1	8.2	2.0	20.2	15.4	1.4	1.2	5.9	2.6	71.0	67.4
Income quintile 5	85.2	18.9	5.6	27.3	17.5	3.8	2.5	32.7	7.2	200.7	190.6

(continued)

Table D.4 (continued)

	Expected annuity from nonhome, nonpension wealth	Expected annuity from home equity	Expected annuity from DC plans	Actual plus expected annual defined benefit	Actual plus expected annual Soc. Sec. benefit	Expected annuity from DCEMP	Expected annuity from DCEMPW	Expected annuity from future gains in NWX	Expected annuity from future gains in DCTOT	Total expected retirement income	Total expected retirement income: Method A
2001											
Aged 47–64	31.3	9.4	8.3	14.2	18.9	2.6	0.8	11.7	5.7	102.8	99.2
Aged 47–55	27.0	8.9	7.4	15.4	19.2	3.2	1.2	14.9	7.7	104.8	99.1
Aged 56–64	37.8	10.2	9.7	12.4	18.4	1.7	0.3	6.7	2.6	99.9	99.3
Aged 47–64											
Non-Hispanic white[a]	37.3	10.8	9.9	15.3	20.5	3.0	0.9	13.7	6.5	117.8	112.9
African American or Hispanic[a]	6.5	3.9	1.9	9.1	12.5	1.3	0.5	3.5	2.3	41.6	39.9
Married couples	43.2	11.9	11.6	17.4	25.0	3.3	1.1	15.7	7.5	136.7	130.7
Single males	18.5	7.3	5.3	15.3	12.0	2.7	0.7	7.8	4.8	74.3	70.4
Single females	11.1	4.9	2.5	5.4	8.9	1.0	0.2	4.6	1.8	40.4	40.5
Less than 12 years of schooling[b]	4.3	4.1	1.4	5.3	12.9	0.5	0.2	1.9	0.8	31.3	31.9
12 years of schooling[b]	10.9	5.7	3.6	8.5	15.6	1.2	0.4	5.0	2.8	53.7	52.1
13–15 years of schooling[b]	17.4	7.9	5.0	10.7	16.4	1.7	0.6	6.9	3.7	70.2	67.3
16 or more years of schooling[b]	71.7	16.2	18.0	25.6	26.3	5.6	1.7	25.6	11.9	202.6	191.4
Income quintile, aged 47–64											
Income quintile 1	2.4	3.0	0.9	3.0	11.0	0.4	0.1	1.3	0.7	22.7	23.2
Income quintile 2	4.3	4.9	1.8	6.9	14.9	0.8	0.3	2.8	1.4	37.9	36.9
Income quintile 3	7.5	6.2	3.3	17.4	17.7	1.4	0.5	3.8	2.6	60.5	57.9
Income quintile 4	18.0	10.3	8.9	14.8	23.1	2.7	1.3	8.3	6.4	93.8	88.0
Income quintile 5	129.3	23.3	27.5	29.8	28.3	8.2	2.1	44.0	17.8	310.3	293.0

305

2007

Aged 47–64	32.5	12.6	9.7	14.2	19.1	2.8	1.5	12.5	6.4	111.3	106.9
Aged 47–55	28.2	12.2	7.9	14.1	19.5	3.3	2.0	16.9	8.6	112.6	106.5
Aged 56–64	38.2	13.2	12.1	14.3	18.7	2.0	1.0	6.7	3.3	109.6	107.4
Aged 47–64											0.0
Non-Hispanic white[a]	38.3	13.8	11.3	15.4	20.3	3.1	1.7	14.3	7.2	125.5	119.9
African American or Hispanic[a]	8.6	7.8	3.2	9.6	14.5	1.3	0.9	5.3	2.7	53.8	52.5
Married couples	45.0	16.1	12.9	17.9	24.7	3.6	2.1	16.9	8.3	147.5	140.8
Single males	22.7	8.2	7.0	10.0	11.7	2.1	1.0	9.6	5.2	77.5	74.6
Single females	7.5	6.7	3.3	7.2	9.4	1.0	0.5	3.7	2.2	41.5	40.5
Less than 12 years of schooling[b]	2.8	4.2	1.1	1.8	12.9	0.4	0.2	2.2	0.8	26.3	27.0
12 years of schooling[b]	9.7	8.4	3.9	8.0	16.1	1.1	0.8	5.3	2.8	56.0	54.2
13–15 years of schooling[b]	16.6	9.6	6.7	12.1	16.4	1.7	1.2	7.6	4.4	76.3	73.3
16 or more years of schooling[b]	70.8	20.7	19.2	24.4	25.2	5.6	2.8	24.9	12.4	206.0	193.9
Income quintile, aged 47–64											
Income quintile 1	4.6	4.0	0.5	2.2	10.2	0.2	0.1	2.1	0.3	24.2	25.3
Income quintile 2	5.8	6.2	2.5	6.1	14.3	0.5	0.3	2.8	1.2	39.8	39.4
Income quintile 3	8.1	9.1	5.6	13.0	18.9	1.9	1.1	4.7	4.5	66.8	62.5
Income quintile 4	11.8	12.8	10.9	19.3	24.1	2.7	2.6	7.5	7.4	99.1	91.6
Income quintile 5	136.1	31.9	29.9	31.1	28.6	8.7	3.6	46.9	18.9	335.8	317.7

NOTE: Households are classified by the age of the head of household. Each column equals the expected annuity (or annual benefit) from the current holdings of the indicated asset plus any future expected gains on the asset. Key: Home equity = net equity in owner-occupied housing. Nonhome, nonpension wealth = net worth − defined contribution − home equity. Defined contribution plans: Total defined contribution wealth = defined contribution wealth + employer contributions to defined contribution pension plans + present discounted value of future employee contributions into employee's defined contribution plan.

[a] Asian and other races are excluded from the table because of small sample sizes.

[b] Households are classified by the schooling level of the head of household.

SOURCE: Author's computations from the 1989, 2001, and 2007 SCF.

Table D.5 Percentage of Households with Expected Retirement Income Less Than the Poverty Line, Based on Wealth Holdings and Expected Pension and Social Security Benefits, 1989, 2001, and 2007

	Nonhome, nonpension wealth	FWX plus half of home equity	Nonpension wealth	NWX plus DC plans (DCTOT)	NWX plus all pensions	Total expected retirement income: NWX + PW + Soc. Sec.	Marginal effect of all pensions, 1989	Marginal effect of all pensions, 2007
1989								
Aged 47–64	67.5	57.0	45.1	40.7	27.5	14.8	−17.6	−17.3
Aged 47–55	64.9	50.8	40.4	32.1	23.6	13.2	−16.8	−16.9
Aged 56–64	70.6	64.1	50.7	50.7	32.1	16.7	−18.6	−17.9
Aged 47–64								
Non-Hispanic white[a]	60.5	47.8	35.1	30.1	15.9	3.2	−19.2	−18.4
African American or Hispanic[a]	91.1	87.5	77.3	74.0	63.0	48.1	−14.4	−16.3
Married couples	64.5	49.8	36.8	33.2	19.0	7.3	−17.8	−16.5
Single males	59.4	56.5	45.9	44.1	23.3	11.4	−22.6	−13.5
Single females	77.5	73.5	63.7	56.3	48.4	33.2	−15.3	−21.4
Less than 12 years of schooling[b]	82.4	75.9	62.9	57.4	42.4	26.7	−20.5	−11.4
12 years of schooling[b]	60.2	47.1	34.9	29.6	16.9	1.6	−18.0	−21.5
13–15 years of schooling[b]	51.9	37.0	22.3	19.8	7.3	0.4	−15.0	−23.1
16 or more years of schooling[b]	42.3	25.8	20.2	18.5	9.7	5.4	−10.4	−12.2
2001								
Aged 47–64	71.7	62.3	50.2	38.9	30.2	10.2		
Aged 47–55	71.6	62.1	49.0	35.9	29.0	10.7		
Aged 56–64	71.7	62.6	52.0	43.5	32.0	9.4		
Aged 47–64								

Non-Hispanic white[a]	67.1	56.9	43.5	31.5	22.8	4.0
African American or Hispanic[a]	86.0	78.5	69.7	59.5	49.7	21.6
Married couples	65.4	55.3	41.3	29.3	21.7	3.9
Single males	77.6	66.7	53.4	44.0	32.0	11.9
Single females	82.9	76.3	69.7	58.7	49.9	24.4
Less than 12 years of schooling[b]	91.8	87.3	78.7	72.2	59.4	23.8
12 years of schooling[b]	83.2	72.5	63.1	48.6	36.6	10.6
13–15 years of schooling[b]	71.8	63.7	47.8	34.2	25.9	6.8
16 or more years of schooling[b]	52.7	41.0	27.9	18.5	14.2	5.7
2007						
Aged 47–64	75.1	59.8	45.2	33.2	27.9	10.2
Aged 47–55	76.6	59.3	45.5	31.7	28.6	11.6
Aged 56–64	72.9	60.4	44.9	35.3	27.0	8.2
Aged 47–64						
Non-Hispanic white[a]	70.6	54.0	38.9	25.9	20.5	4.8
African American or Hispanic[a]	88.4	75.1	60.2	49.7	43.9	13.9
Married couples	70.9	54.0	37.1	24.9	20.6	5.7
Single males	72.1	57.8	50.3	44.0	36.8	12.8
Single females	86.9	74.9	62.4	48.0	41.0	19.7
Less than 12 years of schooling[b]	94.2	92.0	80.1	74.6	68.7	28.1
12 years of schooling[b]	86.3	72.6	54.3	39.9	32.8	9.0
13–15 years of schooling[b]	80.7	62.8	50.4	32.5	27.4	9.0
16 or more years of schooling[b]	56.4	37.5	23.9	15.5	11.7	6.4

NOTE: Households are classified by the age of the head of household. Each column equals the expected annuity (or annual benefit) from the current holdings of the indicated asset plus any future expected gains on the asset. Key: Home equity = net equity in owner-occupied housing. Nonhome, nonpension wealth = net worth − defined contribution − home equity. Defined contribution plans: Total defined contribution wealth = defined contribution wealth + employer contributions to defined contribution pension plans + present discounted value of future employee contributions into employee's defined contribution plan.

[a] Asian and other races are excluded from the table because of small sample sizes.

[b] Households are classified by the schooling level of the head of household.

SOURCE: Author's computations from the 1989, 2001, and 2007 SCF.

Table D.6 Share of Households with Expected Replacement Income Greater Than or Equal to Three-Quarters of Projected Income at Age 64, Based on Wealth Holdings and Expected Pension and Social Security Benefits, 1989, 2001, and 2007 (%)

	Nonhome, nonpension wealth	Nonhome, nonpension wealth plus half of home equity	Nonpension wealth	Nonhome, nonpension wealth plus DC plans	Nonhome, nonpension wealth plus all pensions	Total expected retirement income: NWX + PW + Soc. Sec.
1989						
Aged 47–64	6.8	8.0	10.8	13.0	27.8	45.4
Aged 47–55	6.7	7.7	8.8	11.9	23.6	38.8
Aged 56–64	6.9	8.3	13.1	14.2	32.6	53.0
Aged 47–64						
Non-Hispanic white[a]	8.3	9.5	13.1	16.0	31.7	49.7
African American or Hispanic[a]	1.6	2.8	2.8	2.8	16.4	35.2
Married couples	7.0	8.7	10.8	13.2	26.0	47.3
Single males	10.9	10.9	22.0	22.0	44.2	54.0
Single females	4.8	5.2	6.5	9.1	25.6	37.6
Less than 12 years of schooling[b]	3.9	4.6	6.9	8.9	23.8	42.1
12 years of schooling[b]	11.0	13.7	16.3	17.0	28.0	47.8
13–15 years of schooling[b]	9.5	11.5	12.8	17.6	30.4	44.8
16 or more years of schooling[b]	8.4	8.6	14.1	17.1	37.8	52.7
Income quintile, ages 47–64						
Income quintile 1	2.5	6.3	12.4	12.4	22.9	51.8
Income quintile 2	7.7	7.7	10.1	10.1	23.2	45.8
Income quintile 3	3.6	5.3	6.1	8.6	32.5	56.4
Income quintile 4	5.8	6.4	10.7	15.4	28.2	33.6
Income quintile 5	14.1	14.2	15.1	19.1	32.0	39.2

2001						
Aged 47–64	6.3	8.0	10.5	16.1	26.8	46.5
Aged 47–55	4.9	6.5	8.6	14.0	24.3	40.7
Aged 56–64	8.4	10.4	13.4	19.3	30.7	55.3
Aged 47–64						
Non-Hispanic white[a]	7.6	9.7	12.7	19.5	30.9	50.5
African American or Hispanic[a]	2.0	2.2	3.0	4.9	14.3	37.4
Married couples	6.9	8.4	10.9	17.6	28.5	49.7
Single males	4.9	8.2	10.8	18.0	30.9	47.1
Single females	5.6	6.9	9.4	11.4	19.9	38.2
Less than 12 years of schooling[b]	2.3	4.3	7.6	9.6	17.2	44.3
12 years of schooling[b]	5.1	5.9	7.9	12.4	21.7	44.8
13–15 years of schooling[b]	6.1	9.6	10.8	15.4	24.5	43.1
16 or more years of schooling[b]	9.2	10.3	13.7	22.8	37.4	51.5
Income quintile, aged 47–64						
Income quintile 1	7.5	12.1	17.0	19.2	28.1	62.2
Income quintile 2	5.1	5.3	7.9	12.0	24.4	45.1
Income quintile 3	3.1	3.6	4.5	9.6	20.8	38.4
Income quintile 4	5.0	7.3	9.6	17.6	27.5	41.3
Income quintile 5	10.9	11.8	13.3	22.3	33.7	45.1
2007						
Aged 47–64	5.5	7.3	10.0	16.8	28.5	49.3
Aged 47–55	4.4	6.1	8.1	14.7	26.1	43.7
Aged 56–64	6.9	8.9	12.5	19.6	31.8	57.1
Aged 47–64						
Non-Hispanic white[a]	6.1	8.2	11.0	18.9	31.2	53.6
African American or Hispanic[a]	3.9	5.0	7.8	11.4	23.2	41.5

(continued)

Table D.6 (continued)

	Nonhome, nonpension wealth	Nonhome, nonpension wealth plus half of home equity	Nonpension wealth	Nonhome, nonpension wealth plus DC plans	Nonhome, nonpension wealth plus all pensions	Total expected retirement income: NWX + PW + Soc. Sec.
Single males	9.9	11.2	14.9	20.8	35.8	57.2
Single females	4.1	6.9	10.5	15.4	25.1	44.0
Less than 12 years of schooling[b]	2.2	2.5	3.1	4.4	7.5	34.6
12 years of schooling[b]	3.2	4.6	7.6	11.7	19.9	42.6
13–15 years of schooling[b]	6.1	8.3	10.2	15.2	27.5	45.9
16 or more years of schooling[b]	8.1	10.3	13.9	25.7	42.7	61.4
Income quintile, aged 47–64						
Income quintile 1	6.7	10.4	16.8	19.4	25.6	57.3
Income quintile 2	4.8	6.5	9.3	14.8	25.1	47.0
Income quintile 3	4.0	5.7	7.6	16.0	29.2	47.8
Income quintile 4	2.1	2.8	3.2	12.4	29.2	47.1
Income quintile 5	10.1	11.2	12.9	21.5	33.8	47.3

NOTE: Households are classified by the age of the head of household. Key: Home equity = net equity in owner-occupied housing. Nonhome, nonpension wealth = net worth − defined contribution − home equity. Total defined contribution wealth = defined contribution wealth + employer contributions to defined contribution pension plans + employer contributions to defined contribution pension plans.
[a] Asian and other races are excluded from the table because of small sample sizes.
[b] Households are classified by the schooling level of the head of household.
SOURCE: Author's computations from the 1989, 2001, and 2007 SCF.

References

Aon Consulting. 2001. *Replacement Ratio Study.* Chicago: Aon Consulting.

Bank of America. 2010. "Bank of America Survey Finds Despite Tightening Their Wallets, Americans Are Further from Achieving Their Retirement Goals amidst Weakening Economy." Phoenix, AZ: Bank of America. http://mediaroom.bankofamerica.com/phoenix.zhtml?c=234503&p=irol-newsArticle&ID=1390174&highlight= (accessed February 19, 2011).

Banks, James, Richard Blundell, and Sarah Tanner. 1998. "Is There a Retirement-Savings Puzzle?" *American Economic Review* 88(4): 769–788.

Bernheim, B. Douglas. 1997. "The Adequacy of Personal Retirement Saving: Issues and Options." In *Facing the Age Wave*, David A. Wise, ed. Stanford, CA: Hoover Institute Press, pp. 30–56.

Bernheim, B. Douglas, Jonathan Skinner, and Steven Weinberg. 2001. "What Accounts for the Variation in Retirement Wealth among U.S. Households?" *American Economic Review* 91(4): 832–857.

Blau, Francine D., and John W. Graham. 1990. "Black-White Differences in Wealth and Asset Composition." *Quarterly Journal of Economics* 105(1): 321–339.

Bloom, David E., and Richard B. Freeman. 1992. "The Fall in Private Pension Coverage in the United States." *American Economic Review Papers and Proceedings* 82(2): 539–558.

Brown, Jeffrey R., Julia Lynn Coronado, and Don Fullerton. 2009. "Is Social Security Part of the Social Safety Net?" Working Paper No. 2610. London: CESifo.

Butrica, Barbara A., and Philip Issa. 2010. *Retirement Account Balances (Updated 1/10).* Washington, DC: Urban Institute. http://www.urban.org/publications/411976.html (accessed February 24, 2011).

Butrica, Barbara A., Daniel Murphy, and Sheila R. Zedlewski. 2008. "How Many Struggle to Get By in Retirement?" Urban Institute Discussion Paper No. 08-01. Washington, DC: Urban Institute.

Butrica, Barbara A., Karen E. Smith, and Eric J. Toder. 2009a. "What the Economic Crisis of 2008 Means for Retirement Security." Washington, DC: Urban Institute. http://www.urban.org/uploadedpdf/411876_2008stockmarketcrash.pdf (accessed February 24, 2011).

———. 2009b. "Retirement Security and the Stock Market Crash: What Are the Possible Outcomes?" Urban Institute Discussion Paper No. 09-05. Washington, DC: Urban Institute. http://www.urban.org/publications/411998.html (accessed February 24, 2011).

Chernozhukov, Victor, and Christian Hansen. 2004. "The Effects of 401(k)

Participation on the Wealth Distribution: An Instrumental Quantile Regression Analysis." *Review of Economics and Statistics* 86(3): 735–751.

Coronado, Julia Lynn, Don Fullerton, and Thomas Glass. 2000. "The Progressivity of Social Security." NBER Working Paper No. 7520. Cambridge, MA: National Bureau of Economic Research.

Council of Economic Advisers. 2001. *Economic Report of the President, 2000.* Table B-93, p. 406. Washington, DC: U.S. Government Printing Office,

———. 2009a. *Economic Report of the President: 2009 Spreadsheet Tables.* Table B-47. Washington, DC: U.S. Government Printing Office. http://www.gpoaccess.gov/eop/tables09.html (accessed January 11, 2010).

———. 2009b. *Economic Report of the President: 2009 Spreadsheet Tables.* Table B-96. Washington, DC: U.S. Government Printing Office. http://www.gpoaccess.gov/eop/tables09.html (accessed January 11, 2010).

———. 2009c. *Economic Report of the President: 2009 Spreadsheet Tables.* Table B-33. Washington, DC: U.S. Government Printing Office. http://www.gpoaccess.gov/eop/tables09.html (accessed January 11, 2010).

Engelhardt, Gary V., and Anil Kumar. 2007. "Employer Matching and 401(k) Saving: Evidence from the Health and Retirement Study." *Journal of Public Economics* 91(10): 1920–1943.

Engen, Eric M., and William G. Gale. 1997. "Debt, Taxes, and the Effects of 401(k) Plans on Household Wealth Accumulation." Photocopy. Brookings Institution, Washington, DC.

———. 2000. "The Effects of 401(k) Plans on Household Wealth: Differences across Earnings Groups." Photocopy. Brookings Institution, Washington, DC.

Engen, Eric M., William G. Gale, and Cori E. Uccello. 1999. "The Adequacy of Household Saving." *Brookings Papers on Economic Activity* 1999(2): 65–187.

———. 2005. "Effects of Stock Market Fluctuations on the Adequacy of Retirement Wealth Accumulation." *Review of Income and Wealth* 51(3): 397–418.

Even, William E., and David A. Macpherson. 1994a. "Trends in Individual and Household Pension Coverage." Photocopy. Miami University, Oxford, Ohio.

———. 1994b. "Why Did Male Pension Coverage Decline in the 1980s?" *Industrial and Labor Relations Review* 47(3): 429–453.

———. 1994c. "Why Has the Decline in Pension Coverage Accelerated among Less Educated Workers?" Photocopy. Miami University, Oxford, OH.

———. 1994d. "Gender Differences in Pensions." *Journal of Human Resources* 29(2): 555–587.

Farber, Henry S. 2001. "Job Loss in the United States, 1981–1999." Working Paper No. 453. Princeton, NJ: Princeton University, Industrial Relations Section.

Feldstein, Martin S. 1974. "Social Security, Induced Retirement and Aggregate Capital Accumulation." *Journal of Political Economy* 82(5): 905–926.

————. 1976. "Social Security and the Distribution of Wealth." *Journal of the American Statistical Association* 71(356): 800–807.

Fisher, Jonathan, David S. Johnson, Joseph Marchand, Timothy M. Smeeding, and Barbara Boyle Torrey. 2005. "The Retirement-Consumption Conundrum: Evidence from a Consumption Survey." Working Paper No. 2005-14. Boston, MA: Center for Retirement Research at Boston College.

Friedberg, Leora, and Michael Owyang. 2004. "Explaining the Evolution of Pension Structure and Job Tenure." NBER Working Paper No. 10714. Cambridge, MA: National Bureau of Economic Research.

Gale, William G. 1995. "The Effects of Pensions on Wealth: A Reevaluation of Theory and Evidence." Photocopy. Brookings Institution, Washington, DC.

Gale, William G., and John Karl Scholz. 1994. "IRAs and Household Saving." *American Economic Review* 84(3):1233–1260.

Ghilarducci, Teresa, Wei Sun, and Steve Nyce. 2004. "Employer Pension Contributions and 401(k)s: A Note." *Industrial Relations* 43(2): 473–479.

Gittleman, Maury, and Edward N. Wolff. 2004. "Racial Differences in Patterns of Wealth Accumulation." *Journal of Human Resources* 39(1): 193–227.

Goldin, Claudia, and Lawrence F. Katz. 2008. *The Race between Education and Technology.* Cambridge, MA: Harvard University Press.

Gustman, Alan L., Olivia S. Mitchell, Andrew A. Samwick, and Thomas L. Steinmeier. 1997. "Pension and Social Security Wealth in the Health and Retirement Study." NBER Working Paper No. 5912. Cambridge, MA: National Bureau of Economic Research.

Gustman, Alan L., and Thomas L. Steinmeier. 1992. "The Stampede toward Defined Contribution Pension Plans: Fact or Fiction?" *Industrial Relations* 31(2): 361–369.

————. 1998. "Effects of Pensions on Saving: Analysis with Data from the Health and Retirement Study." NBER Working Paper No. 6681. Cambridge, MA: National Bureau of Economic Research.

————. 1999. "What People Don't Know about Their Pensions and Social Security: An Analysis Using Linked Data from the Health and Retirement Study." NBER Working Paper No. 7368. Cambridge, MA: National Bureau of Economic Research.

————. 2000. "Pensions and Retiree Health Benefits in Household Wealth." *Journal of Human Resources* 35(1): 30–50.

Gustman, Alan L., Thomas L. Steinmeier, and Nahid Tabatabai. 2009. "How Do Pension Changes Affect Retirement Preparedness? The Trend to Defined Contribution Plans and the Vulnerability of the Retirement Age Population to the Stock Market Decline of 2008–2009." Working Paper No. 2009-206.

Ann Arbor, MI: University of Michigan, Michigan Retirement Research Center.

Haveman, Robert, Karen Holden, Barbara Wolfe, and Shane Sherlund. 2003. "Have Newly Retired Workers in the U.S. Saved Enough to Maintain Well-Being through Retirement Years?" Paper presented at the annual meetings of the Association for Public Policy Analysis and Management (APPAM), held in Washington, DC, November 6–8.

Hurd, Michael. 1994. "The Economic Status of the Elderly in the United States." In *Aging in the United States and Japan*, Yukio Noguchi and David A. Wise, eds. Chicago: University of Chicago Press, pp. 63–83.

Hurst, Erik. 2008. "The Retirement of a Consumption Puzzle." NBER Working Paper No. 13789. Cambridge, MA: National Bureau of Economic Research.

Johnson, Richard W., Usha Sambamoorthi, and Stephen Crystal. 2000. "Pension Wealth at Midlife: Comparing Self-Reports with Provider Data." *Review of Income and Wealth* 46(1): 59–83.

Karamcheva, Nadia, and Geoffrey Sanzenbacher. 2010. "Is Pension Inequality Growing?" Issue Brief No. 10-1. Boston, MA: Center for Retirement Research at Boston College.

Kennickell, Arthur B. 2001. "Modeling Wealth with Multiple Observations of Income: Redesign of the Sample for the 2001 Survey of Consumer Finances." Photocopy. Federal Reserve Board, Washington, DC. http://www.federalreserve.gov/pubs/oss/oss2/method.html (accessed February 24, 2011).

Kennickell, Arthur B., and Annika E. Sundén. 1999. "Pensions, Social Security, and the Distribution of Wealth." Photocopy. Federal Reserve Board, Washington, DC.

Kennickell, Arthur B., and R. Louise Woodburn. 1999. "Consistent Weight Design for the 1989, 1992, and 1995 SCFs, and the Distribution of Wealth." *Review of Income and Wealth* 45(2): 193–216.

Kopczuk, Wojciech, and Emmanuel Saez. 2004. "Top Wealth Shares in the United States, 1916–2000: Evidence from Estate Tax Returns." *National Tax Journal* 57(2, Part 2): 445–488.

Kotlikoff, Laurence J., and Daniel E. Smith. 1983. *Pensions in the American Economy.* Chicago: University of Chicago Press.

Kuznets, Simon. 1953. *Shares of Upper Income Groups in Income and Savings.* Cambridge, MA: National Bureau of Economic Research.

Leimer, Dean R. 2003. "Historical Redistribution under the Social Security Old-Age and Survivors Insurance Program." ORES Working Paper Series No. 101. Washington, DC: Social Security Administration.

———. 2004. "Historical Redistribution under the Social Security Old-Age and Survivors Insurance Program." ORES Working Paper Series No. 102. Washington, DC: Social Security Administration.

Leonhardt, David. 2002. "For Executives, Nest Egg Is Wrapped in a Security Blanket." *New York Times*, March 5, C:1.

Liebman, Jeffrey B. 2002. "Redistribution in the Current U.S. Social Security System." In *The Distributional Aspects of Social Security and Social Security Reform,* Martin S. Feldstein and Jeffrey B. Liebman, eds. Chicago: University of Chicago Press, pp. 11–47.

Love, David A., Paul A. Smith, and Lucy C. McNair. 2008. "A New Look at the Wealth Adequacy of Older U.S. Households." *Review of Income and Wealth* 54(4): 616–642.

Mandell, Lewis, Pamela Perun, Lisa Mensah, and Raymond O'Mara III. 2009. *Real Savings+: An Automatic Investment Option for the Automatic IRA.* Washington, DC: Aspen Institute.

McGarry, Kathleen, and Andrew Davenport. 1997. "Pensions and the Distribution of Wealth." NBER Working Paper No. 6171. Cambridge, MA: National Bureau of Economic Research.

McGill, Dan M., Kyle N. Brown, John J. Haley, and Sylvester J. Schieber. 1996. *Fundamentals of Private Pensions*, 7th ed. Philadelphia: University of Pennsylvania Press.

Mitchell, Olivia S., and James Moore. 1998. "Can Americans Afford to Retire? New Evidence on Retirement Saving Adequacy." *Journal of Risk and Insurance* 65(3): 371–400.

Modigliani, Franco. 1954. "Utility Analysis and the Consumption Function: An Interpretation of Cross-Section Data." In *Post-Keynesian Economics*, Kenneth Kurihara, ed. New Brunswick, NJ: Rutgers University Press, pp. 388–436.

Mok, Wallace, and Zahra Siddique. 2009. "Racial Differences in Fringe Benefits and Compensation." IZA Discussion Paper No. 4435. Bonn, Germany: IZA.

Moore, James F., and Olivia S. Mitchell. 2000. "Projected Retirement Wealth and Saving Adequacy." In *Forecasting Retirement Needs and Retirement Wealth*, Olivia S. Mitchell, P. Brett Hammond, and Anna M. Rappaport, eds. Philadelphia: University of Pennsylvania Press, pp. 68–94.

Morin, Rich. 2009. "Most Middle-Aged Adults Are Rethinking Retirement Plans: The Threshold Generation." Pew Research Center Publication No. 1234. Washington, DC: Pew Research Center. http://pewresearch.org/pubs/1234/ (accessed February 24, 2011).

Munnell, Alicia H. 1996. "Private Pensions and Saving: New Evidence." *Journal of Political Economy* 84(51): 1013–1031.

Munnell, Alicia H., Alex Golub-Sass, Richarad A. Kopcke, and Anthony

Webb. 2009. "What Does It Cost to Guarantee Returns?" Issue Brief No. 9-4. Boston, MA: Center for Retirement Research at Boston College.

Munnell, Alicia H., Alex Golub-Sass, Pamela Perun, and Anthony Webb. 2007. "Households 'At Risk': A Closer Look at the Bottom Third." Working Paper No. 2007-2. Boston, MA: Center for Retirement Research at Boston College.

Munnell, Alicia H., and Pamela Perun. 2006. "An Update on Private Pensions." Issue Brief No. 50. Boston, MA: Center for Retirement Research at Boston College.

Munnell, Alicia H., and Laura Quinby. 2009. "Pension Coverage and Retirement Security." Issue Brief No. 9-26. Boston, MA: Center for Retirement Research at Boston College.

———. 2010. "Why Did Some Employers Suspend Their 401(k) Match?" Issue Brief No. 10-2. Boston, MA: Center for Retirement Research at Boston College.

Munnell, Alicia H., and Christopher Sullivan. 2009. "401(k) Plans and Race." Issue Brief No. 9-24. Boston, MA: Center for Retirement Research at Boston College.

Munnell, Alicia H., Anthony Webb, and Luke Delorme. 2006. "Retirement at Risk: A New National Retirement Risk Index." Issue in Brief No. 48. Boston, MA: Center for Retirement Research at Boston College.

New York Times. 2009. "About Your 401(k)." Editorial, August 23, A:18.

Oliver, Melvin L., and Thomas M. Shapiro. 1997. *Black Wealth, White Wealth: A New Perspective on Racial Inequality*. New York: Routledge.

Popke, Leslie E. 1999. "Are 401(k) Plans Replacing Other Employer-Provided Pensions?" *Journal of Human Resources* 34(2): 346–368.

Poterba, James M. 2004. "Valuing Assets in Retirement Savings Accounts." *National Tax Journal* 57(2, Part 2): 489–512.

Poterba, James M., Joshua Rauh, Steven F. Venti, and David A. Wise. 2007. "Defined Contribution Plans, Defined Benefit Plans, and the Accumulation of Retirement Wealth." *Journal of Public Economics* 91(10): 2062–2086.

Poterba, James M., Steven F. Venti, and David A. Wise. 1992. "401(k) Plans and Tax-Deferred Saving." NBER Working Paper No. 4181. Cambridge, MA: National Bureau of Economic Research.

———. 1993. "Do 401(k) Contributions Crowd Out Other Personal Savings?" NBER Working Paper No. 4391. Cambridge, MA: National Bureau of Economic Research.

———. 1995. "Targeted Retirement Saving and the Net Worth of Elderly Americans." *American Economic Review Papers and Proceedings* 84(2): 180–185.

———. 1998. "401(k) Plans and Future Patterns of Retirement Saving." *American Economic Review Papers and Proceedings* 87(2): 179–184.

———. 2001. "The Transition to Personal Accounts and Increasing Retirement Wealth: Micro and Macro Evidence." NBER Working Paper No. 8610. Cambridge, MA: National Bureau of Economic Research.

———. 2007a. "Rise of 401(k) Plans, Lifetime Earnings, and Wealth at Retirement." NBER Working Paper No. 13091. Cambridge, MA: National Bureau of Economic Research.

———. 2007b. "The Changing Landscape of Pension in the United States." NBER Working Paper No. 13381. Cambridge, MA: National Bureau of Economic Research.

———. 2008. "New Estimates of the Future Path of 401(k) Assets." In *Tax Policy and the Economy*, Vol. 22, James M. Poterba, ed. Cambridge, MA: National Bureau of Economic Research, pp. 43–80.

Purcell, Patrick. 2009a. *Pension Sponsorship and Participation: A Summary of Recent Trends*. CRS Report RL30122. Washington, DC: Congressional Research Service.

———. 2009b. *Income and Poverty among Older Americans in 2008*. CRS Report RL32697. Washington, DC: Congressional Research Service.

———. 2009c. *Income of Americans Aged 65 and Older, 1968 to 2008*. CRS Report RL33387. Washington, DC: Congressional Research Service.

Sanzenbacher, Geoffrey. 2006. "Estimating Pension Coverage Using Different Data Sets." Issue Brief No. 51. Boston, MA: Center for Retirement Research at Boston College.

Sass, Steven A., Courtney Monk, and Kelly Haverstick. 2010. "Workers' Response to the Market Crash: Save More, Work More?" Issue Brief No. 10-3. Boston, MA: Center for Retirement Research at Boston College. http://www.globalaging.org/pension/us/2010/CrashRetire.pdf (accessed February 24, 2011).

Scholz, John Karl, and Ananth Seshadri. 2009. "What Replacement Rates Should Households Use?" Working Paper No. 2009-214. Ann Arbor: Michigan Retirement Research Center.

Sherraden, Michael. 1991. *Assets and the Poor: A New American Welfare Policy*. Armonk, NY: M.E. Sharpe.

Skinner, Jonathan. 2007. "Are You Sure You're Saving Enough for Retirement?" *Journal of Economic Perspectives* 21(3): 59–80.

Smith, James P. 1997. "The Changing Economic Circumstances of the Elderly: Income, Wealth, and Social Security." Syracuse University Public Policy Brief No. 8. Syracuse, NY: Syracuse University.

———. 2003. "Trends and Projections in Income Replacement during Retirement." *Journal of Labor Economics* 21(4): 755–781.

Smith, Karen, Mauricio Soto, and Rudolph G. Penner. 2009. "How Seniors Change Their Asset Holdings during Retirement." Working Paper No. 2009-31. Boston, MA: Center for Retirement Research at Boston College.

Smith, Karen, Eric Toder, and Howard Iams. 2001. "Lifetime Redistribution of Social Security Retirement Benefits." Photocopy. Social Security Administration, Washington, DC.

Sorokina, Olga, Anthony Webb, and Dan Muldoon. 2008. "Pension Wealth and Income: 1992, 1998, and 2004." Issue Brief No. 8-1. Boston, MA: Center for Retirement Research at Boston College.

Turner, John A. 2009. *Pension Policy: The Search for Better Solutions*. Kalamazoo, MI: W.E. Upjohn Institute for Employment Research.

U.S. Census Bureau. 1975. *Historical Statistics of the United States, Colonial Times to 1970*, Bicentennial Edition, Part I. Washington, DC: U.S. Government Printing Office.

———.1999. *Statistical Abstract of the United States, 1999*, 119th ed. Table No. 1203. Washington, DC: U.S. Government Printing Office, p. 725.

———. 2009. *Statistical Abstract of the United States, 2009.* Table No. 935. Washington, DC: U.S. Government Printing Office.

U.S. Department of Labor, Pension and Welfare Benefits Administration. 2000. *Coverage Status of Workers under Employer Provided Pension Plans: Findings from the Contingent Work Supplement to the February 1999 Current Population Survey.* Washington, DC: U.S. Department of Labor.

Venti, Steven F., and David A. Wise. 1998. "The Cause of Wealth Dispersion at Retirement: Choice or Chance?" *American Economic Review Papers and Proceedings* 88(2): 185–191.

Weller, Christian, and Edward N. Wolff. 2005. *Retirement Income: The Crucial Role of Social Security*. Washington, DC: Economic Policy Institute.

Wolff, Edward N. 1980. "Estimates of the 1969 Size Distribution of Household Wealth in the United States from a Synthetic Database." In *Modeling the Distribution and Intergenerational Transmission of Wealth*, James P. Smith, ed. Chicago: University of Chicago Press, pp. 223–271.

———. 1987a. "Estimates of Household Wealth Inequality in the United States, 1962–1983." *Review of Income and Wealth* 33(3): 231–256.

———. 1987b. "The Effects of Pensions and Social Security on the Distribution of Wealth in the United States." In *International Comparisons of the Distribution of Household Wealth*, Edward N. Wolff, ed. New York: Oxford University Press, pp. 208–247.

———. 1990. "Wealth Holdings and Poverty Status in the United States." *Review of Income and Wealth* 36(2): 143–165.

———. 1992. "Methodological Issues in the Estimation of Retirement

Wealth." In *Research in Economic Inequality*, Vol. 2, Daniel J. Slottje, ed. Stamford, CT: JAI Press, pp. 31–56.

———. 1993a. "The Distributional Implications of Social Security Annuities and Transfers on Household Wealth and Income." In *Research in Economic Inequality*, Vol. 4, Edward N. Wolff, ed. Stamford, CT: JAI Press, pp. 131–157.

———. 1993b. "Social Security Annuities and Transfers: Distributional and Tax Implications." In *Poverty and Prosperity in the USA in the Late Twentieth Century*, Dimitri B. Papadimitriou and Edward N. Wolff, eds. Houndsmill, Hampshire, UK: Macmillan Publishers, pp. 211–239.

———. 1994. "Trends in Household Wealth in the United States, 1962–1983 and 1983–1989." *Review of Income and Wealth* 40(2): 143–174.

———. 1996. *Top Heavy: A Study of Increasing Inequality of Wealth in America and What Can Be Done about It*. New York: New Press.

———. 1998. "Recent Trends in the Size Distribution of Household Wealth." *Journal of Economic Perspectives* 12(3): 131–150.

———. 2001. "Recent Trends in Wealth Ownership, from 1983 to 1998." In *Assets for the Poor: The Benefits of Spreading Asset Ownership*, Thomas M. Shapiro and Edward N. Wolff, eds. New York: Russell Sage Foundation, pp. 34–73.

———. 2002a. *Top Heavy: A Study of Increasing Inequality of Wealth in America*. Newly updated and expanded edition. New York: New Press.

———. 2002b. *Retirement Insecurity: The Income Shortfalls Awaiting the Soon-to-Retire*. Washington, DC: Economic Policy Institute.

———. 2003. "The Devolution of the American Pension System: Who Gained and Who Lost?" *Eastern Economics Journal* 29(4): 477–495.

———. 2007a. "The Retirement Wealth of the Baby Boom Generation." *Journal of Monetary Economics* 54(1): 1–40.

———. 2007b. "The Adequacy of Retirement Resources among the Soon-to-Retire, 1983–2001." In *Government Spending on the Elderly,* Dimitri B. Papadimitriou, ed. Houndsmill, Hampshire, UK: Palgrave Macmillan, pp. 315–342.

———. 2007c. "The Unraveling of the American Pension System, 1983–2001." In *Work Options for Mature Americans,* Teresa Ghilarducci and John A. Turner, eds. Notre Dame, IN: University of Notre Dame Press, pp. 175–211.

———. 2007d. "Recent Trends in Household Wealth in the United States: Rising Debt and the Middle-Class Squeeze." Levy Institute Working Paper No. 502. Annandale-on-Hudson, New York: Levy Economics Institute of Bard College.

Wolff, Edward N., and Ajit Zacharias. 2009. "A New Look at the Economic Well-Being of the Elderly in the United States, 1989–2001." *Journal of Income Distribution* 18(1): 146–179.

Wolff, Edward N., Ajit Zacharias, and Thomas Masterson. 2009. "Trends in American Living Standards and Inequality, 1959–2004." Photocopy. Levy Economics Institute of Bard College, Annandale-on-Hudson, NY.

Wolman, William, and Anne Colamosca. 2002. *The Great 401(k) Hoax: Why Your Family's Financial Security Is at Risk, and What You Can Do about It.* Oxford: Perseus Publishing.

Author

Edward N. Wolff received his PhD from Yale University in 1974 and is professor of economics at New York University, where he has taught since 1974, and a senior scholar at the Levy Economics Institute of Bard College. He is also a research associate at the National Bureau of Economic Research and has been a council member of the International Association for Research in Income and Wealth since 1987. Dr. Wolff is an associate editor of *Structural Change and Economic Dynamics* and is on the editorial board of *Economic Systems Research*, the *Journal of Economic Inequality*, and the *Journal of Socio-Economics*; he was managing editor of the *Review of Income and Wealth* from 1987 to 2004. He was a visiting scholar at the Russell Sage Foundation in New York (2003–2004); president of the Eastern Economics Association (2002–2003); a council member of the International Input-Output Association (1995–2003); and has acted as a consultant with the Economic Policy Institute, the World Bank, the United Nations, the WIDER Institute, and Mathematica Policy Research.

Dr. Wolff's principal research areas are productivity growth and income and wealth distribution. He is the author (or coauthor) of *Growth, Accumulation, and Unproductive Activity: An Analysis of the Post-War U.S. Economy* (1987); *Productivity and American Leadership: The Long View* (1989); *The Information Economy: The Implications of Unbalanced Growth* (1989); *Competitiveness, Convergence, and International Specialization* (1993); *TOP HEAVY: A Study of Increasing Inequality of Wealth in America* (1995, 1996, 2002); *Economics of Poverty, Inequality, and Discrimination* (1997); *Retirement Insecurity: The Income Shortfalls Awaiting the Soon-to-Retire* (2002); *Downsizing in America: Reality, Causes, and Consequences* (2003); *Retirement Income: The Crucial Role of Social Security* (2005); and *Does Education Really Help? Skill, Work, and Inequality* (2006).

His edited volumes are *International Comparisons of the Distribution of Household Wealth* (1987); *International Perspectives on Profitability and Accumulation* (1992); *Poverty and Prosperity in the USA in the Late Twentieth Century* (1993); *Research in Economic Inequality*, Vol. 4 (1993); *Convergence of Productivity: Cross-National Studies and Historical Evidence* (1994); *The Economics of Productivity* (1997); *Assets of the Poor: The Benefits of Spreading Asset Ownership* (2001); and *What Has Happened to the Quality of Life in the Advanced Industrialized Nations?* (2004).

He is also the author of many articles published in books and professional journals and provides frequent commentary on radio and television.

Index

The italic letters *f, n,* and *t* following a page number indicate that the subject information of the heading is within a figure, note, or table, respectively, on that page. Double italics indicate multiple but consecutive elements.

About the Institute

The W.E. Upjohn Institute for Employment Research is a nonprofit research organization devoted to finding and promoting solutions to employment-related problems at the national, state, and local levels. It is an activity of the W.E. Upjohn Unemployment Trustee Corporation, which was established in 1932 to administer a fund set aside by Dr. W.E. Upjohn, founder of The Upjohn Company, to seek ways to counteract the loss of employment income during economic downturns.

The Institute is funded largely by income from the W.E. Upjohn Unemployment Trust, supplemented by outside grants, contracts, and sales of publications. Activities of the Institute comprise the following elements: 1) a research program conducted by a resident staff of professional social scientists; 2) a competitive grant program, which expands and complements the internal research program by providing financial support to researchers outside the Institute; 3) a publications program, which provides the major vehicle for disseminating the research of staff and grantees, as well as other selected works in the field; and 4) an Employment Management Services division, which manages most of the publicly funded employment and training programs in the local area.

The broad objectives of the Institute's research, grant, and publication programs are to 1) promote scholarship and experimentation on issues of public and private employment and unemployment policy, and 2) make knowledge and scholarship relevant and useful to policymakers in their pursuit of solutions to employment and unemployment problems.

Current areas of concentration for these programs include causes, consequences, and measures to alleviate unemployment; social insurance and income maintenance programs; compensation; workforce quality; work arrangements; family labor issues; labor-management relations; and regional economic development and local labor markets.